HAMMOND'S
Family Reference
WORLD ATLAS

SPACE AGE EDITION

DOUBLEDAY & COMPANY, INC.

GARDEN CITY   NEW YORK

Contents

GAZETTEER-INDEX OF THE WORLD

ABBREVIATIONS

Country	Area (Square Miles)	Population	Index Ref.	Plate No.
Afghanistan	250,000	13,799,037	H 3	57
Africa	11,850,000	261,000,000	......	62,65
Alabama, U.S.A.	51,060	3,266,740	......	82,83
Alaska, U.S.A.	586,400	226,167	......	84,85
Albania	11,096	1,625,378	E 5	50
Alberta, Canada	248,800	1,331,944	......	190,191
Aleutian Islands, Alaska....	6,800	......	D 4	80
Algeria	919,353	11,020,000	G 5	62
American Samoa	76	20,051	J 7	69
Andaman & Nicobar Is. (India)	3,215	63,438	E 3	59
Andorra	175	10,000	G 1	46
Angola (Port.)	481,351	4,832,677	K14	64
Antarctica	5,500,000	......		35
Antigua (Br.) (incl. Barbuda and Redonda)...	171	63,000	G 3	75
Antilles, Greater and Lesser..........			D 3	75
Arabia	1,000,000	11,000,000	D 5	56
Arctic Ocean	......		......	36
Argentina	1,078,266	20,008,945	......	70,72
Arizona, U.S.A.	113,575	1,302,161	......	86,87
Arkansas, U.S.A.	52,499	1,786,272	......	88,89
Armenian S.S.R. (U.S.S.R.)	11,500	1,768,000	F 6	53
Ascension Island (Br.)	34	429	D13	64
Asia	16,500,000	1,750,000,000	......	54
Australia	2,974,581	10,508,186	......	66
Australian Capital Territory	939	58,828	J 7	67
Austria	32,369	7,073,807	B 3	48
Azerbaidzhan S.S.R. (U.S.S.R.)	33,100	3,700,000	G 6	53
Azores Islands (Port.)	890	336,933	H 4	34
Bahama Islands (Br.)	4,404	107,000	C 1	75
Bahrein	231	143,135	F 4	57
Balearic Islands (Sp.)	1,936	443,327	H 3	46
Barbados	166	232,085	G 4	75
Barbuda and Redonda Is. (Br.)	63	1,145	G 3	75
Basutoland	11,716	697,000	M17	65
Bechuanaland Prot.	222,000	350,000	L16	65
Belgium	11,775	9,189,741	C 6	44
Bermuda (Br.)	21	42,640	G 2	75
Bhutan	18,000	400,000	E 2	59
Bismarck Archipelago (Aust. Trust.)	19,660	155,173	E 6	68
Bolivia	412,777	3,549,000	G 7	70
Bonin-Volcano Is. (U.S. Adm.)	105	210	E 3	68
Brazil	3,286,170	70,967,185	......	71,73
British Columbia, Canada..	359,279	1,629,082	......	192,193
British Honduras	8,867	90,381	B 1	76
Brunei	2,226	83,877	E 5	61
Bulgaria	42,796	7,981,000	G 4	50
Burma	261,610	22,342,000	E 2	59
Burundi	10,747	2,246,186	N12	65
Byelorussian S.S.R. (White Russian S.S.R.) (U.S.S.R.)	80,100	8,055,000	C 4	53
California, U.S.A.	156,573	15,717,204	......	90,91
Cambodia	69,884	4,952,000	C 3	61
Cameroon	178,368	4,097,000	J10	62
Canada	3,621,616	18,238,247	......	178,179
Canal Zone (U.S.A.)	362	42,122	E 3	76
Canary Islands (Sp.)	2,894	944,448	B 4	46
Cape of Good Hope, S. Afr.	277,169	5,321,407	L18	65
Cape Verde Islands (Port.)	1,557	201,549	H 5	34
Caroline Islands (U.S. Trust.)	525	36,789	E 5	68
Cayman Is. (Br.)	104	8,511	B 3	75
Celebes (Indon.)	72,986	7,079,349	G 6	61
Central African Rep.	239,382	1,227,000	K10	63
Central America	217,813	10,311,128	......	76
Ceylon	25,332	10,167,000	D 4	59
Chad	455,598	2,674,990	K 8	63
Channel Islands (Br.)	75	110,543	B 3	40
Chatham Islands (N.Z.)	372	487	J10	68
Chile	286,396	7,340,249	G 8	70,72
China (Mainland)	3,745,296	669,000,000	E 1	59,60
China (Taiwan)	22,440	11,031,341	K 7	60
Christmas Island (Australia)	64	3,099	O11	55
Colombia	439,828	14,132,000	F 3	70
Colorado, U.S.A.	103,884	1,753,947	......	92,93
Comoro Is. (Is. Comores) (Fr.)	849	183,133	P14	65
Congo, Rep. of	175,676	900,000	J 2	64
Congo, Rep. of the	902,274	14,150,000	L12	65
Connecticut, U.S.A.	4,899	2,535,234	......	94,95
Cook Islands (N.Z.)	99	18,378	K 7	69
Corsica (Corse) (Fr.)	3,367	165,000	G 6	41
Costa Rica	19,238	1,251,397	C 3	76
Crete (Krētē), Greece	3,232	483,075	E 6	51
Cuba	42,857	7,068,000	B 2	75
Curaçao (Netherlands Antilles)	173	125,181	E 4	75
Cyprus	3,572	577,615	B 2	56
Czechoslovakia	49,356	13,741,529	D 2	48
Dahomey	42,471	2,002,521	G10	62
Daito Is., Ryukyu Is. (U.S. Adm.)	18	4,396	M 6	60
Delaware, U.S.A.	1,978	446,292	......	119
Denmark	16,556	4,585,256	B 3	43
District of Columbia, U.S.A.	61	763,956	B 5	114
Dominica (Br.)	305	59,916	G 4	75
Dominican Republic	19,129	3,013,525	D 3	75
Ecuador ...approx.	115,000	4,396,300	E 4	70
Egypt	386,000	26,059,000	M 6	63
England and Wales	58,344	46,071,604	......	39
Estonia (Estonian S.S.R.) (U.S.S.R.)	17,400	1,196,000	C 3	52
Ethiopia	365,754	20,000,000	O 9	63
Europe	4,129,908	575,000,000	......	37
Faeröe Islands (Den.)	540	34,596	D 2	37
Falkland Islands (Br.) (incl. S. Georgia)	4,618	2,127	J14	73
Fernando Po (Spain)	785	62,612	H11	62
Fiji (Br.)	7,036	414,000	H 8	68
Finland	130,500	4,446,222	E 2	43

Country	Area (Square Miles)	Population	Index Ref.	Plate No.
Florida, U.S.A.	54,252	4,951,560	......	96,97
Formosa (Taiwan) (China)	22,440	11,031,341	K 7	60
France	212,736	46,300,000	......	40
Franz Josef Land (Zemlya Frantsa Iosifa)	......	......	A 7	36
Gabon	90,733	447,880	J12	64
Galápagos Islands, Ecuador	3,042	1,900	F 6	34
Gambia (Br.)	4,033	294,942	C 9	62
Georgia, U.S.A.	58,274	3,943,116	......	98,99
Georgian S.S.R. (U.S.S.R.)	29,400	4,049,000	F 6	53
Germany, East (German Democratic Rep.)	41,535	16,117,000	......	42
Germany, West (Federal Republic of)	95,914	56,173,184	......	42
Ghana	91,844	6,726,815	F10	62
Gibraltar (Br.)	2	24,502	D 4	46
Gilbert, Ellice and Phoenix Islands	196	46,186	J 6	69
Great Britain and Northern Ireland	94,214	52,834,249	......	38
Greece	51,182	8,387,201	......	51
Greenland (Den.)	839,999	33,113	B12	36
Grenada (Br.)	133	88,617	F 4	75
Guadeloupe and Dependencies (Fr.)	688	278,864	F 3	75
Guam (U.S.A.)	209	67,044	E 4	68
Guatemala	45,452	3,980,000	B 2	76
Guiana, British	89,480	560,620	J 2	70
Guiana, French	35,135	31,000	K 3	71
Guiana, Netherlands (Surinam)	54,300	302,400	J 3	71
Guinea	96,525	3,000,000	D 9	62
Guinea, Portuguese	13,948	544,184	C 9	62
Haiti	10,714	4,346,000	D 3	75
Hawaii, U.S.A.	6,415	632,772	......	100,101
Holland (Netherlands)..land	12,883	11,797,000	E 4	44
Honduras	45,000	1,883,362	C 2	76
Honduras, British	8,867	90,381	B 1	76
Hong Kong (Br.)	391	3,133,131	J 7	60
Hungary	35,875	10,050,000	E 3	48
Iceland	39,709	180,058	C 2	37
Idaho, U.S.A.	82,708	667,191	......	102,103
Ifni, Spain	676	49,889	D 5	62
Illinois, U.S.A.	55,930	10,081,158	......	104,105
India	1,127,345	439,072,893	C 2	59
Indiana, U.S.A.	36,185	4,662,498	......	106,107
Indonesia	735,268	97,085,348	C 6	61
Iowa, U.S.A.	56,032	2,757,537	......	108,109
Iran (Persia)	628,000	20,678,000	F 3	57
Iraq	116,600	7,263,000	D 3	56
Ireland	26,601	2,814,703	B 4	39
Ireland, Northern	5,238	1,425,462	C 3	38
Isle of Man (Br.)	221	48,150	D 3	39
Israel	7,978	2,183,332	B 3	58
Italy	116,286	50,463,762	......	47
Ivory Coast	183,397	3,300,000	E10	62
Jamaica	4,411	1,613,880	C 3	75
Japan	142,743	93,418,501	N 4	60
Java and Madura (Indon.)	51,032	63,059,575	K 2	61
Jordan	34,750	1,752,095	D 4	58
Kalimantan (Indon. Borneo)	211,175	4,101,475	E 5	61
Kansas, U.S.A.	82,048	2,178,611	......	110,111
Kentucky, U.S.A.	39,863	3,038,156	......	112,113
Kenya	219,730	7,287,000	O11	65
Kerguélen Arch. (Fr.)	......	......	M 8	34
Korea, North	49,096	10,030,000	L 4	60
Korea, South	36,152	24,994,117	L 4	60
Krētē (Crete), Greece	3,232	483,075	E 6	51
Kuria Muria Is. (Aden Prot.)	......	100	G 6	57
Kuril Is. (U.S.S.R.)	5,700	19,000	T 5	54
Kuwait	8,000	321,621	E 4	56
Laccadive, Minicoy and Amindivi Is. (India)	746	24,108	C 3	59
Laos	89,343	2,000,000	C 2	61
Latvia (Latvian S.S.R.) (U.S.S.R.)	24,600	2,094,000	B 3	52
Lebanon	3,475	1,646,000	C 3	56
Liberia	43,000	1,290,000	E10	62
Libya	679,358	1,216,000	J 6	62
Liechtenstein	65	16,628	E 1	45
Lithuania (Lithuanian S.S.R.) (U.S.S.R.)	25,200	2,713,000	B 3	52

Country	Area (Square Miles)	Population	Index Ref.	Plate No.
Louisiana, U.S.A.	45,106	3,257,022	......	114,115
Luxembourg	999	314,889	H 8	44
Macao (Port.)	6	169,299	P 7	55
Madagascar	241,094	5,486,713	R16	65
Madeira Islands (Port.)	308	282,678	A 2	46
Maine, U.S.A.	31,012	969,265	......	116,117
Malagasy Rep.	241,094	5,486,713	R16	65
Malawi	36,829	2,920,000	N14	65
Malaya, Fed. of	50,690	7,137,000	C 4	61
Malaysia, Fed. of	127,368	10,048,950	C 5	61
Maldive Islands	115	89,000	L 9	55
Mali	584,942	4,307,113	F 8	62
Malta	122	329,000	E 7	47
Manitoba, Canada	219,723	921,686	......	186,187
Mariana Islands (U.S. Trust.)	142	9,134	E 4	68
Marquesas Is. (Fr.)	480	3,936	N 6	69
Marshall Islands (U.S. Trust.)	61	14,907	G 4	68
Martinique (Fr.)	425	277,000	G 4	75
Maryland, U.S.A.	9,874	3,100,689	......	118,119
Massachusetts, U.S.A.	7,867	5,148,578	......	120,121
Mauritania	328,185	791,000	D 8	62
Mauritius (Br.)	720	667,000	S19	65
Mexico	760,373	34,923,129	......	77
Michigan, U.S.A.	57,019	7,823,194	......	122,123
Midway Islands (U.S.A.)	2	416	J 3	69
Minnesota, U.S.A.	80,009	3,413,864	......	124,125
Mississippi, U.S.A.	47,223	2,178,141	......	126,127
Missouri, U.S.A.	69,138	4,319,813	......	128,129
Moldavian S.S.R. (U.S.S.R.)	13,100	2,880,000	C 5	53
Molucca Islands (Indonesia)	30,168	789,534	C 5	68
Monaco	370 Acres	22,297	G 6	41
Mongolia	625,946	998,000	O 5	54
Montana, U.S.A.	145,736	674,767	......	130,131
Montserrat	32	12,157	G 3	75
Morocco	171,583	11,626,470	E 5	62
Mozambique (Port.)	297,731	6,592,994	N16	65
Muscat and Oman	82,000	565,000	G 6	57
Natal, So. Africa	35,284	2,933,447	N17	65
Nauru (Aust.-N.Z.-Br. Tr. Terr.)	8	4,613	G 6	68
Nebraska, U.S.A.	76,612	1,411,330	......	132,133
Nepal	54,000	9,387,661	D 2	59
Netherlands (Holland)..land	12,883	11,797,000	E 4	44
Netherlands Antilles	383	194,000	E 4	75
Nevada, U.S.A.	109,788	285,278	......	134,135
New Britain (island) (Aust. Trust.)	14,600	100,873	F 6	68
New Brunswick, Canada	27,473	597,936	C 3	180
New Caledonia (Fr.)	7,201	77,000	G 8	68
Newfoundland, Canada	42,734	457,853	J 4	181
New Guinea, Territory of (Aust. Trust.)	93,000	1,386,808	B 7	61
New Hampshire, U.S.A.	9,014	606,921	......	136,137
New Hebrides Islands (Br. and Fr.)	5,700	55,713	G 7	68
New Ireland (island) (Aust. Trust.)	3,800	37,225	F 6	68
New Jersey, U.S.A.	7,521	6,066,782	......	138,139
New Mexico, U.S.A.	121,510	951,023	......	140,141
New South Wales, Australia	309,432	3,917,013	H 6	67
New York, U.S.A.	47,939	16,782,304	......	142,143
New Zealand	103,934	2,414,984	K 6	67
Nicaragua	57,143	1,883,000	C 2	76
Niger	501,930	3,112,000	H 8	62
Nigeria	356,093	36,473,000	H10	62
Niue I. (Br.)	100	4,864	K 7	69
North America	9,124,000	278,303,000	......	74
North Borneo (Sabah)	29,387	454,421	F 4	61
North Carolina, U.S.A.	49,067	4,556,155	......	144,145
North Dakota, U.S.A.	69,457	632,446	......	146,147
Northern Ireland (Br.)	5,459	1,425,462	C 3	38
Northern Territory, Australia	523,620	27,095	E 3	66
Northwest Territories, Canada	1,258,217	22,998	......	194,195
Norway	124,560	3,596,211	B 2	43
Nova Scotia, Canada	20,743	737,007	D 5	180,181
Ohio, U.S.A.	40,972	9,706,397	......	148,149
Oklahoma, U.S.A.	69,283	2,328,284	......	150,151
Ontario, Canada	363,282	6,236,092	......	184,185
Orange Free State, South Africa	49,647	1,373,790	M17	65
Oregon, U.S.A.	96,248	1,768,687	......	152,153
Orkney Islands, Scotland	376	18,743	E 1	38

Country	Area (Square Miles)	Population	Index Ref.	Plate No.
Pacific Islands, U.S. Trust Terr.	680	81,000	D,F 5	68
Pakistan	364,218	93,831,982	B2,D2	59
Palau Islands (U.S. Trust.)	189	15,006	D 5	68
Panama (excl. Canal Zone)	28,575	1,075,541	D 3	76
Papua Territory (Aust.)	90,600	523,000	B 7	61
Paraguay	150,518	1,857,000	H 8	70
Pennsylvania, U.S.A.	45,007	11,319,366		154,155
Persia (Iran)	628,000	20,678,000	F 3	57
Peru	513,000	10,524,000	E 5	70
Philippines, Republic of the	115,600	27,455,799	H 3	61
Phoenix Is. (U.S. and Br.)	16	984	J 6	69
Pitcairn Island (Br.)	2	126	O 8	69
Poland	119,734	29,731,009		49
Portugal	35,413	9,130,410	B 3	46
Prince Edward Island, Canada	2,184	104,629	F 3	180,181
Principe and S. Tomé (Port.)	372	63,676	H11	64
Puerto Rico	3,421	2,349,544	G 2	75
Qatar	5,000	55,000	F 4	57
Québec, Canada	523,860	5,259,211		182,183
Queensland, Australia	670,500	1,518,828	G 4	67
Réunion (Fr.)	970	336,000	R20	65
Rhode Island, U.S.A.	1,058	859,488	H 5	120,121
Rhodesia	150,333	3,200,000	M15	65
Río de Oro, Spain	71,585	24,105	D 7	62
Río Muni (Spain)	10,045	183,377	H11	64
Rumania	91,671	18,567,000	G 3	50
Russian S.F.S.R. (U.S.S.R.)	6,501,500	117,494,000	F 3	52
Rwanda	10,169	2,707,186	N12	65
Ryukyu Islands (U.S. Adm.)	921	883,122	L 6	60
Sabah (North Borneo)	29,387	454,421	F 4	61
Saguia el Hamra, Sp.	31,661	14,298	D 6	62
St. Croix, Virgin Is. (U.S.A.)	80	12,103	H 2	75
St. Helena I. (Br.)	47	5,000	E15	64
St. John, Virgin Is. (U.S.A.)	20	749	H 1	75
St. Lucia	233	86,108	G 4	75
St-Pierre and Miquelon Is. (Fr.)	93	4,822	H 6	177
St. Thomas, Virgin Is. (U.S.A.)	32	16,201	G 1	75
St. Vincent	150	79,948	G 4	75
Sakhalin (U.S.S.R.)	35,400	632,000	T 4	54
Salvador, El	8,060	2,501,278	B 2	76
Samoa, Western	1,133	113,567	J 7	69
Samoa (U.S.A.)	76	20,051	J 7	69
San Marino	38	17,000	D 3	47
Sarawak	47,071	744,529	E 5	61
Sardinia (Sardegna) (It.)	9,301	1,413,289	B 4	47
Saskatchewan, Canada	237,975	925,181		188,189
Saudi Arabia	350,000	6,036,000	D 4	56
Scotland	30,411	5,178,490		38
Senegal	77,401	2,973,285	D 9	62
Seychelles	157	41,425	M 6	34
Shetland Islands, Scotland	550	17,809	G 1	38
Siam (Thailand)	200,148	26,257,848	C 2	61
Sicily, Italy	9,926	4,711,783	D 6	47
Sierra Leone	27,925	2,450,000	D10	62
Sikkim	2,745	162,189	D 2	59
Singapore	220	1,713,000	C 5	61
Sinkiang, China	660,977	4,012,330	D 1	59
Society Islands (Fr.)	650	41,798	L 7	69
Socotra (Aden Prot.)	1,400	14,000	J 8	55
Solomon Islands (Aust. Tr.)	4,070	51,928	F 6	68
Solomon Islands Prot. (Br.)	14,600	124,100	G 6	68
Somali Republic	262,000	2,030,000	P11	63,65
Somaliland, French	8,492	67,300	P 9	63
South Africa	472,494	15,853,696	L18	65
South America	6,894,000	148,000,000		70,73
South Arabia	110,000	1,000,000	E 7	56
South Australia, Australia	380,070	969,340	E 5	66
South Carolina, U.S.A.	30,272	2,382,594		156,157
South Dakota, U.S.A.	76,378	680,514		158,159
South-West Africa (S. Afr. Mand.)	317,725	512,496	K16	64
Spain	195,258	30,430,698		46
Spanish Sahara	103,243	23,793	C 7	62
Sudan	967,500	12,650,000	M 9	63
Sumatra (Indon.)	164,148	14,982,910	C 6	61
Surinam (Netherlands Guiana)	54,300	302,400	J 3	71
Svalbard, Norway (Spitsbergen)	24,294	3,769	A 1	43
Swaziland (Br.)	6,704	275,000	N17	65
Sweden	173,394	7,495,129	C 2	43
Switzerland	15,944	5,429,061		45
Syria	72,587	4,555,267	C 2	56
Tahiti (island) (Fr.)	600	25,156	L 7	69
Taiwan (Formosa) (China)	22,440	11,031,341	K 7	60
Tanzania	343,726	9,875,000	N13	65
Tasmania, Australia	26,215	350,340	H 8	67
Tennessee, U.S.A.	41,762	3,567,089		160,161
Texas, U.S.A.	262,840	9,579,677		162,163
Thailand (Siam)	200,148	26,257,848	C 2	61
Tibet, China	469,413	2,000,000	D 1	59
Timor (Port.)	7,332	517,079	H 7	61
Timor (Indon.)	24,450	702,638	H 7	61
Togo	20,733	1,439,772	G10	62
Tokelau (Union Group) (N.Z. and U.S.)	4	1,870	J 6	69
Tonga (Friendly) Is. (Br.)	269	63,874	J 8	69
Transvaal, S. Afr.	110,450	6,225,052	M17	65
Trinidad and Tobago	1,864	827,957	G 5	75
Tristan da Cunha (Br.)	38	264	J 7	34
Trucial Oman	12,000	110,000	F 5	57
Tuamotu (Low) Arch. (Fr.)	332	8,237	M 7	69
Tunisia	48,300	4,254,000	H 5	62
Turkey	296,185	27,829,198	B 2	56
Turks and Caicos Is. (Br.)	202	5,668	D 2	75
Uganda (Br.)	80,301	6,536,616	N11	65
Ukrainian S.S.R. (U.S.S.R.)	220,600	41,869,046	C 5	53
Union of Soviet Socialist Republics	8,570,600	219,700,000		52
United Arab Republic	386,000	26,059,000	M 6	63
United Kingdom	94,214	52,834,249		38,39
United States of America.. land	3,554,609	179,323,175		78
land and water	3,615,221			
Upper Volta	105,841	4,400,000	F 9	62
Uruguay	72,172	2,846,000	J10	73
Utah, U.S.A.	82,339	890,627		164,165
Vatican City	109 Acres	1,010	C 4	47
Venezuela	352,143	7,523,999	G 2	70
Vermont, U.S.A.	9,276	389,881		166,167
Victoria, Australia	87,884	2,930,113	G 7	67
Vietnam, North	63,370	15,916,955	D 2	61
Vietnam, South	65,726	14,520,000	D 2	61
Virgin Islands (Br.)	58	7,340	H 1	75
Virgin Islands (U.S.A.)	132	32,099	H 1	75
Virginia, U.S.A.	39,838	3,966,949		168,169
Wake Island (U.S.A.)	3	349	G 4	68
Wales (including Monmouthshire)	8,017	2,640,632	E 4	39
Walvis Bay (S. Afr.)	430	12,568	J16	64
Washington, U.S.A.	66,709	2,853,214		170,171
Western Australia, Australia	975,920	736,629	C 4	66
West Irian (Indon. Adm.)	161,514	700,000	K 6	61
West Virginia, U.S.A.	24,079	1,860,421		172,173
White Russian S.S.R. (Byelorussian S.S.R.) (U.S.S.R.)	80,100	8,055,000	C 4	53
Wisconsin, U.S.A.	54,705	3,951,777		174,175
World land area	57,500,000	3,061,000,000		34
Wyoming, U.S.A.	97,411	330,066		176,177
Yap (U.S. Trust.)	87	5,686	D 5	68
Yemen	75,000	5,000,000	D 7	56
Yugoslavia	99,079	18,538,150	C 3	50
Yukon Territory, Canada	205,346	14,628		194
Zambia	290,320	2,510,000	M14	65

SOCIAL AND ECONOMIC TABLES

POLITICAL DIVISION	GOVERNMENT	MONETARY UNIT	LANGUAGE	MAJOR PRODUCTS
ADEN PROTECTORATE†	Ruled by local sultans, advised by and responsible to the British High Commissioner at Aden.	East African shilling	Arabic	Dates, gums, tobacco, fish oil, butter, wheat, barley, sesame, millet, sorghum, aloes, ghee; goats, sheep, camels, cattle.
AFGHANISTAN	A constitutional monarchy ruled by a king, a cabinet and a bicameral legislative assembly.	Afghani rupee	Afghan (Pushtu) Persian	Wheat, barley, millet, corn, sorghum, lentils, vegetables, fruits, nuts, castor beans, madder, asafetida, cotton, tobacco, fat-tailed sheep (karakul), camels, zebus; wool, skins; sheepskin, leather, carpets, rugs; gold, iron, lapis lazuli, coal, copper, lead, silver.
ALBANIA	A Soviet-type republic with president, cabinet and one house legislature. Actually ruled by the Communist party politburo.	lek	Albanian	Corn, tobacco, wheat, flax, oats, barley, rye, rice, olives, fruit; cattle, sheep; fish; wool, hides; dairy products, furs; bitumen, salt, lignite, aluminum, petroleum, copper, chromite; flour, olive oil, cheese, cement, leather.
ALGERIA	Formerly an integral part of France, Algeria became an independent republic in 1962.	franc	Arabic French Berber	Wheat, barley, oats, corn, grapes, olives, tobacco, dates, figs, flax, pomegranates, prunes, apricots, legumes, potatoes; sheep, goats, cattle, mules, horses, pigs, camels; sardines, anchovies, tuna; forestry products; iron, phosphates, zinc, petroleum; wine, olive oil, distilling, flour, carpet weaving, alcohol, cotton weaving, tobacco products, wool, cork.
ANDORRA	A republic under the joint suzerainty of the French State and the Bishop of Urgel, with a council general of 24 elective members. Executive authority is vested in the First Syndic.	franc and peseta	Catalan	Tobacco, potatoes, barley; sheep, cattle; lumber.
ANGOLA	Portuguese overseas province with a governor-general.	angolar	Bantu languages Portuguese	Coffee, corn, sugar, palm oil and kernels, cotton, sisal, wax, tobacco; diamonds; whale oil, fish oil, sugar, palm oil.
ARGENTINA	A republic with a president, vice-president, appointive cabinet, elective senate and house of deputies.	Argentine peso	Spanish	Wheat, corn, oats, barley, linseed, rye, grapes and other fruit, tobacco, vegetables; yerba maté; cattle, sheep; quebracho, lumber; petroleum, natural gas, gold, lead, silver, tungsten; vegetable oils, wines, hides, wool, meats, textiles, metal products, vehicles and machinery, chemicals, wood and paper products, leather, clothing and shoes.
ASCENSION ISLAND	Possession of Great Britain administered through the government of St. Helena by a resident magistrate and a Justice of the Peace.	pound	English	
AUSTRALIA	Member of the British Commonwealth of Nations with a governor-general, prime minister and cabinet. Parliament consists of a senate and house of commons.	Australian pound	English	Wheat, oats, rice and other grains, fruits, vegetables, honey; sheep, cattle; gold, coal, copper, iron, lead, silver, tin, zinc; iron and steel, wool, textiles, electrical and radio equipment and appliances, drugs and chemicals, paints, optical instruments, agricultural implements and machinery, metal work and machinery, clothing, leather, furniture, airplanes, engines, ships, processed fruit and vegetables, building materials, confectionery, automobiles.
AUSTRIA	Republic with a president, chancellor and vice-chancellor, cabinet of ministers, and two-house assembly.	schilling	German	Rye, wheat, oats, barley, corn, potatoes, sugar beets, hops, grapes, rapeseed, flax, hemp, tobacco; iron, copper, lead, magnesite, graphite, coal, aluminum, petroleum, lignite, salt; timber, pulp, poultry and livestock; steel, machinery, machine tools, chemicals, textiles, paper, building materials, processed foods, leather.
BAHAMA ISLANDS	British colony with governor, executive and legislative council and house of assembly.	pound	English	Tomatoes, pineapples, okra, vegetables, citrus fruits, bananas, sisal; crawfish, shells; lumber; salt; handcraft products.
BAHREIN	Arab sheikhdom protected by Great Britain and advised by British political agent.	rupee	Arabic	Pearl fishing, petroleum, boat building, fishing; reed mats, dates, lucerne; donkeys; textiles.
BARBADOS	British colony with governor, executive and legislative council and house of assembly.	B.W.I. dollar	English	Sugar cane, cotton; flying fish; manjak (asphalt); sugar, molasses, rum, edible oil, margarine.
BASUTOLAND	British protectorate governed by resident commissioner under High Commissioner for Basutoland, Bechuanaland and Swaziland.	pound	Bantu languages Afrikaans English	Corn, wheat, sorghum, barley, oats, beans, peas; cattle, sheep, goats, horses, donkeys, pigs, mules; wool, mohair.
BECHUANALAND PROTECTORATE	British protectorate. Governed by a resident commissioner under High Commissioner for Basutoland, Bechuanaland and Swaziland.	pound	Bantu languages Bushman English	Kaffir, wheat and wheatmeal; cattle, sheep, goats, pigs; hides, gold.
BELGIUM	Constitutional, hereditary monarchy. King appoints a cabinet of ministers. Parliament consists of a senate and chamber of deputies.	franc	French and Flemish	Wheat, rye, oats, barley, potatoes, sugar beets, flax, tobacco, vegetables, fruit, hops, hemp, bulbs, livestock, fish; coal, iron, zinc, lead, copper, tin, silver; coke, steel, machinery, textiles, lace, glass, chemicals, uranium refining, sugar, margarine, cheese, vinegar, alcohol, beer, matches, paper, foods, beverages, wool, cut diamonds, dairy products.
BERMUDA	British colony with governor, executive and legislative council and house of assembly.	pound	English	Lily bulbs, onions, bananas, cabbage, tomatoes, beans; coral; fish; perfume.
BHUTAN	Ruled by a Maharaja and advised by India in foreign relations.	rupee	Bhutia (Tibetan dialect)	Rice, corn, millet, lac, wax, musk; elephants, ponies, chowries; cloth, baskets, mats, metalwork, guns, swords.
BISMARCK ARCHIPELAGO	A part of the Territory of New Guinea administered by Australia as a U.N. trust territory.	Australian pound	Papuan English Chinese	Coconuts, cocoa, coffee, kapok, rubber, grains; cattle, goats, pigs; fish.
BOLIVIA	A republic with a president, vice-president, appointive ministers of state, and an elective senate and chamber of deputies.	boliviano	Spanish Indian	Potatoes, corn, barley, quinoa, nuts, coca, vanilla, rubber, quinine; tin, zinc, lead, copper, silver, antimony, tungsten, sulphur, petroleum; cattle; textiles, flour, cement, tobacco products, hides, beer, earthenware.
BONIN & VOLCANO IS.	Administered by the United States.	dollar yen	Japanese	Vegetables, sugar, coca; poultry, pigs, cattle; fish.

† A part of the Prot. of South Arabia.

POLITICAL DIVISION	GOVERNMENT	MONETARY UNIT	LANGUAGE	MAJOR PRODUCTS
BRAZIL	Federal republic with a president, vice-president, appointive secretaries of state and a bicameral legislature.	cruzeiro	Portuguese	Coffee, corn, rice, cotton, cacao, sugar cane, cassava, beans, carnauba wax, medicinal plants, oranges, balata, tobacco, fibers, castor oil; livestock; timbo, brazil nuts; iron, manganese, gold, rutile, zirconium, diamonds, mica, bauxite, quartz, beryllium, chrome, tungsten, silver; foods, textiles, chemicals, pharmaceuticals, metallurgical products, paper and wood products, hides, vegetable oils, machinery.
BRITISH HONDURAS	British colony with governor, council of ministers and legislative assembly.	Br. Honduras dollar	English and Spanish	Rice, maize, beans, bananas, coconuts, citrus fruits, sugar cane; mahogany, chicle, pine, cedar; fish; rum, food products.
BRUNEI	A sultanate with a chief minister, executive and legislative councils and an advisory British High Commissioner.	Malayan dollar	Malay English	Rice, sago, rubber, jelutong, cutch, sugar cane, tapioca, bananas, pineapples; timber; domestic birds, buffalo, pigs, cattle; petroleum, natural gas; boat building, cloth, brass and silverware.
BULGARIA	Soviet-type republic with a one-house legislature, which elects a presidium whose president is the nominal chief of state. Actual power is Communist politburo.	lev	Bulgarian	Wheat, corn, barley, oats, rye, tobacco, fruit, cotton, sugar beets, potatoes; livestock, silkworm cocoons; fish; coal, salt, bauxite, copper, iron, lead, manganese, silver, kaolin; tobacco products, attar of roses, sugar, flour, textiles, leather goods, shoes, lead concentrates, wines and spirits.
BURMA, UNION OF	A republic with a president elected by a bicameral legislature.	kyat	Burmese Karen Shan	Rice, sesame, peanuts, corn, cotton, millet, tobacco, sugar, beans, fruit, vegetables, pulses, rubber; teak wood, lumber; cattle, buffalo, pigs, goats, sheep; petroleum, silver, lead, zinc, tin, copper, tungsten, rubies, sapphires, amber, jade, nickel, gold, antimony, cobalt, salt; textiles, hides, matches, lacquer ware.
BURUNDI	Independent republic established in 1962.	Belgian franc	Bantu languages Flemish French	Agricultural products; cattle; hides.
CAMBODIA	Constitutional monarchy with a national assembly.	riel	Khmer Lao	Rice, tobacco, kapok, cotton, pepper, coin, sugar, rubber; timber; cattle; fish; silk, cotton, textiles, pottery, rush mats, precious stones, phosphates.
CAMEROON	Independent republic.	franc	Sudanese and Bantu languages Arabic French	Cocoa, palm kernels, bananas, caoutchouc, coffee, cacao, palm oil; timber; cattle, sheep, pigs, horses, asses; rubber, tobacco.
CANADA	Member of the British Commonwealth with a governor-general, prime minister and cabinet. Parliament consists of a senate and house of commons.	dollar	English French	Wheat, oats, barley, flax, rye, potatoes, turnips, vegetables, sugar beets, tobacco, fruits, dairy products, livestock; fish; forestry products; furs; gold, copper, nickel, zinc, lead, silver, platinum, iron ore, titanium, cobalt, radium, uranium, petroleum, natural gas, coal, asbestos, salt, gypsum, quartz, sulphur, cement, clay; hydro-electric power; foods, beverages, transportation equipment, iron and steel products, aluminum, metal products, pulp, paper and wood products, textiles, electrical apparatus, chemicals.
CAPE VERDE ISLANDS	Portuguese overseas province, ruled by a governor.	escudo	Portuguese	Coffee, castor beans, corn, fruit, grains, tobacco; goats, oxen, pigs, asses; hides, skins; preserved fish, salt, lime, sugar.
CAROLINE ISLANDS	A group in the United States trust Territory of the Pacific Islands and administered by a high commissioner.	dollar	Micronesian dialects Malayo-Polynesian languages	Copra, breadfruit, cassava, taro, sweet potatoes; pigs, cattle, poultry, fish; phosphates.
CENTRAL AFRICAN REPUBLIC	Equatorial African republic within the French Community with a legislative assembly.	franc	Bantu and Sudanese languages Arabic, French	Coffee, cotton, sisal, groundnuts, millet, sorghum; gold, diamonds; rubber; palm products, beeswax.
CEYLON	Dominion of the British Commonwealth ruled by a governor-general, a prime minister, a cabinet and a bicameral legislature.	Celanese rupee	Singhalese Tamil	Tea, coconuts, rubber, rice, millet, tobacco, cacao, cinnamon, citronella, cloves, fruits, palmyra, fish; cattle, buffalo, goats, swine, sheep; graphite, plumbago, mica, ilmenite, monazite, iron ore; salt, pearls, zircon, glass sands, copra, plywood, leather, shoes, glass, steel, acetic acid, ceramics, quinine, strychine, shark-liver oil, coconut oil, textiles.
CHAD	Equatorial African republic within the French Community with a legislative assembly.	franc	Bantu and Sudanese languages Arabic, French	Millet, sesame, vegetables; livestock, hides; ivory, ostrich feathers; cotton, dates.
CHILE	A republic with a president, vice-president, appointive cabinet of ministers of state, elective senate and chamber of deputies.	Chilean escudo	Spanish	Wheat, potatoes, oats, rice, barley, corn, kidney beans, lentils, fruits; fish; livestock; copper, silver, nitrates, iodine, iron, sulphur, gold, manganese, coal; foods, textiles, leather, wood products, cement, chemicals and pharmaceuticals, wines and beer, wool.
CHINA: MAINLAND (COMMUNIST)	In theory, governmental power resides in the National People's Congress and the State Council. In practice, power resides in the Communist Party's Central Committee.	Chinese dollar	Chinese Mongol Turki	Rice, wheat, sweet potatoes, corn, barley, millet, kaoliang, soybeans, cotton, tea, sugar cane, tobacco, peanuts, peas, beans, opium, tung, silk; pigs, oxen, sheep, goats, buffalo, donkeys, horses, mules, poultry; timber; fish; iron, coal, tungsten, tin, antimony, mercury, copper, lead, zinc, silver, salt, soda, gold, petroleum, bismuth, molybdenum; foodstuffs, textiles, chemicals, machinery, metal work, metallurgical products, bristles, cement, clothing, embroideries, ceramics.
CHINA: TAIWAN (NATIONALIST)	A republic whose supreme organ of government is the popularly elected National Assembly. The Assembly elects the president and vice-president. Legislative powers reside with the Legislative Yuan.	new Taiwan dollar	Chinese (Amoy dialect) Formosan	Rice, tea, sugar, sweet potatoes, ramie, jute, tumeric, pineapples, bananas, camphor; pigs, buffalo, cattle, goats, horses.
COLOMBIA	A centralized federal republic with a president, vice-president, appointive cabinet, elective senate and house of representatives.	Colombian peso	Spanish	Coffee, sugar cane, corn, rice, root crops, cotton, bananas, cacao, wheat, tobacco, cinchona; cattle; rubber, fibers; petroleum, gold, silver, platinum, emeralds, salt; textiles, beer, sugar, cement, flour, tobacco products.
COMORO ISLANDS	An overseas territory of France with an administrator, privy council and an elective general council.	franc	Arabic French	Sugar cane, vanilla, rice, sweet potatoes, yams, copra, sisal, cacao, perfume plants; rum distilling.
CONGO, REPUBLIC OF	Equatorial African republic within the French Community with a legislative assembly.	franc	Bantu and Sudanese languages Arabic, French	Palm oil and kernels, hardwoods, kola nuts, copal, rubber, tobacco; lead, gold; livestock; rice.
CONGO, REPUBLIC OF THE	Independent republic.	franc	Bantu languages French Flemish	Palm oil and kernels, cotton, coffee, oil cakes, copal, rice, groundnuts; rubber, manioc, fibers; copper, cement, coal, silver, cassiterite (tin), diamonds, gold, cobalt, radium, uranium, tantalum, zinc.

POLITICAL DIVISION	GOVERNMENT	MONETARY UNIT	LANGUAGE	MAJOR PRODUCTS
COOK ISLANDS	Territory of New Zealand administered by a resident commissioner.	New Zealand pound	Polynesian dialects English	Citrus fruits, coconuts, copra, tomatoes, arrowroot, pineapples, breadfruit, taro, kumaras, plantains, yams; mother-of-pearl.
COSTA RICA	Republic with president, cabinet and one-house legislature.	colon	Spanish	Coffee, bananas, cocoa, abaca, sugar cane, maize, rice, tobacco; cattle; tuna; gold, silver; cigars and cigarettes, textiles, furniture and woodwork, sugar.
CUBA	Formal republic with dictatorial aspects. Government by decree of Prime Minister.	Cuban peso	Spanish	Sugar cane, tobacco, coffee, pineapples, citrus fruits, bananas, henequen; cattle; cedar, mahogany and other woods; fish; chromite, iron, manganese, copper, nickel, asphalt; sugar, textiles, alcohol, molasses, chemicals, tobacco products, electrical goods, clothing.
CURACAO (NETH. ANTILLES)	Self-governing part of Netherlands Union with governor, executive council and one-house legislature.	guilder	Dutch and Papiamento	Fish; dividivi (tannin), crude salt, phosphates; refined petroleum.
CYPRUS	Independent republic and member of British Commonwealth.	pound	Greek Turkish	Wheat, barley, oats, grapes, raisins, olives, fodder crops, potatoes, carobs, cotton, tobacco, linseed, hemp, flax, citrus fruits, bread beans, corn, sesame, melons; sponges, fish; sheep, goats, donkeys, cattle, pigs, horses, mules; copper pyrites, asbestos, chromite, gypsum, amber, copper concentrates; tobacco products, buttons, wines, spirits, false teeth, lace, gum, boots and shoes, dried fruits, cheese.
CZECHOSLOVAKIA	Soviet-type republic with a president and a one-house elective parliament. Actual power resides in politburo, highest body of Communist party.	koruna	Czech and Slovak	Wheat, rye, barley, oats, corn, hops, sugar beets, grapes, potatoes; poultry, livestock; timber; coal, lignite, iron, graphite, garnets, silver, copper, lead, salt, manganese, zinc; beer, spirits, malt, metals, munitions, machinery, iron and steel, porcelain, shoes, textiles, wood products, pulp and paper, sugar, leather, foods, chemicals, rubber products.
DAHOMEY	West African republic with a legislative assembly.	franc	Sudanese languages French	Palm oil, shea nuts, groundnuts, cotton fiber, copra, castor oil, kapok, millet; gold, diamonds, bauxite, iron ore.
DENMARK	Constitutional, hereditary monarchy with a two-house, elective legislature and an appointive council of ministers.	krone	Danish	Barley, mixed grains, oats, rye, wheat, potatoes, sugar beets; livestock, fish; clay; ships and transportation equipment, butter, bacon, eggs, cheese, milk, footwear, clothing, machines, chemicals, tobacco products, metal goods, leather goods, beverages; stone, earthenware and glassware, electrical goods.
DOMINICAN REPUBLIC	Republic with president, cabinet and two-house legislature.	Dominican peso	Spanish	Sugar cane, cacao, coffee, tobacco, bananas, rice, corn; cattle; lumber; gold; starch, alcohol, molasses, sugar, chocolate, meats, cigars, cigarettes, leather.
ECUADOR	A centralized republic with a president, a cabinet and an elective bicameral legislature, the senate including representatives of various social, economic and governmental groups.	sucre	Spanish, Indian	Rice, cacao, coffee, bananas, rubber, kapok, cotton, tagua (ivory) nuts, cinchona; livestock; gold, petroleum, salt, balsa wood; textiles, toquilla (panama) hats, buttons, sugar, flour, shoes, beer and liquors, chemicals, pharmaceuticals, cement, soap, candles.
EGYPT	This country, officially called the United Arab Republic, is a republic with a president, cabinet and unicameral legislature.	Egyptian pound	Arabic	Cotton, barley, wheat, rice, sugar cane, onions, corn, millet, fruits, vegetables; sheep, goats, cattle, buffalo, donkeys, pigs, horses, mules; fish; petroleum, cement, phosphates, asbestos, chromite, cotton ginning, milling, pottery, perfume, soap.
ENGLAND AND WALES	England is governed directly by the government of Great Britain and Northern Ireland. Executive power resides nominally in the Crown but actually in the prime minister and cabinet. Parliament consists of two houses.	pound sterling	English and Welsh (Celtic)	Potatoes, turnips, beets, oats, wheat, barley, rye, hay, beans, peas, cabbage, vetches, hops, fruits; sheep, cattle, pigs, horses, poultry; fish; coal, coke, gas, iron, copper, lead, nickel, tin, clay; dairy products, wool, cotton and linen textiles; electrical goods, vehicles, steel, scientific instruments, cutlery, foods and beverages, tobacco products, clothing and shoes, chemicals, pottery, china, machinery, locomotives, carpets, knitwear, lace, pharmaceuticals.
ETHIOPIA	Constitutional monarchy with an emperor assisted by a council of ministers and a bicameral legislature.	Ethiopian dollar	Amharic Hamitic languages Arabic	Coffee, teff, barley, durra, wheat, cotton, sugar cane; cattle, sheep, goats, horses, mules; hides, skins; wax, gold, rocksalt.
FALKLAND ISLANDS	British colony with a governor and an executive and a legislative council.	pound	English	Forage crops, sheep; wool, skins, tallow, whale oil, whale-meat meal.
FERNANDO PO	Spanish province ruled by a governor.	peseta	Bantu languages Spanish	Cocoa, coffee, bananas, palm oil and kernels, copra; cabinet woods.
FIJI	British colony ruled by a governor with an executive and legislative council.	Fiji pound	English Fijian Hindustani Chinese	Sugar cane, coconuts, bananas, pineapples, rice, root vegetables, citrus fruits, cotton, rubber, castor oil seeds, taro, yams, cassava, sweet potatoes, groundnuts, pulses, corn, fodder crops, tobacco; cattle, pigs; tuna, bêche-de-mer, trochus shell; gold, silver; sugar, copra, coconut oil, soap, biscuits, molasses, paint, butter, ghee, candlenut oil.
FINLAND	A republic with a president, a one-house elective diet and appointive council of state.	markka	Finnish and Swedish	Hay, potatoes, wheat, oats, barley, rye, sugar beets, flax, hemp, vegetables; cattle, horses, sheep, pigs, poultry, reindeer; wood and timber; fish; copper; lumber, plywood, furniture, pulp and paper, cardboard, textiles, butter, eggs, cheese, flour, leather, chemicals, china and glass, foodstuffs.
FRANCE	A republic with a president, a two-house elective parliament and an appointive council of ministers.	franc	French	Sugar beets, potatoes, wheat, oats, barley, rye; corn, turnips, fruits, nuts, wine grapes, buckwheat; cattle, sheep, pigs, horses; fish; coal, iron ore, lignite, salt, bauxite, pyrites, potash salts, leeks, kaolin, natural gas, iron and steel, chemicals; silk, cotton, rayon, wool and linen, textiles; clothing, lace, perfumes and cosmetics, automobiles, machinery, dairy products, beet sugar, wines, porcelain, aluminum, foods, leather, spirits.
GABON	Equatorial African republic within the French Community with a legislative assembly.	franc	Bantu and Sudanese languages Arabic, French	Mahogany, ebony, okumé wood; gold; fishing; cocoa; rubber, kapok, waxes, kola nuts; manioc, sweet potatoes, corn, plantains.
GAMBIA	Crown colony and protectorate of Great Britain administered by a governor, executive and legislative councils.	pound	Sudanese languages English	Groundnuts, palm kernels; hides and skins; beeswax.

POLITICAL DIVISION	GOVERNMENT	MONETARY UNIT	LANGUAGE	MAJOR PRODUCTS
IRAN	Constitutional monarchy governed by a shah, prime minister, cabinet and a bicameral legislature.	rial	Persian Arabic Kurdish	Wheat, cotton, gums, opium, fruit, rice, barley, sugar beets, tobacco, tea, corn, millet, legumes, vegetables, nuts; sheep, goats, cattle, asses, horses, mules; fish; petroleum oil, red oxide, copper, sulphur, arsenic, coal, salt, marble, nickel, manganese, lead, cobalt, turquoise, iron ore; carpets, rugs, textiles, leather, glass, matches, chemicals, jute, tobacco products, oil refining, casings, wood, oils.
IRAQ	Independent republic.	Iraqi dinar	Arabic Turkish Kurdish	Dates, other fruits, barley, wheat, rice, tobacco, cotton, beans, corn, sorghum, sesame; sheep, goats, asses, camels, horses, buffalo; oil, salt, wool, textiles, cigarettes, distilling.
IRELAND	A republic with a president, premier and an elective, two-house parliament.	Irish pound	English and Gaelic	Hay, potatoes, turnips, fodder, beets, sugar beets, oats, wheat, barley, cabbage, rye, flax; cattle, sheep, pigs, horses, poultry; fish; coal, peat, gypsum; tobacco, dairy products, foodstuffs, beer, malt, clothing, meats, textiles, boots and shoes, wood and paper products.
ISRAEL	Republic with president, prime minister, cabinet and elective unicameral legislature.	Israeli pound	Hebrew Arabic	Dairy products, vegetables, eggs, fruits, green fodder, wheat, hay, barley, corn, durra; goats, sheep, cattle, camels, poultry; fish; textiles, clothing, foods, beverages, tobacco, diamond polishing, shoes, metal and woodwork, furniture, building materials, leather, dairy products, electrical products, paper, printing, false teeth, pharmaceuticals, chemicals, dyes, soap, radios, oil refining, wines.
ITALY	A republic with a president, a two-house, elective legislature and an appointive cabinet.	lira	Italian	Wheat, corn, oats, sugar beets, potatoes, tomatoes, rice, olives, grapes, lemons and other fruits, hemp, tobacco, nuts; fish; sheep and goats, cattle, pigs, horses, donkeys; iron ore, sulphur, zinc, bauxite, lead, mercury, barite, copper, marble, manganese, lignite; textiles, chemicals, wines, automobiles and machinery, electrical goods, beet sugar, olive oil, cheese, clothing, processed foods.
IVORY COAST	West African republic with a legislative assembly.	French franc	Sudanese languages French	Coffee, cocoa, bananas, manioc, corn, rice, yams, kola, coconuts, palm oil, groundnuts, cotton, millet, tobacco; mahogany, caoutchouc; sheep, cattle, goats, pigs; gold, diamonds, manganese, iron ore, ilmenite.
JAMAICA	Independent member of the British Commonwealth of Nations.	Jamaican pound	English	Sugar cane, bananas, tobacco, coconuts, cacao, pimentoes, coffee, ginger; bauxite; honey; logwood; rum, textiles, cigars.
JAPAN	Constitutional monarchy with the executive power vested in prime minister and cabinet, the legislative power residing in a two-house parliament. The duties of the emperor are merely ceremonial.	yen	Japanese	Rice, wheat, barley, mulberry trees, potatoes, sweet potatoes, fruits, rape, vegetables, oats, tobacco, soy beans, tea, flax, hemp, camphor; timber, bamboo; horses, cattle, sheep, goats, pigs, rabbits; fish, agar, pearl oysters; silk worms; coal, pyrites, gold, copper, pyrethrum, manganese, silver, sulphur, chromite, zinc, salt, tin, lead, iron, petroleum; textiles, steel, paper, porcelain, earthenware, lacquer ware, vegetable oil, toys, slippers, shoes, machinery.
JORDAN	Constitutional monarchy with cabinet and bicameral legislature.	Jordan dinar	Arabic	Wheat, barley, legumes, vegetables, fruits, olives; sheep, goats, camels; salt, phosphate, potash; wool, tobacco products, flour milling, building materials, olive oil.
KENYA	Independent member of the British Commonwealth, headed by a president, a prime minister and a bicameral legislature.	East African shilling	Swahili English Sudanese Hamitic Bantu	Sisal, wheat, tea, coffee, pyrethrum, cotton, corn, sugar cane, sesame, groundnuts, wattle; hides and skins; sodium carbonate, gold, kyanite, salt, silver, lime, bags, butter, sugar, sisal products.
KOREA	Divided into two parts by Armistice Line of August, 1953, pending final decisions of peace treaty. Communist "people's republic" in North Korea; South Korea headed by a president, a prime minister, a cabinet and a bicameral legislature.	hwan	Korean	Rice, barley, millet, wheat, soya beans, red beans, cotton, tobacco, hemp, ginseng, fruit, radishes; timber; draft cattle, pigs, horses, mules, donkeys, sheep, goats, rabbits; fish; gold, iron ore, coal, tungsten, copper, silver, graphite, salt, kaolin, talc, bismuth, flourite, minerals (N. Korea), textiles, fertilizer, chemicals, cement, heavy industries (N. Korea); textiles, cement, tobacco, silkworms, chemicals, machinery, metal, rubber, wood, paper and tobacco products (S. Korea).
KUWAIT	Constitutional sheikhdom, with a Sheikh, a cabinet and a unicameral national assembly.	Kuwaiti dinar	Arabic	Petroleum, shipbuilding (dhows), pearls, skins, wool.
LAOS	Constitutional monarchy with a cabinet and a national assembly.	kip	Khmer (Annamese) Lao	Rice, coffee, tea, citrus fruits, corn, cinchona, gum, benzoin, cardamon; stick-lac; teak; tin.
LEBANON	Independent republic governed by a president, cabinet and an elective legislature.	Lebanese pound	Arabic French	Wheat, barley, corn, potatoes, citrus and other fruits, onions, olives, tobacco (Latakia); goats, asses, cattle, buffalo, sheep, horses, mules; iron, lignite; textiles, cement, olive oil, tobacco products, soap, matches, petroleum refining, gasoline, leather.
LIBERIA	Republic with president, cabinet, senate and house of representatives.	Liberian dollar	English Sudanese languages	Rubber, rice, coffee, cassava, sugar cane, cacao, palm oil and kernels, piassava, groundnuts; rum; iron ore.
LIBYA	A kingdom with a prime minister, a cabinet and a bicameral legislature.	Libyan pound	Arabic	Barley, wheat, olives, grapes, dates, almonds, figs, tobacco, esparto; goats, sheep, camels, cattle, donkeys, mules and horses; sponge and tuna fishing; matting, carpets, leather articles, embroidered fabrics.
LIECHTENSTEIN	A principality headed by a prince and an elective, one-house legislature.	Swiss franc	German	Grain, fruit, grapes, wood; cattle, pigs, chickens; cotton textiles, wine, leather, false teeth, pottery, wood-carving.
LUXEMBOURG	A grand duchy and hereditary, constitutional monarchy with an elective chamber of deputies and appointive minister of state and cabinet.	Luxembourg franc	Mosel-frankisch (German dialect)	Oats, potatoes, wheat, rye, grapes; livestock; iron ore, slate, gypsum, sand and gravel; iron, steel and metal working; chemicals, non-metallic minerals, beverages, tobacco, leather, wines, dairy products, quarrying.
MACAO	Portuguese overseas province ruled by a governor.	pataca	Chinese Portuguese	Fish; preserves, firecrackers, vegetable oil, cement, metal work, lumber, tobacco (processed), matches, wine.
MALAGASY REPUBLIC	Independent republic. Member of the French Community.	French franc	French Malagasy and Bantu languages	Cassava, rice, corn, potatoes, coffee, sugar cane, haricot beans, groundnuts, sisal, castor oil, tobacco, raffia; cattle, pigs, goats, sheep; graphite, mica, gold, rock crystal, corundum, phosphates, agate; textiles, sugar and rice factories, tapioca.
MALAWI	An indepedent member of the British Commonwealth, with a prime minister, a cabinet and a unicameral legislature.	Malawi pound	Bantu languages English	Tobacco, tea, cotton, pulses, tung oil, sisal, corn, cassava, wheat, rice, millet, groundnuts, rubber, beeswax, timber; goats, cattle, pigs, sheep; hides, skins, meat, ghee, soap; gold, mica, corundum.

POLITICAL DIVISION	GOVERNMENT	MONETARY UNIT	LANGUAGE	MAJOR PRODUCTS
IRAN	Constitutional monarchy governed by a shah, prime minister, cabinet and a bicameral legislature.	rial	Persian Arabic Kurdish	Wheat, cotton, gums, opium, fruit, rice, barley, sugar beets, tobacco, tea, corn, millet, legumes, vegetables, nuts; sheep, goats, cattle, asses, horses, mules; fish; petroleum oil, red oxide, copper, sulphur, arsenic, coal, salt, marble, nickel, manganese, lead, cobalt, turquoise, iron ore; carpets, rugs, textiles, leather, glass, matches, chemicals, jute, tobacco products, oil refining, casings, wood, oils.
IRAQ	Independent republic.	dinar	Arabic Turkish Kurdish	Dates, other fruits, barley, wheat, rice, tobacco, cotton, beans, corn, sorghum, sesame; sheep, goats, asses, camels, horses, buffalo; oil, salt, wool, textiles, cigarettes, distilling.
IRELAND	A republic with a president, premier and an elective, two-house parliament.	pound	English and Gaelic	Hay, potatoes, turnips, fodder, beets, sugar beets, oats, wheat, barley, cabbage, rye, flax; cattle, sheep, pigs, horses, poultry; fish; coal, peat, gypsum; tobacco, dairy products, foodstuffs, beer, malt, clothing, meats, textiles, boots and shoes, wood and paper products.
ISRAEL	Republic with president, prime minister, cabinet and elective unicameral legislature.	Israeli pound	Hebrew Arabic	Dairy products, vegetables, eggs, fruits, green fodder, wheat, hay, barley, corn, durra; goats, sheep, cattle, camels, poultry; fish; textiles, clothing, foods, beverages, tobacco, diamond polishing, shoes, metal and woodwork, furniture, building materials, leather, dairy products, electrical products, paper, printing, false teeth, pharmaceuticals, chemicals, dyes, soap, radios, oil refining, wines.
ITALY	A republic with a president, a two-house, elective legislature and an appointive cabinet.	lira	Italian	Wheat, corn, oats, sugar beets, potatoes, tomatoes, rice, olives, grapes, lemons and other fruits, hemp, tobacco, nuts; fish; sheep and goats, cattle, pigs, horses, donkeys; iron ore, sulphur, zinc, bauxite, lead, mercury, barite, copper, marble, manganese, lignite; textiles, chemicals, wines, automobiles and machinery, electrical goods, beet sugar, olive oil, cheese, clothing, processed foods.
IVORY COAST	West African republic with a legislative assembly.	franc	Sudanese languages French	Coffee, cocoa, bananas, manioc, corn, rice, yams, kola, coconuts, palm oil, groundnuts, cotton, millet, tobacco; mahogany, caoutchouc; sheep, cattle, goats, pigs; gold, diamonds, manganese, iron ore, ilmenite.
JAMAICA	Independent member of the British Commonwealth of Nations.	pound	English	Sugar cane, bananas, tobacco, coconuts, cacao, pimentoes, coffee, ginger; bauxite; honey; logwood; rum, textiles, cigars.
JAPAN	Constitutional monarchy with the executive power vested in prime minister and cabinet, the legislative power residing in a two-house parliament. The duties of the emperor are merely ceremonial.	yen	Japanese	Rice, wheat, barley, mulberry trees, potatoes, sweet potatoes, fruits, rape, vegetables, oats, tobacco, soy beans, tea, flax, hemp, camphor; timber, bamboo; horses, cattle, sheep, goats, pigs, rabbits; fish, agar, pearl oysters; silk worms; coal, pyrites, gold, copper, pyrethrum, manganese, silver, sulphur, chromite, zinc, salt, tin, lead, iron, petroleum; textiles, steel, paper, porcelain, earthenware, lacquer ware, vegetable oil, toys, slippers, shoes, machinery.
JORDAN	Constitutional monarchy with cabinet and bicameral legislature.	Jordan dinar	Arabic	Wheat, barley, legumes, vegetables, fruits, olives; sheep, goats, camels; salt, phosphate, potash; wool, tobacco products, flour milling, building materials, olive oil.
KENYA	Colony and protectorate of Great Britain with a governor, a council of ministers, an appointive executive and a partly elective legislative council.	East African shilling	Swahili English Sudanese Hamitic Bantu	Sisal, wheat, tea, coffee, pyrethrum, cotton, corn, sugar cane, sesame, groundnuts, wattle; hides and skins; sodium carbonate, gold, kyanite, salt, silver, lime, bags, butter, sugar, sisal products.
KOREA	Divided into two parts by Armistice Line of August, 1953, pending final decisions of peace treaty. Communist "people's republic" in North Korea; South Korea headed by a president, a prime minister, a cabinet and a bicameral legislature.	hwan	Korean	Rice, barley, millet, wheat, soya beans, red beans, cotton, tobacco, hemp, ginseng, fruit, radishes; timber; draft cattle, pigs, horses, mules, donkeys, sheep, goats, rabbits; fish; gold, iron ore, coal, tungsten, copper, silver, graphite, salt, kaolin, talc, bismuth, flourite, minerals (N. Korea), textiles, fertilizer, chemicals, cement, heavy industries (N. Korea); textiles, cement, tobacco, silkworms, chemicals, machinery, metal, rubber, wood, paper and tobacco products (S. Korea).
KUWAIT	An independent and sovereign state on the Persian Gulf, ruled by an hereditary sheikh.	Kuwaiti dinar	Arabic	Petroleum, shipbuilding (dhows), pearls, skins, wool.
LAOS	Constitutional monarchy with a cabinet and a national assembly.	kip	Khmer (Annamese) Lao	Rice, coffee, tea, citrus fruits, corn, cinchona, gum, benzoin, cardamon; stick-lac; teak; tin.
LEBANON	Independent republic governed by a president, cabinet and an elective legislature.	Lebanese pound	Arabic French	Wheat, barley, corn, potatoes, citrus and other fruits, onions, olives, tobacco (Latakia); goats, asses, cattle, buffalo, sheep, horses, mules; iron, lignite; textiles, cement, olive oil, tobacco products, soap, matches, petroleum refining, gasoline, leather.
LIBERIA	Republic with president, cabinet, senate and house of representatives.	dollar	English Sudanese languages	Rubber, rice, coffee, cassava, sugar cane, cacao, palm oil and kernels, piassava, groundnuts; rum; iron ore.
LIBYA	A federal kingdom with a bicameral legislature, constituted under U. N. auspices and comprising the three provinces of Cyrenaica, Tripolitania and the Fezzan.	Libyan pound	Arabic	Barley, wheat, olives, grapes, dates, almonds, figs, tobacco, esparto; goats, sheep, camels, cattle, donkeys, mules and horses; sponge and tuna fishing; matting, carpets, leather articles, embroidered fabrics.
LIECHTENSTEIN	A principality headed by a prince and an elective, one-house legislature.	Swiss franc	German	Grain, fruit, grapes, wood; cattle, pigs, chickens; cotton textiles, wine, leather, false teeth, pottery, wood-carving.
LUXEMBOURG	A grand duchy and hereditary, constitutional monarchy with an elective chamber of deputies and appointive minister of state and cabinet.	franc	Mosel-frankisch (German dialect)	Oats, potatoes, wheat, rye, grapes; livestock; iron ore, slate, gypsum, sand and gravel; iron, steel and metal working; chemicals, non-metallic minerals, beverages, tobacco, leather, wines, dairy products, quarrying.
MACAO	Portuguese overseas province ruled by a governor.	pataca	Chinese Portuguese	Fish; preserves, firecrackers, vegetable oil, cement, metal work, lumber, tobacco (processed), matches, wine.
MALAGASY REPUBLIC	Independent republic. Member of the French Community.	franc	French Malagasy and Bantu languages	Cassava, rice, corn, potatoes, coffee, sugar cane, haricot beans, groundnuts, sisal, castor oil, tobacco, raffia; cattle, pigs, goats, sheep; graphite, mica, gold, rock crystal, corundum, phosphates, agate; textiles, sugar and rice factories, tapioca.

POLITICAL DIVISION	GOVERNMENT	MONETARY UNIT	LANGUAGE	MAJOR PRODUCTS
MALAYSIA, FEDERATION OF	Independent federation of the British Commonwealth, with a head of state, a council of rulers, a bicameral legislature and 14 state assemblies.	Malayan dollar	Malay Chinese English Indonesian languages Hindi	Rubber, rice, coconuts, coffee, pineapples, tapioca, pepper, sugar, tobacco, fibers, gambier, vegetables, tea; buffalo, swine, oxen, goats, sheep; fish; tin, coal, iron ore, bauxite, petroleum, antimony, manganese, copra, palm oil, timber, gold, rubber products, canning, shipping, milling, bricks, gasoline, wood products, textiles.
MALDIVE ISLANDS	An independent sultanate, with a bicameral legislature advised by the high commissioner in Ceylon.	Celanese rupee	Singhalese Arabic Dravidian	Coconuts, copra, coir, fruit, nuts; fish, cowries; cloth, mats, boats.
MALI	West African republic with a legislative assembly.	French franc	Sudanese and Hamitic languages Arabic French	Millet, rice, groundnuts, corn, sweet potatoes, cotton, manioc, tobacco, karite, shea nuts, yams, kopak, sisal; cattle, goats, sheep, horses, asses, camels; hides and skins; pottery, bricks, jewelry, weaving, leather, rice mills, soap.
MALTA	An independent member of the British Commonwealth, with a prime minister, a cabinet and a unicameral legislature.	Maltese pound	Maltese and English	Wheat, barley, potatoes, onions, grapes and other fruits, cumin seed, cotton; goats, sheep, pigs, cattle; fish; lace, filigree, wine, footwear, beer, cigarettes, buttons, pipes, gloves.
MARIANA ISLANDS	A group of islands in the United States trust Territory of the Pacific administered by a high commissioner.	American dollar	Micronesian dialects Spanish	Fruits, corn, sweet potatoes, vegetables, breadfruit, cacao; fish; phosphates.
MARQUESAS ISLANDS	A group of islands in French Polynesia administered from Tahiti.	French franc	Marquesan French	Bananas, breadfruit, yams, bamboo, coconuts, sugar cane.
MARSHALL ISLANDS	A group of islands in the United States trust Territory of the Pacific administered by a high commissioner.	American dollar	Micronesian dialects	Arrowroot, breadfruit, coconuts, pandanus, taro, vegetables, copra, bananas; poultry, pigs; fish.
MARTINIQUE	Overseas department of France with a prefect and elective general council.	French franc	Creole, French	Sugar cane, cocoa, pineapples, bananas, coffee; rum, sugar.
MAURITANIA	West African republic within the French Community with a legislative assembly.	French franc	Arabic Hamitic and Sudanese languages French	Millet, gum, dates, corn, watermelons, wheat, henna; sheep and goats, cattle, camels, asses, horses; hides and skins; salt.
MAURITIUS	British colony ruled by a governor, an executive council and a legislative council.	Mauritius rupee	English Hindustani French	Sugar, aloe fiber, rice, vanilla beans, hemp, sisal, groundnuts, tea, yams, manioc, pineapples, tobacco, coconuts; alcohol, molasses, rum, copra.
MEXICO	Federative republic with a president, council of ministers and a two-house legislature.	Mexican peso	Spanish	Corn, wheat, beans, chick peas, sugar bananas, barley, cotton, coffee, vegetables; cattle; henequen; fish; silver, petroleum, lead, gold, zinc, copper; textiles, sugar, alcohol, foundry products.
MONACO	A principality. The prince's authority exercised through a state ministry and 3 government counsellors. The one-house legislative body is elective.	French franc	French	Principal revenue derived from Monte Carlo gambling casino. Tobacco, postage stamps, perfume, liqueurs, olive oil, oranges.
MONGOLIA	Communist republic, whose prime minister is also head of Communist party politburo, which is the actual ruler.	tugrik	Mongolian Russian	Stock raising (sheep, goats, cattle, horses, camels); milk, butter, cheese; wool, hides, skins, horns, bricks, machinery; coal, lead, gold.
MOROCCO	Constitutional monarchy with an appointed cabinet and a bicameral elected parliament.	dirham	Arabic Berber French	Wheat, barley, olives, almonds, citrus fruits, dates, beans, grapes, vegetables, linseed; cork, cedar; sheep, goats, cattle, asses, camels, horses, mules, pigs; fish; phosphate, iron ore, anthracite, manganese, lead, zinc, cobalt, copper, antimony; leather, carpets.
MOZAMBIQUE	Portuguese overseas province ruled by a governor and a government council.	Portuguese escudo	Bantu languages Portuguese	Sugar, corn, cotton, copra, sisal, cashew nuts, bananas, coffee, kapok, sorghum, manioc, beeswax, tea, tobacco, vegetable oils; mangrove bark; timber; oxen, goats, pigs, sheep, cattle; gold, silver, asbestos, uranium, bauxite, samerskite.
MUSCAT AND OMAN	An independent sultanate.	rupee (official) Maria Theresa dollar	Arabic	Dates, pomegranates, limes and other fruits, sugar cane; dried fish.
NEPAL	An independent kingdom governed by a maharaja, prime minister and a national council acting as a unicameral elected legislature.	Nepalese rupee	Indo-Aryan languages Tibetan	Rice, grains, jute, sugar cane, tea, vegetables, tobacco, cotton, potatoes, medicinal herbs; timber; cattle, hides, skins, ghee; iron, coal, copper, lead, zinc; cotton cloth, pottery, paper.
NETHERLANDS	A constitutional, hereditary monarchy governed by the queen, her ministers and a two-house legislature, partly elective and partly chosen by provincial councils.	guilder	Dutch	Potatoes, sugar beets, rye, wheat, oats, barley, flax, legumes, flower bulbs, seeds, vegetables, fruit; cattle, pigs, sheep, horses, poultry; fish; coal, petroleum, salt; leather, rubber, footwear; metal products, textiles, paper, building materials, chemicals, foods and beverages, clothing, shipbuilding, cheese and other dairy products, fertilizers, ceramics, cement, tobacco products.
NEW CALEDONIA	French overseas territory administered by high commissioner assisted by an appointive executive council and an elective general council.	French franc	Melanesian dialects French	Coconuts, copra, coffee, cotton, manioc, corn, tobacco, bananas, pineapples, wheat, rice, kauri logs; cattle, pigs, horses, goats, sheep, hides; guano, trochus shell; nickel, chrome, manganese, iron, cobalt, copper, lead, platinum; canned meat.
NEW GUINEA, TERR. OF	Trust territory of Australia governed by administrator of Papua.	Australian pound	Papuan Pidgin English English	Coconuts, copra, cocoa, dairying; timber; gold, silver, platinum; boat making.
NEW HEBRIDES	British and French condominium administered by British and French resident commissioners, with a partly elected advisory council.	Australian currency Bank of Indo-china Notes	Melanesian dialects Pidgin English English French	Coconuts, copra, cocoa, coffee, yams, taro, manioc, fruits; kauri pine; cattle, pigs; trochus shells.

POLITICAL DIVISION	GOVERNMENT	MONETARY UNIT	LANGUAGE	MAJOR PRODUCTS
NEW ZEALAND	An independent member of the British Commonwealth governed by a governor-general, a prime minister, a cabinet and a unicameral assembly.	New Zealand pound	English Maori	Wheat, oats, barley, seeds, kauri, gum; sheep, cattle, pigs, horses; hides, skins; fish; gold, silver, coal, copper, limestone, manganese, iron, tungsten; dairy products, meats, wool, clothing, lumber, woodwork, furniture, electrical and radio goods, motor assembly, printing, publishing, biscuits, confections, footwear, rubber products, chemical fertilizers, tobacco products, brewing.
NICARAGUA	Republic with a president, cabinet and a two-house legislature.	córdoba	Spanish	Coffee, sugar cane, sesame, corn, bananas, rice, cacao, cotton, beans; cattle; hardwoods; gold, silver; sugar, wood products.
NIGER	West African republic with a legislative assembly.	French franc	Sudanese Hamitic Arabic French	Millet, manioc, groundnuts, rice, wheat, cotton, gum arabic, kapok, kidney beans, corn, onions, sorghum, dates, sugar cane; goats, sheep, cattle, asses, camels, horses; hides and skins, leather; natron, sodium sulphate, salt.
NIGERIA	Independent federal republic within British Commonwealth with a president, cabinet and a bicameral central legislature.	West African pound	Sudanese languages Arabic English	Palm oil and kernels, cacao, groundnuts, cotton, rubber, bananas, benni seeds, shea nuts, yams, cassava, corn, rice, fruits, millet, coffee; cattle, sheep, goats; hides and skins; timber; tin, coal, columbite, lead, gold, silver, zinc; cigarettes, soap, sugar.
NIUE	Dependency of New Zealand administered by a resident commissioner.	New Zealand pound	Mixed Melanesian and Polynesian dialects English	Copra, sweet potatoes, bananas; hats, baskets.
NORFOLK ISLAND	An Australian territory governed by an administrator.	Australian pound	English	Citrus, passion fruits, bananas, cherry guavas; hides; fish.
NORTHERN IRELAND	Executive power vested in appointed governor and cabinet responsible to legislative two-house parliament.	pound sterling	English and Gaelic	Potatoes, oats, flax, turnips, hay; cattle, sheep, pigs, poultry; basalt and igneous rocks, sand and gravel, grit and conglomerate, chalk, clays; linen, rayon, woolen goods, carpets, hosiery, cotton goods, shirts, collars, shipbuilding, aircraft, marine machinery, rope, tobacco, whiskey.
NORWAY	A constitutional, hereditary monarchy headed by the king, his council of state and a two-house, elective legislature.	krone (crown)	Norwegian	Hay, potatoes, oats, barley, wheat, rye, fruits, vegetables; dairy products, livestock; herring, cod and other fish; sulphur, iron, copper, zinc, silver, nickel, molybdenum; timber, pulp, cellulose, paper, canned foods, electro-chemical products, transportation equipment, salted, dried and canned fish, leather, basic metals, textiles, fertilizers, shipbuilding.
PAKISTAN	Self-governing republic within the British Commonwealth ruled by a president, cabinet and unicameral legislature.	Pakistani rupee	Indo-Aryan languages (Urdu, Bengali, Punjabi, etc.)	Rice, wheat, corn, jute, cotton, sugar cane, fruit, oilseeds, tobacco, tea, fibers; timber; cattle, goats, sheep, horses, camels, poultry; hides, skins, wool; fish; salt, copper, petroleum, chromite, gypsum, magnisite, sulphur, antimony; textiles, flour milling, cement, iron and steel foundries, sugar, leather, chemicals, glass, sportsgoods, handicrafts, surgical instruments.
PALAU ISLANDS	A civil administrative district in the Western Carolines and part of the United States trust Territory of the Pacific Islands, with locally elected native councils.	American dollar	Micronesian dialects	Coconuts, manioc, taro, pineapples, sweet potatoes, papayas; poultry, pigs, goats; fish; phosphate; handcrafts.
PANAMA	A constitutional republic with a president, two vice-presidents, a cabinet of ministers and a one-house legislature.	balboa	Spanish	Bananas, cacao, abaca, coconuts, rice, sugar cane, coffee, pineapples; cattle; hardwoods; gold; hides, sugar, wood products.
PAPUA TERRITORY	Australian territory governed by an administrator and a house of assembly.	Australian pound	Papuan Pidgin English English	Coconuts, rubber, sweet potatoes, yams, taro, sago, rice, bananas, coffee, kapok, bamboo, sisal hemp, copra; shells, sponges; cattle, goats, poultry; gold, copper, manganese.
PARAGUAY	A centralized republic with a president, an appointed cabinet and a one-house legislature.	guaraní	Spanish, Indian	Cotton, tobacco, sugar cane, rice, cassava, yerba maté, corn, citrus fruits; cattle, hides; lumber, quebracho; iron, manganese, copper; canned meats, vegetable oils, petit-grain oil, tobacco products.
PERU	A republic with a president, two vice-presidents, appointive cabinet and a two-house legislature.	sol	Spanish, Indian	Cotton, sugar, potatoes, barley, corn, rice, wheat, coca, quinoa, cacao, tobacco, coffee, quinine, flax, rubber, balata, guano; fish; livestock; petroleum, lead, zinc, copper, silver, gold, vanadium; textiles, foodstuffs, cement, leather, wool, hides, pharmaceuticals, paper products, clothing, metal.
PHILIPPINES	Republic governed by a president, cabinet and a bicameral legislature.	Philippine peso	Malayan languages (Tagalog, Visayan, etc.) English Spanish	Rice, sugar cane, copra, manila hemp (abacá), corn, tobacco, maguey, rubber, bananas, pineapples, mangoes, papaya, citrus fruits, other fruits; hogs, carabaos, cattle, horses, goats, sheep; fish; timber, gum resins, tan and dye barks, dye woods; gold, iron, copper, chromite, silver, manganese, asbestos, asphalt, guano, silica, coal, petroleum; sugar, textiles, distilling, dessicated coconuts, tobacco products, rice milling, cocoa, coconut oil, embroideries.
PITCAIRN ISLANDS	British colony administered by a chief magistrate responsible to the governor of Fiji.	Fiji pound	English Tahitian	Fruits, vegetables, goats, poultry; handicraft.
POLAND	A Soviet-type "People's Republic" headed by a one-party legislative Sejm which elects an executive Council of Ministers. Actual power in the hands of politburo, highest organ of Communist party.	zloty	Polish	Potatoes, straw and hay, rye, sugar beets, mangolds, oats, barley, wheat, peas, beans, flax, hemp, rapeseed; livestock; fish; zinc, lead, coal, salt, iron ore, petroleum, natural gas, phosphates, lignite; iron and steel products, coke, foods and beverages, textiles, cement, lime, bricks, electrical goods, chemicals, wood, timber, paper, cellulose, leather and leather products, glass.
PORTUGAL	A "unitary corporative republic" with a president, premier, and a one-house elective legislature.	escudo	Portuguese	Wheat, corn, oats, barley, rye, rice, French beans, potatoes, grapes, olives; livestock; cork, lumber, resin; sardines, tuna and other fish; copper pyrites, coal, copper, tin, kaolin, cement, wolfram, sulphur, tungsten, iron; wines, olive oil, canned sardines, textiles, porcelain, tiles, embroideries, lace.

POLITICAL DIVISION	GOVERNMENT	MONETARY UNIT	LANGUAGE	MAJOR PRODUCTS
PUERTO RICO	A self-governing commonwealth associated with the United States, with a governor, an executive council and a bicameral legislature.	American dollar	Spanish, English	Sugar cane, tobacco, fruits, pineapples, grapefruit, coconuts, coffee, cotton, livestock, vegetables; molasses, embroideries, rum, canned fruit and juice, alcohol, cordials, tobacco products.
QATAR	British protected Sheikhdom.	rupee; riyal	Arabic	Dates; pearl fishing, dried fish; camels; petroleum.
RÉUNION	French overseas department administered by a prefect.	French franc	French	Sugar, rum, vanilla, tapioca, essences, fruit and vegetable preserves.
RHODESIA	A self-governing state and member of Br. Commonwealth with governor and elective executive and legislative councils.	Rhodesian pound	Bantu languages English	Corn, tobacco, groundnuts, wheat, potatoes, citrus and other fruits; cattle, sheep, pigs, goats; meats, hides; gold, asbestos, chromite, coal; footwear, apparel, cigarettes, flour, groundnut oil, wood products.
RÍO MUNI	Internally autonomous Spanish province ruled by a governor.	Spanish peseta	Bantu languages Spanish	Cocoa, coffee, palm oil and kernels; cabinet woods.
RUMANIA	A Soviet-type "People's Republic" with a 17-member State Council, cabinet of ministers and a one-house legislature. Supreme power resides in Communist party polit-buro.	leu	Rumanian	Wheat, barley, rye, corn, oats, potatoes, sugar beets, hemp, flax, grapes, fruits, tobacco; lumber; sheep, cattle, pigs, horses; petroleum, natural gas, salt, coal, lignite, iron and copper ores, gold, silver, bauxite, lead, manganese, zinc; flour, brewing and distilling, iron and steel, metal products, textiles, wood and paper products.
RWANDA	An independent republic with a president, a council of ministers and a legislative assembly.	Belgian franc	Bantu languages Flemish French	Foods; cattle; hides.
RYUKYU IS.	Administered by the United States.	American dollar	Luchuan Japanese English	Sweet potatoes, sugar cane, rice, fruits, mulberries; swine, cattle, goats, horses, poultry; silkworms; fish; Panama hats, textiles, lacquer, pottery, china, glassware, tiles, plywood.
SABAH	State in the Federation of Malaysia, with a head of state, a cabinet and a unicameral legislature.	Malayan dollar	Malay Indonesian languages English Chinese	Rubber, coconuts, copra, tobacco, manila hemp, sago, rice, cutch, sugar, pepper, kapok, groundnuts, derris root, vegetables, timber, fish.
ST. HELENA	British colony with a governor, executive and advisory councils.	pound sterling	English	Hemp, lily bulbs, potatoes, tow, rope and twine, lace; sheep, goats, cattle, donkeys, poultry.
ST. PIERRE AND MIQUELON	French overseas territory with a governor and a general council.	French franc	French	Fish, silver fox; dried cod and cod liver oil; sienna earth, yellow ocher.
SALVADOR, EL	Republic with a president and a one-house legislature.	colón	Spanish	Coffee, cotton, corn, tobacco, henequen, sugar cane, rice; balsam and other woods; gold, silver; cotton textiles, henequen bags, sugar.
SAMOA, AMERICAN	U.S. territory with a governor and a bicameral legislature.	American dollar	English Samoan	Copra, taro, breadfruit, yams, bananas, arrowroot, pineapples, oranges; mats.
SAMOA, WESTERN	Independent member of the British Commonwealth of Nations.	New Zealand pound	Samoan English	Copra, cocoa beans, bananas, taro; fish; pigs, poultry.
SAN MARINO	Republic with two regents, council of state, one-house legislature.	lira	Italian	Cattle, hides, wines, quarrying.
SÃO TOMÉ AND PRÍNCIPE	Portuguese overseas province administered by a governor.	Portuguese escudo	Bantu languages Portuguese	Cacao, coffee, coconuts, copra, palm oil, cinchona, bananas.
SARAWAK	State in the Federation of Malaysia, with a governor, a chief minister, a cabinet and a unicameral legislature.	Malayan dollar	Malay Indonesian languages Chinese English	Rice, rubber, sago, pepper, coconuts, pineapples, tobacco, coffee, fruits, vegetables; timber, rattan canes, guttas; buffalo, cattle, pigs, goats; fish; petroleum, gold, antimony, phosphates, cutch.
SAUDI ARABIA	Absolute monarchy, with premier and cabinet responsible to the king and advisory councils.	riyal	Arabic	Dates, sorghum, wheat, rice, henna, coffee, fruits, nuts, vegetables, honey, gum, sesame oil; fish; camels, sheep, goats, cattle, donkeys, poultry, horses; hides, wool, clarified butter, charcoal, pottery, tile, salt, soap, weaving; petroleum, gold, pearls.
SCOTLAND	A secretary of state for Scotland in the British cabinet has in his charge four departments for Scotland (agriculture, education, health and home.) Authority in other matters is exercised by other members of the British cabinet.	pound sterling	English and Gaelic	Turnips, potatoes, wheat, barley, sugar beets, flax, vegetables, forage crops, fruits; sheep, cattle, pigs, horses; coal, iron ore, granite, sandstone, limestone, slate, lead, clay; steel, machinery, tools, locomotives, electronic equipment, linoleum, shipbuilding and repair, watches, clocks, jute, bagging, burlap, textiles, hosiery, thread, lace, carpet, yarn, chemicals, whiskey, ale, paper, bricks and other clay products, preserves, boots and shoes, furniture.
SENEGAL	West African republic within the French Community with a president and an elected legislative assembly.	French franc	Sudanese languages Arabic French	Millet, groundnuts, manioc, rice, corn, gum arabic, palm nuts, honey, sweet potatoes, sisal, indigo; sheep, goats, cattle, asses, horses; fish; titanium, zircon; brick, pottery, weaving, jewelry, oil cakes.
SEYCHELLES	A British colony ruled by a governor and councils.	Seychelles rupee	English French	Coconuts, cinnamon, patchouli, copra, vanilla, corn; guano; salted fish, tortoise shell, calipee.
SIERRA LEONE	Independent Commonwealth member, with prime minister and a unicameral legislature.	leone	Sudanese languages English	Palm oil and kernels, kola nuts, ginger, piassava, groundnuts, cocoa; diamonds, iron ore, chrome ore.
SINGAPORE	State in the Federation of Malaysia, with a head of state, a prime minister, a cabinet and a unicameral legislature.	Malayan dollar	Chinese Malay Hindi English	Rubber, coconuts, fruits, vegetables, rice, coffee, tapioca, tobacco, sweet potatoes, pepper, pineapples; pigs, poultry, cattle; fish; tin; tin smelting, rubber milling, coconut milling, soap, beer, pineapple canning, biscuits, brick making, shipping, textiles, palm oil, cigarettes, gasoline, kerosene.
SOCIETY ISLANDS	Part of French Polynesia governed from Tahiti.	French franc	Polynesian French	Copra, vanilla, pearls, mother of pearl, vanilla, phosphates, sugar, rum.
SOLOMON ISLANDS	British protectorate, with appointed legislative and executive councils.	Australian pound	Melanesian Pidgin English English	Copra, pigs, poultry; trochus shell, turtle shell, bêche-de-mer.

POLITICAL DIVISION	GOVERNMENT	MONETARY UNIT	LANGUAGE	MAJOR PRODUCTS
SOMALI REPUBLIC	Independent republic with a prime minister, a parliament and territorial assemblies.	Somali shilling	Somali Arabic Italian	Sugar, cotton, tobacco, bananas, aromatic gums, resin, kapok, grains, beans; camels, goats, sheep, cattle; skins, hides; tunny, mother-of-pearl.
SOMALILAND, FRENCH	Overseas territory of France with a governor and an elective representative assembly.	Djibouti franc	Hamitic languages Arabic French	Boats, sheep; salt.
SOUTH AFRICA	A republic with president, prime minister, cabinet, elective senate and house of assembly.	rand	Afrikaans English Bantu languages Bushman	Corn, wheat, potatoes, oats, kaffir-corn, barley, tobacco, sugar cane, tea, citrus fruits, rye, groundnuts, grapes, pineapples; cattle, sheep, goats, pigs, horses, donkeys, mules; gold, coal, diamonds, copper, asbestos, manganese, lime, limestone, platinum, chrome, iron, silver, tungsten, mercury, vanadium, tin, antimony, silver, scheelite, talc; hides, chemicals, wool, footwear, rubber, machinery, clothing, textiles, food, vehicles, printing, furniture, building materials.
SOUTH ARABIA	British protectorate and federation, under a high commissioner and a supreme council, respectively.	East African shilling	Arabic	Dates, gums, tobacco, salt, fish oil, butter; wheat, barley, sesame, millet, sorghum, aloes, ghee; goats, sheep, camels, cattle; dhow building, ship bunkering.
SPAIN	A nominal monarchy governed by a chief of state. The legislative Cortés prepares laws subject to the veto of the chief of state. A king is to be chosen by a regency council upon the death or incapacitation of the present chief of state.	peseta	Spanish Catalan	Wheat, barley, potatoes, oranges, olives, oats, rye, rice, corn, peas, beans, grapes, onions, sugar beets, esparto, flax, hemp, pulse, cork, nuts; pigs, sheep, goats, donkeys, mules, horses, poultry; sardines, tuna, cod and other fish; coal, lignite, iron ore, lead, iron pyrites, potash, zinc, mercury, sulphur, copper; textiles, wines, olive oil, paper, cement, hides, preserved and canned fish and shellfish, paper.
SPANISH SAHARA	Spanish province with a high commissioner, a cabinet and a general assembly.	Spanish peseta	Arabic Spanish	Barley, corn; goats, sheep, camels; fish.
SUDAN	A republic with a bicameral parliament and council of ministers. Executive power resides temporarily in a council of state.	Sudanese pound	Arabic Sudanese Hamitic languages English	Cotton, cotton seed, gum arabic, Senna leaves and pods, groundnuts, sesame, millet, dates, dom nuts (vegetable ivory), wheat, shea nuts; sheep, goats, cattle, camels, asses; mahogany; hides and skins, ivory, gold, salt, trochus shell, mother-of-pearl.
SURINAM	Self-governing part of the Netherlands Union with an appointed governor, an appointive council of ministers, an advisory council and an elective legislative body.	Dutch guilder	Dutch	Rice, citrus fruits, coconuts, coffee, bananas, sugar cane, cacao, balata, corn, tobacco; lumber; gold, bauxite; sugar, rum, plywood, molasses.
SWAZILAND	British protectorate governed by a resident commissioner and a legislative council.	pound sterling	Bantu languages English	Tobacco, corn, groundnuts, kaffir-corn, wheat, oats, rye, barley, fruits; cattle, goats, sheep, pigs; butter; hides, skins; asbestos, gold, tin.
SWEDEN	A constitutional hereditary monarchy with a prime minister, council of state and a two-house elective legislature.	krona (crown)	Swedish	Hay, sugar beets, potatoes, fodder crops, oats, wheat, rye, barley; forest products, cattle, pigs, sheep, horses, poultry; fish; iron ore, sulphur, arsenic, zinc, copper, silver, gold, lead, manganese; lumber and wood products, machinery, textiles, iron and steel and metal goods, chemicals, dairy products, electric power, tobacco products, brick, porcelain and glass, shipbuilding, matches.
SWITZERLAND	A republic with a president, vice-president, an executive federal council and a two-house, elective legislature.	Swiss franc	German French Italian Romansch	Wheat, potatoes, sugar beets, rye, oats, barley, fruits, tobacco; livestock; salt, iron, manganese; dairy products, textiles, watches and clocks, chemicals, foods, wines, dyes.
SYRIA	Independent republic.	Syrian pound	Arabic Turkish Kurdish	Wheat, barley, sorghum, corn, cotton, lentils, chickpeas, sesame, vegetables, olives, grapes, tobacco (Latikia); sheep, goats, cattle, donkeys, camels, horses, poultry; wool, hides, skins; gypsum; leather, textiles, food, tobacco, wine, flour.
TANZANIA	An independent united republic of the British Commonwealth, with a central parliament, a president and two vice-presidents. It was formed by the two former possessions of Tanganyika and Zanzibar.	East African shilling	Bantu languages Swahili English	Sisal, cotton, cloves, coffee, bananas, tobacco, papain, beeswax, grains, sugar; cattle, goats, sheep; hides, skins; wood, timber, wax, gum arabic; diamonds, gold, tin, mica, salt, camphor, tungsten.
THAILAND (SIAM)	Constitutional monarchy ruled by a king, prime minister and a legislative assembly.	baht	Thai Khmer	Rice, rubber, coconuts, tobacco, cotton, corn, beans; teak and other woods; bullocks, buffalo, horses, elephants; fish; tin, wolfram.
TIBET	Theocracy. Nominally independent but under effective Chinese Communist control.	sang	Tibetan	Barley, wheat, pulse, corn, vegetables, rice; yaks, asses, sheep, goats, donkeys; hides, wool, furs, musk; borax, salt, gold; cult objects.
TIMOR, PORTUGUESE	Portuguese overseas province ruled by a governor.	Portuguese escudo	Malay Portuguese	Coffee, copra, sandalwood, wax, cocoa; hides, shells.
TOGO	Independent republic.	French franc	Sudanese languages French	Palm oil and kernels, tapioca, cocoa, yams, coffee, plantains, corn, groundnuts, cotton, copra, kola, cassava, rubber; sheep, goats, pigs, cattle, asses, horses.
TOKELAU ISLANDS	An island territory of New Zealand governed by a high commissioner.	New Zealand pound	Samoan	Coconuts, fiber, taro, copra; pigs, chickens; fish; hats, mats.
TONGA	Constitutional monarchy ruled by queen with cabinet and legislative assembly, and advised by British Resident, with local autonomy.	Tongan pound	Tongan English	Copra, bananas, fungus, candlenuts; pigs, cattle, goats.
TRINIDAD AND TOBAGO	Independent member of the British Commonwealth.	B.W.I. dollar	English	Coffee, cocoa, sugar cane, citrus fruits; cattle; petroleum, asphalt; rum, canned grapefruit juice, sugar.
TRISTAN DA CUNHA	Possession of Great Britain governed by an administrator and an island council under St. Helena.	pound sterling	English	Potatoes, fruit; cattle, sheep; fish.

POLITICAL DIVISION	GOVERNMENT	MONETARY UNIT	LANGUAGE	MAJOR PRODUCTS
TRUCIAL OMAN	Seven sheikhdoms under British protection with a British agent.	rupee riyal	Arabic	Dates, grains, vegetables; fishing, pearl fishing.
TUNISIA	A republic with a president, a cabinet of secretaries of state, and an assembly.	Tunisian dinar	Arabic French Berber	Wheat, barley, oats, corn, sorghum, beans, grapes, olives, citrus fruits, dates, alfa grass, almonds, oranges, shaddocks, pistachios, cork; sheep, goats, cattle, horses, asses, mules, camels, pigs; fish, sponges; flour milling, oil refining, wool spinning, pottery, leather, silk weaving; phosphates, iron ore, lignite, lead, zinc.
TURKEY	A republic with a president and a two-house legislature.	Turkish pound (lira)	Turkish	Tobacco, cereals, olives, cotton, figs, nuts, fruits; cattle, livestock; fish; chromium, iron ore, copper, coal, lignite, meerschaum, manganese; textiles, iron and steel, paper, rugs, olive oil.
UGANDA	An independent member of the British Commonwealth with a president, cabinet and a unicameral legislature.	East African shilling	Bantu and Sudanese languages English	Cotton, coffee, plantains, millet, cotton seed, tobacco, chilies, sugar cane, rubber; cattle, sheep, goats; hides, skins; tin; cigarettes.
U.S.S.R.	A federation of 15 socialist republics with a two-chamber legislative assembly (Supreme Soviet) which elects the executive presidium and council of ministers. The policy of the state is largely defined by the Central Committee of the Communist party, the only legal party.	ruble	Russian, Ukrainian, White Russian, Uzbek, Tatar, Azerbaidzhani, Georgian, Lithuanian, Armenian, Yiddish, Latvian, Mordvinian, Chuvash, Tadzhik, Estonian, Kazakh, etc.	Wheat, rye, oats, barley, corn, sugar beets, sunflower seeds, cotton, forage crops, flax, hemp, potatoes, tobacco; cattle, sheep, goats, pigs, horses; lumber, furs; fish; coal, peat, petroleum, iron, lignite, copper, lead, zinc, nickel, aluminum, phosphates, manganese, gold, sulphur, potash, asbestos, platinum, salt, chromite; steel, machinery, textiles, sugar, flour, meats, automobiles, paper, synthetic rubber, foods, wines, chemicals.
UNITED ARAB REP.	See Egypt.			
UNITED STATES	Federal republic with a president, vice-president and two-house legislature (senate and house of representatives), and an appointed cabinet. It consists of 50 states, each with a governor and state legislature.	dollar	English	Corn, hay, tobacco, wheat, cotton, oats, soy beans, potatoes, barley, sorghums, peanuts, rye, rice, citrus fruits, fruits, sugar beets, sugar cane, vegetables, tree nuts, feed grains and hay; livestock; fish; lumber; petroleum, coal, cement, iron, natural gas, copper, sand and gravel, zinc, lead, stone, gold, silver, molybdenum, bauxite, phosphates, mica, sulphur; foods, transportation equipment, machinery, primary metal products, electrical machinery, textiles, chemicals, paper and wood products, beverages, dairy products.
UPPER VOLTA	West African republic with a legislative assembly.	French franc	Sudanese languages French	Millet, groundnuts, corn, karite nuts and butter (shea nut), vegetables, rice, tapes, cotton, kapok, sesame, sorghum, tea; sheep, goats, cattle, asses, pigs; gold, manganese, copper, silver, chrome, lignite, iron.
URUGUAY	A republic governed by a National Council, an appointed cabinet and a two-house elective legislature.	Uruguayan peso	Spanish	Wheat, corn, linseed, oats, sunflower seeds, peanuts, barley, rice, citrus fruits, peaches, grapes, vegetables, tobacco; sheep, cattle; gold; meat, hides, wool, textiles, leather, boots and shoes, wines.
VATICAN CITY	The Pope, who is elected for life by the cardinals of the Roman Catholic Church, exercises absolute legislative, executive and judicial power. He appoints a governor of the state and delegates diplomatic and judicial power.	Italian lira	Italian Latin	
VENEZUELA	A republic with a president, appointive cabinet, and elective two-house legislature.	bolívar	Spanish	Coffee, cacao, sugar cane, cotton, tobacco, coconuts, tonka beans, balata, dividivi, rubber; livestock; fish and pearls; petroleum, iron, gold, coal, copper, phosphates, magnesite, asphalt, salt, diamonds; textiles, leather, sugar, cement, wood products, foodstuffs, beverages, soap, tobacco products, meats, milk; refined petroleum.
VIETNAM	Divided in two parts by Armistice Line Sept. 1954. North of 17th parallel is Communist controlled "republic". South is a republic with a president and an assembly.	piaster	Khmer (Annamese) Lao	Rice, corn, sugar, tobacco, coffee, fruits, manioc, betel nuts, arrowroot, tea, cotton, areca nut, medicinal plants, cardamom, soya, rubber, copra, groundnuts, haricots, sweet potatoes, cinnamon; mulberries, bamboo, silk; cattle, buffalo, pigs; lumber; gold, tin, copper, coal, zinc, iron, cement, limestone, calamine, tungsten, manganese, phosphate, lead, bauxite.
VIRGIN ISLANDS (BR.)	British colony with an administrator, an executive and a legislative council.	B.W.I. dollar	English, Creole	Poultry and livestock, fish, fruit, vegetables.
VIRGIN ISLANDS (U. S.)	Territory of the U. S. with an appointed governor.	American dollar	English, Creole	Sugar cane, vegetables, citrus fruits, coconuts; cattle; fish; rum, bay rum, bay oil, molasses, handicrafts, sugar, lime juice, hides, bitters.
WEST IRIAN	Former Dutch colony now under Indonesian administration, with independence to be scheduled before 1969.	Indonesian rupiah	Papuan Dutch Indonesian	Sago, coconuts, sweet potatoes, wild nutmeg, mace, copra; bird of paradise plumes; petroleum.
YAP	Administered by a civil administrator of the Palau district as a part of the United States Trust Territory of the Pacific Islands.	American dollar	Micronesian dialects	Coconuts, breadfruit, sweet potatoes, taro, manioc, vegetables; poultry, pigs; fish.
YEMEN	Independent republic.	bakcha	Arabic	Coffee, barley, wheat, millet, sesame; cattle, hides; fish.
YUGOSLAVIA	A Soviet-type republic combining six republics under a central government with a president, fed. executive council and two-house elective legislature. Actually ruled by Communist League.	Yugoslav dinar	Serbian-Croatian, Slovenian Macedonian	Wheat, barley, rye, oats, corn, sugar beets, hemp, hops, opium, tobacco, flax, alfalfa, vegetables, fruits; sheep, cattle, pigs, goats, horses, poultry; coal, lignite, iron, copper, lead, salt, zinc, mercury, antimony, petroleum, bauxite, chrome, cement; lumber, textiles, foods, beverages, sugar, wood-distillates, wines.
ZAMBIA	Independent republic within the British Commonwealth, with a president, a cabinet and a unicameral legislature.	Zambia pound	Bantu languages English	Corn, wheat, potatoes, tobacco, sorghum, millet, groundnuts, cassava, rice, beans, cowpeas, cotton; lumber; cattle; copper, lead, manganese, zinc, cobalt.

UNIVERSE and EARTH

A man looking up at the sky on a clear night sees as much of the universe as a protozoan might see of the ocean in which it drifts. The moon, the planets, and the few thousand stars which are visible to him are as a single drop of water in the boundless sea of the universe.

While emotionally man cannot begin to grasp the magnitude of space, intellectually he has done so. His computations and the use of magnificent instruments which have enabled him to probe deeper and deeper into the cosmos, have indicated that we live in a universe with a diameter of 7,000,000,000 to 8,000,000,000 . . . not miles, but light-years, the distance light travels, at 186,000 miles a second, in one year.

In this sea of space are star atolls . . . the galaxies, billions of them, each containing billions of stars, clouds of hydrogen and dust. While the average size of these stars is that of the sun, a star in which a million earths could fit, there are stars in which a million suns could fit.

And where in the vastness of all this is our earth? In an aggregation of twenty galaxies known as the "Local Group" is one called the "Milky Way," an elliptical pinwheel of 100 billion stars. At a position 30,000 light-years from its center, among the countless stars in just one of the spiral arms, is our sun. Spinning upon its axis and rotating around this star which, in turn, is circling the far distant center of the Milky Way once every 200,000,000 years as the great galaxy rushes through space . . . is the planet earth.

This is man's home, upon which he wheels through the universe.

THE UNIVERSE: TIM

GREAT SPIRAL GALAXY
IN THE CONSTELLATION
OF ANDROMEDA

ISLANDS
IN THE
UNIVERSE

Principal Types of Galaxies

ELLIPTICAL galaxies have no clearly defined limits or definite structure.

NORMAL SPIRAL galaxies are characterized by a bright central area from which spiral arms emanate.

BARRED SPIRAL galaxies are identified by two spiral arms which seem to originate from bright stars in the extremities of arms projecting from either side of the central area.

EARTH'S POSITION IN THE MILKY WAY GALAXY

From earth we cannot observe the Milky Way's glowing center which is obscured by clouds of interstellar dust. Our "window on the universe" is at right angles to the plane of our galaxy.

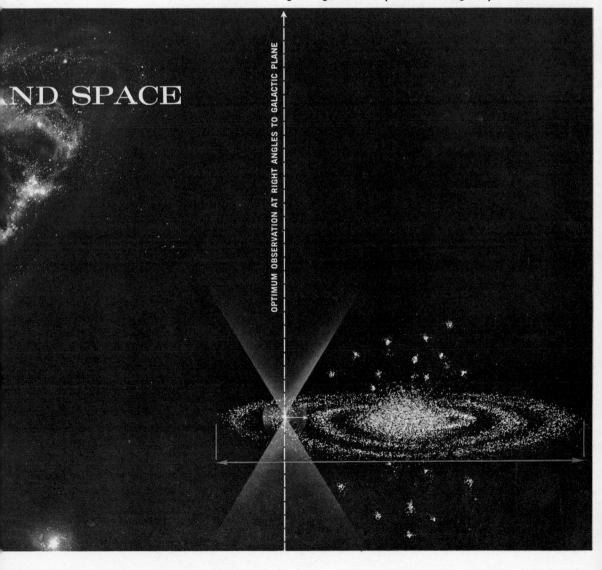

ND SPACE

OPTIMUM OBSERVATION AT RIGHT ANGLES TO GALACTIC PLANE

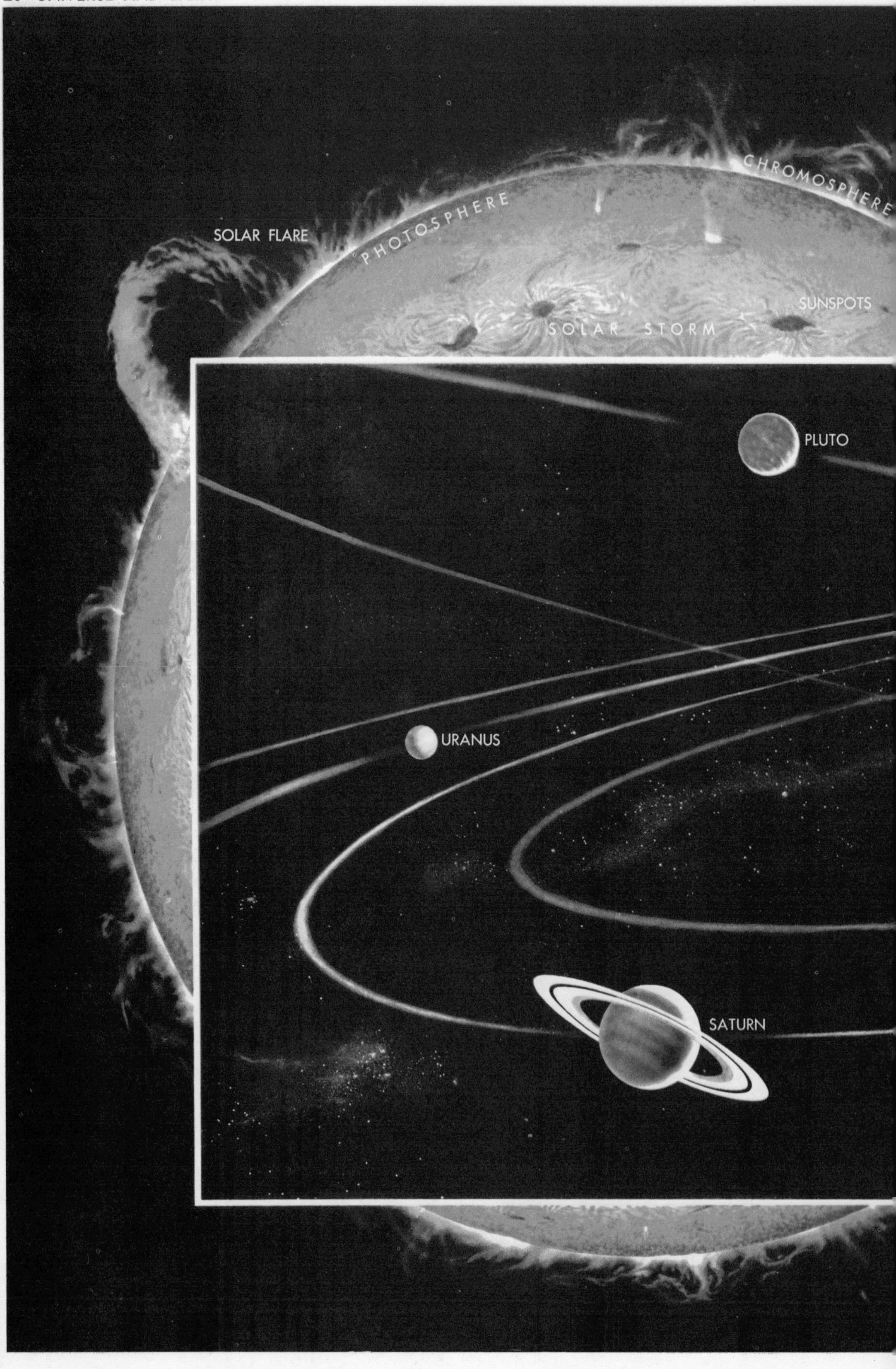

SOLAR FLARE

PHOTOSPHERE

CHROMOSPHERE

SOLAR STORM

SUNSPOTS

PLUTO

URANUS

SATURN

OUR FAMILY OF PLANETS

Among the billions of stars in the universe, we believe that there are millions of solar systems similar to our own. Ours is not a close family, but extends three and a half billion miles in space. If the sun were a pumpkin, the earth would be a pea over two hundred feet away and the furthest planet, Pluto, another pea two miles beyond.

Just beyond the four inner "dwarf" planets, Mercury, Venus, Earth and Mars, is a girdle of much tinier ones, the asteroids. Beyond these are the four giants, Jupiter, Saturn, Uranus and Neptune, and finally Pluto, another dwarf. In this array of planets, only Mars gives the barest chance of being able to support life. A total of thirty-one moons circle the various planets while throughout the solar system fly comets, fiery interplanetary wanderers scattering their embers, the meteors we call shooting stars.

THE SUN — The intense light of the sun is the fire produced by the nuclear conversion of hydrogen into helium. The surface temperature is about 11,000 degrees F., but the interior is millions of degrees hotter. Periodically, storms erupt from the surface and tongues of flame are hurled into space and bombard the earth's atmosphere with high energy radiation.

EARTH'S HOSTILE ENVIRONMENT

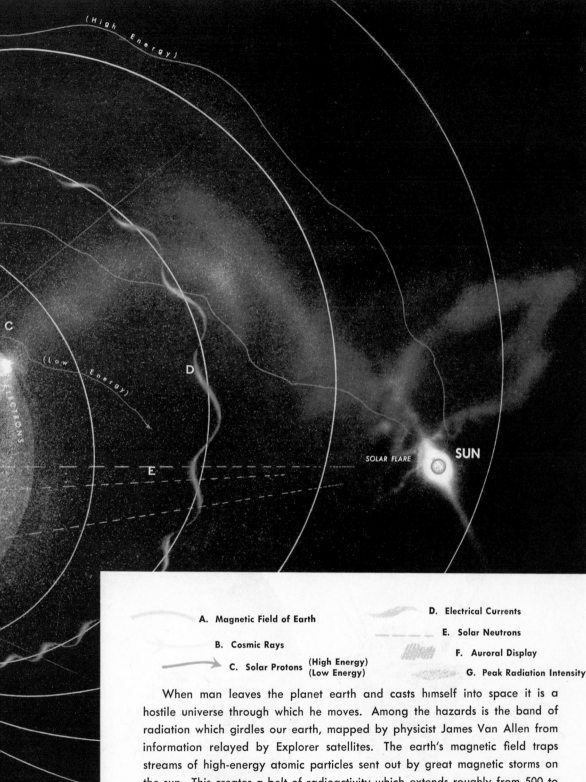

(High Energy)

ELECTRONS

C

(Low Energy)

D

E

SOLAR FLARE **SUN**

A. Magnetic Field of Earth

B. Cosmic Rays

C. Solar Protons (High Energy)
(Low Energy)

D. Electrical Currents

E. Solar Neutrons

F. Auroral Display

G. Peak Radiation Intensity

When man leaves the planet earth and casts himself into space it is a hostile universe through which he moves. Among the hazards is the band of radiation which girdles our earth, mapped by physicist James Van Allen from information relayed by Explorer satellites. The earth's magnetic field traps streams of high-energy atomic particles sent out by great magnetic storms on the sun. This creates a belt of radioactivity which extends roughly from 500 to 40,000 miles into space. In arctic latitudes some particles come close enough to interact with the upper atmosphere creating shimmering auroral displays. Study of the Van Allen belt continues as levels of intensity are measured and limits of exposure are determined before man can breach this celestial barrier in safety.

The familiar face of the moon (right), and detailed photograph (below) show the moon as observed by man since the earliest days when he thought the plains of dust were seas between lunar mountain ranges.

THE MOON

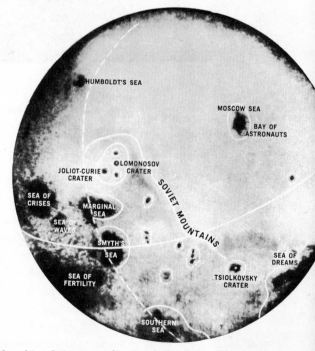

The far side of the moon (to the right of the dotted line) as photographed by the Satellite Lunik which circled the moon in 1959.

The moon is a gigantic stone in the sky . . . an airless, waterless sphere of towering mountain ranges, broad craters, great plains of powdery, gray-brown dust. It rotates around the earth keeping its far side always hidden from our sight. One-quarter the size of the earth and one-sixth its gravity, this neighbor only 238,000 miles away was formed, we speculate, when a cloud of cosmic gas and particles separated into eddies which contracted to become the sun, the planets and their satellites. Unshielded by protective air, temperatures on its surface range over 200° F. by day to −200° F. after dark. Yet some day we shall launch space vehicles from there, virtually without gravitational drag and, because it has no atmosphere, observe the furthest stars.

The gravitational pull exerted by the moon on the waters of the earth is a major cause of tides, the pulse of the seas which affects the creatures of the sea and the men who live by it.

In its eccentric but predictable orbit, the moon on occasion crosses directly between the earth and the sun, casting its shadow on the earth's surface. (A) This is the solar eclipse which permits astronomers to acquire certain invaluable data about the area in the sun's vicinity. When the earth passes between sun and moon, hiding it from the sun's light, the eclipse is lunar. (B)

The superstitions and legends of the moon are still with us but in the days to come the main image of the moon in the minds of men will be that of a stepping stone to space.

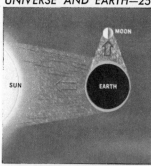

NEAP TIDE is the low monthly tide produced when the sun offsets the pull of the moon.

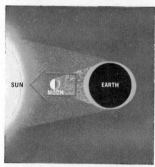

SPRING TIDE is the high monthly tide when sun and moon gravitational pull is combined.

Earth's Natural Satellite

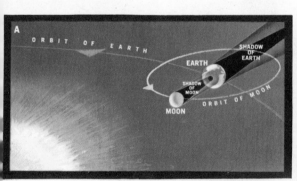

SOLAR ECLIPSE

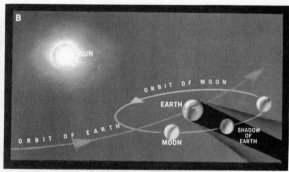

LUNAR ECLIPSE

PHASES OF THE MOON

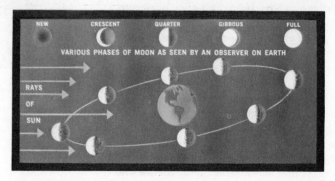

NEW   CRESCENT   QUARTER   GIBBOUS   FULL

VARIOUS PHASES OF MOON AS SEEN BY AN OBSERVER ON EARTH

RAYS OF SUN

Continuing Evolution

Point of Extinction

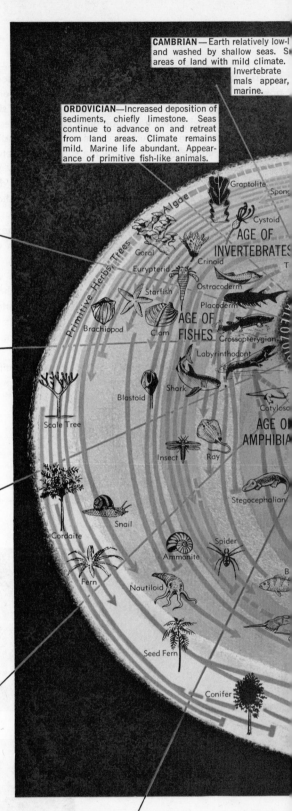

CAMBRIAN — Earth relatively low-l and washed by shallow seas. S areas of land with mild climate. Invertebrate mals appear, marine.

ORDOVICIAN—Increased deposition of sediments, chiefly limestone. Seas continue to advance on and retreat from land areas. Climate remains mild. Marine life abundant. Appearance of primitive fish-like animals.

SILURIAN — Land areas slightly uplifted or depressed. Mountain ranges begin to form. Climate generally warm with some areas quite arid. Beginning of plant life on land. Sea scorpions appear, possibly first air breathers. Coral reefs widespread.

DEVONIAN — Volcanic activity and extensive mountain-building on land areas. Climates become diversified due to changes in relief and air and water currents. Heavy seasonal rains in tropical regions. Fishes abound in seas. Emergence of primitive amphibians and spread of land plants.

MISSISSIPPIAN — Intermittent stages of uplift, erosion and submersion. Climate varied but generally warmer and wetter. Great volcanic activity toward close of period. Further evolution of amphibians. Scale trees prominent.

PENNSYLVANIAN — Formation of great swamp areas. Decayed plants accumulate as peat . . . later form large coal deposits. Marked earth disturbances in Europe and Asia. Lavish growth of plants and abundance of insects. Primitive reptiles appear.

Of the nature of our earth's origin we are uncertain, but radioactive elements found in some rocks have fixed its origin in time. These elements decay into others at fixed rates as centuries go by. By weighing each element which is present today, the age of the rock can be approximated as well as that of any fossilized plant or animal within.

The three to five billion years estimated for the earth's age have been divided by geologists into a chronology of events organized according to cycles of earth upheaval and quiescence. At times certain organisms flourished and can be associated with specific rock structures. In the changing world some creatures could not adapt and became extinct while others evolved into new forms better suited to survival. And so it was that in the primordial sea a microscopic bit of matter began to live as a single-celled organism which, by a series of mutations virtually infinite in number and complexity, become, at last, homo sapiens . . . modern man.

PERMIAN — Widespread cor tinental uplift and formation of Appalachians and Urals. Glaciation in Southern Hemisphere. Reptiles grow in number and variety.

TRIASSIC — Continents almost completely emergent . . . local volcanic activity. Extensive spread of non-marine deposits, largely redbeds. Climate predominantly hot and dry. Shoreline areas well-watered. Conifers dominate land plants. Rapid growth of reptiles.

THE GEOLOGIC RECORD

RE-CAMBRIAN — Formation of oldest acces-ble rocks which have been greatly altered metamorphism. Intermittent volcanic ac-ity followed by periods of erosion and position. Possible existence of rudimentary e in the warm seas.

PRE-CAMBRIAN ERA

70 Million Years Ago

CENOZOIC ERA

Million rs Ago

MESOZOIC ERA

Archaeopteryx

Pantotheres

Toothed Bird

Tiny Primitive Mammals

Whale

Primitive Man

Modern Man

Monkey

Ape

osaur

Dinosaurs

Pterosaur

Eohippus

Miohippus

Horse

Multituberculate

Mastodon

Trachodon

Creodont

AGE OF MAMMALS

Elephant

Brontosaurus

Tyrannosaurus

Oreodon

Cat

Stegosaur

Toothless Bird

Bat

Dog

Crocodile

AGE OF REPTILES

Turtle

Bear

Snake

Kangaroo

Opossum

Frog

Lizard

MODERN BIRDS

Salamander

MODERN REPTILES

MODERN AMPHIBIANS

MODERN FISHES

MODERN ARTHROPODS

MODERN LOWER INVERTEBRATES

Squid

MODERN

Cycad

Angiosperm

PLANTS

IC — Seas again cover as of land. Deforma-the West of United erosion in the East. humid. Coal beds laid Siberia. Cycad-like ominant.

CRETACEOUS — Initially, continental submergence and thick sedimentation. Later, uplift and folding to form Rockies and Andes. Climate mild. Deciduous trees and flowering plants evolve. Reptiles still dominant but mammals increasing. Most reptiles, including dinosaurs die out at end of period.

QUATERNARY — Successive glacial and inter-glacial stages affect Eurasia and North America. Present features of the earth develop. Evolution of man.

TERTIARY — Distinctive continental outlines begin to form. Submergence in Europe. Further elevation of existing North American mountains. Formation of Alps and Himalayas. Climate varied. Mammals dominant.

STRUCTURE OF THE EARTH

Between the loftiest mountain peaks on earth and the lowest ocean deeps, the vertical distance is perhaps twelve miles. Comfortably between these extremes, we pursue our daily affairs . . . on the outermost crust of a dense sphere, nearly four thousand miles above its center, an area as mysterious to us as the distant stars.

We believe this core to be of a nickel-iron substance which has continued to cool and contract since the earth was born. Around it is the mantle, a layer of still-molten rock that under tremendous pressure twists, bends and flows in a viscous tide. The upper layer, the crust, is constantly shifting, moving and reshaping itself, sometimes imperceptibly, sometimes with the violence and catastrophic suddenness of an earthquake or volcano. In the rocks of the Matterhorn are remains of molluscs, thousands of feet higher than the sea in which they once lived. It is even believed by many scientists that the continents once were part of a single landmass which broke apart, the pieces being carried upon the tides of the mantle to where they lie today.

Much of what we do know of the earth's interior has been determined by studying the speed and direction of earthquake shock waves which radiate from seismic disturbances. In this manner, Andrija Mohorovicic in 1909 "discovered" the Moho, the boundary between crust and mantle. An expedition presently is engaged in drilling through the bottom of the Pacific, in an area where the crust is thin, to the Moho. Project Mohole is man's first serious attempt to reach earth's middle layer, the dark unknown which at that point is only a scant six miles below us.

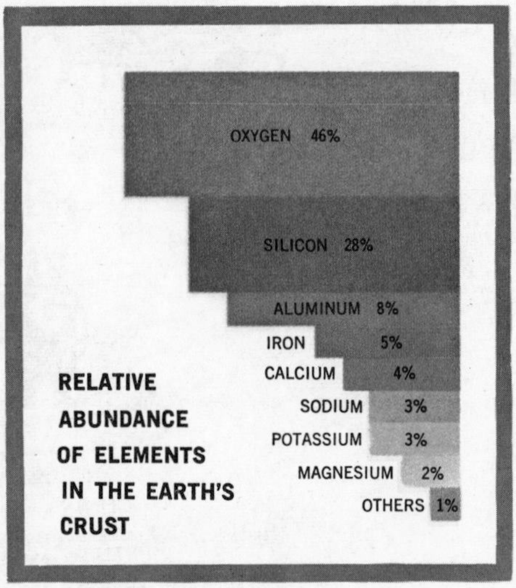

RELATIVE ABUNDANCE OF ELEMENTS IN THE EARTH'S CRUST

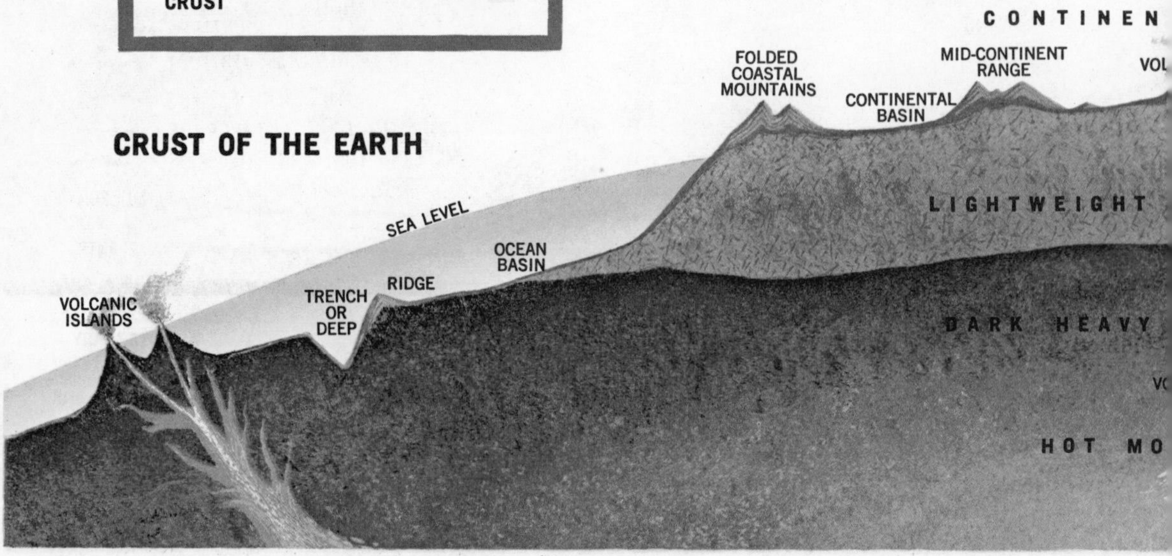

OXYGEN 46%
SILICON 28%
ALUMINUM 8%
IRON 5%
CALCIUM 4%
SODIUM 3%
POTASSIUM 3%
MAGNESIUM 2%
OTHERS 1%

CRUST OF THE EARTH

CONTINEN

FOLDED COASTAL MOUNTAINS
MID-CONTINENT RANGE
VOL
CONTINENTAL BASIN
SEA LEVEL
OCEAN BASIN
RIDGE
TRENCH OR DEEP
VOLCANIC ISLANDS
LIGHTWEIGHT
DARK HEAVY
HOT MO

PRIOR

THEORY OF CONTINENTAL DRIFT
At an early point in geologic time evidence suggests that all land areas were part of one great landmass.

INTERIOR OF THE EARTH
Shown in section are the principal structural layers of the earth. Crustal thickness exaggerated for purposes of clarity.

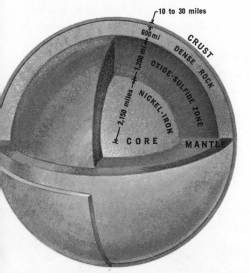

10 to 30 miles

600 mi

1,200 mi

2,150 miles

CRUST

DENSE ROCK

OXIDE-SULFIDE ZONE

NICKEL-IRON

CORE

MANTLE

PRESENT

PROJECT MOHOLE

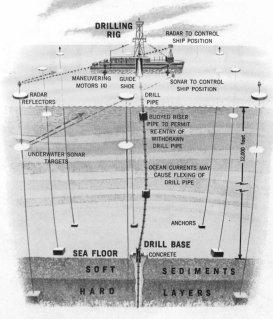

DRILLING RIG

RADAR TO CONTROL SHIP POSITION

MANEUVERING MOTORS (4)

GUIDE SHOE

SONAR TO CONTROL SHIP POSITION

RADAR REFLECTORS

DRILL PIPE

BUOYED RISER PIPE TO PERMIT RE-ENTRY OF WITHDRAWN DRILL PIPE

UNDERWATER SONAR TARGETS

OCEAN CURRENTS MAY CAUSE FLEXING OF DRILL PIPE

12,000 feet

ANCHORS

DRILL BASE

SEA FLOOR

CONCRETE

SOFT SEDIMENTS

HARD LAYERS

AND MASS

FOLDED MOUNTAINS

INTERIOR LOWLANDS

COASTAL PLAIN

E-TYPE ROCKS

CONTINENTAL SHELF

CONTINENTAL SLOPE

TROUGH

BANK

-TYPE ROCKS

SUBMARINE MOUNTAINS

MID-OCEAN RISE

RE

NTERIOR

"Business as usual despite alterations" is, geologically speaking, the story of our earth, for around us nature's carpenters and wrecking crews continuously are building anew and simultaneously tearing down the old world. No point on the earth's surface remains unaffected by these forces which seem to maintain a balance between the high and low areas of the earth's crust. Over a period of centuries, as a coastline slips beneath the sea, somewhere else a mountain range is slowly rising.

Under interior compressive stresses, perhaps resulting from the cooling of the earth's core, perhaps from movement within the mantle, perhaps from the accumulation of vast silt deposits on the ocean floor . . . we don't know . . . flat lands fold into gently rolling hills and valleys. Sometimes the pressure continues to increase. The mountains become higher and the valleys deeper. Finally the rock yields and buckles. Great rock masses shear along a break, or fault. Deeply buried layers of age-old sedimentary strata are forced higher and higher along the fault, reach the top and fold back until the lowest layers have become the mountain peaks.

The building of a mountain range can take ten billion years, but the forces that create it can level great cities within seconds. By fracturing rock deep beneath the surface of the earth, they cause everything that stands above it to slip, slide, tumble and shift in a cataclysmic moment of horror. This is the earthquake, one of the historic scourges of mankind.

Another scourge is the volcano. In the mantle, magma, molten rock with its content of compressed gases, probes for weak spots in the earth's crust and bursts forth through the ground in an eruption of fiery lava, gas and steam that does not stop until a mountain is made.

The major forces at work in rebuilding the face of the earth are violent ones. The erosive forces engaged in destroying it are far gentler.

EARTH DYNAMICS

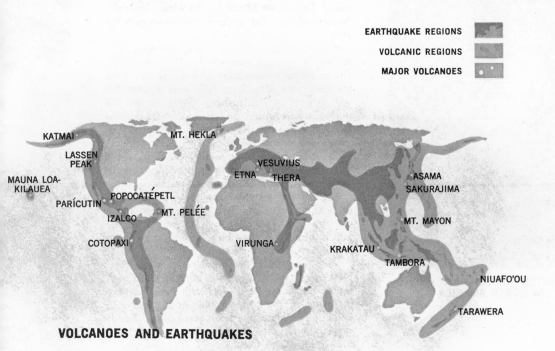

EARTHQUAKE REGIONS
VOLCANIC REGIONS
MAJOR VOLCANOES

KATMAI   MT. HEKLA
LASSEN PEAK
MAUNA LOA-KILAUEA
PARÍCUTIN
POPOCATÉPETL
IZALCO   MT. PELÉE
COTOPAXI
VESUVIUS
ETNA   THERA
VIRUNGA
KRAKATAU
ASAMA
SAKURAJIMA
MT. MAYON
TAMBORA
NIUAFO'OU
TARAWERA

VOLCANOES AND EARTHQUAKES

Mountain Building

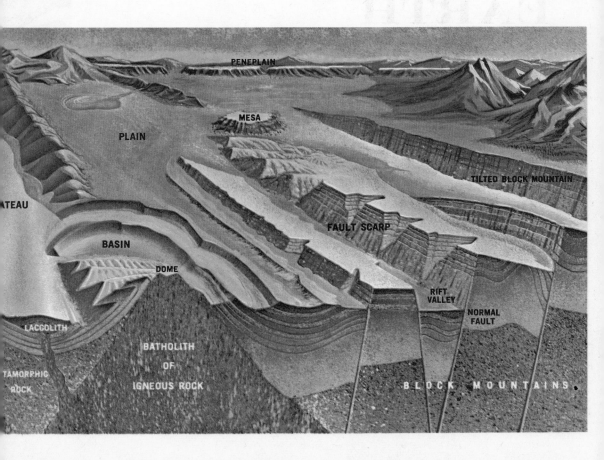

PENEPLAIN
MESA
PLAIN
TILTED BLOCK MOUNTAIN
FAULT SCARP
ATEAU
BASIN
DOME
RIFT VALLEY
NORMAL FAULT
LACCOLITH
BATHOLITH OF IGNEOUS ROCK
TAMORPHIC ROCK
BLOCK MOUNTAINS

**EXTENT OF GLACIATION
IN NORTH AMERICA**

SEATTLE
GREAT FALLS
PIERRE   NEW YORK
              CINCINNATI
KANSAS CITY

SEA ICE
GLACIAL ICE

What levels the face of the land as the ages pass? The air we breathe. The wind. The rain. Snow and ice. The streams, the rivers and the seas.

Water seeps into the rocky crevices of a mountain, freezes, expands and splits the rock. The chemical combination with the air crumbles the rock into soil. Rain falls and washes the soil downhill. The rushing water carves out gullies which widen and deepen into streams which become the rivers that bear the sediment to the sea.

In arid regions, the wind sweeps up loose dust and sand, stripping bedrock bare and sandblasting all that stands in its path.

In frozen mountain regions, never-melting snow compresses into great sheets of ice. These are the glaciers . . . ice rivers that plow the earth before them and grind smooth the valleys through which they creep.

The icecaps of the polar regions are remnants of the ice sheets which once covered one-fourth of all the land. In North America they hollowed out the basins of the Great Lakes and, when they melted, the lakes were filled. Sands deposited by retreating glaciers formed Long Island and Cape Cod.

The sea, too, plays its part in leveling the land. The hammerblows of the surf have pounded to sand many of the coastal areas of the world.

EARTH DYNAMICS: Erosion

GROU
MORA

YOUNG STR

RA

SEA
CAVE
SEA
ARCH

SAND DUNE FORMATION
Desert sand, fine rock granules, formed by erosive processes, is shaped by the wind into constantly changing formations.

WIND ERODED ROCK
A rocky formation from which the softer rock has been ground away by wind-blown sand, dust and moisture.

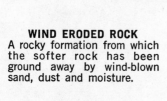

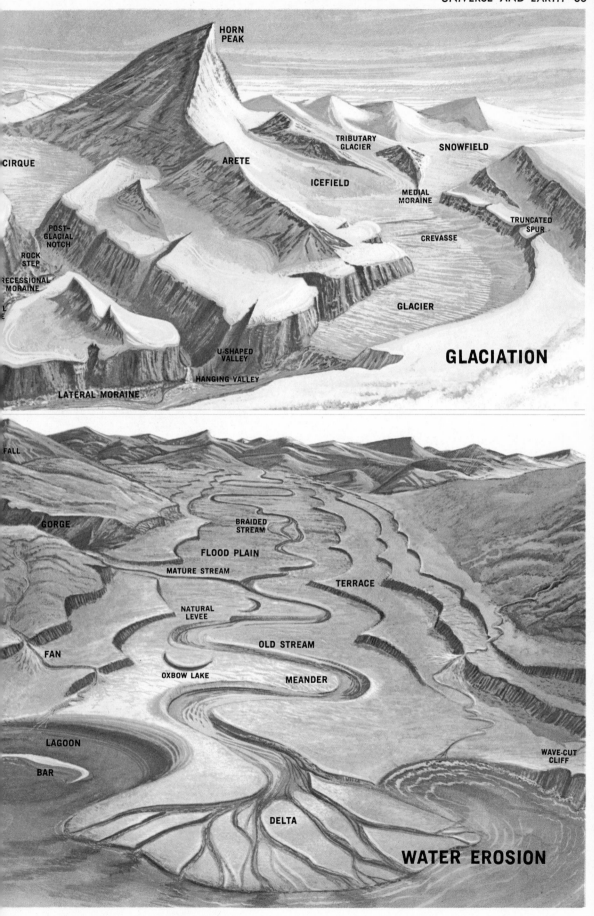

GLACIATION

WATER EROSION

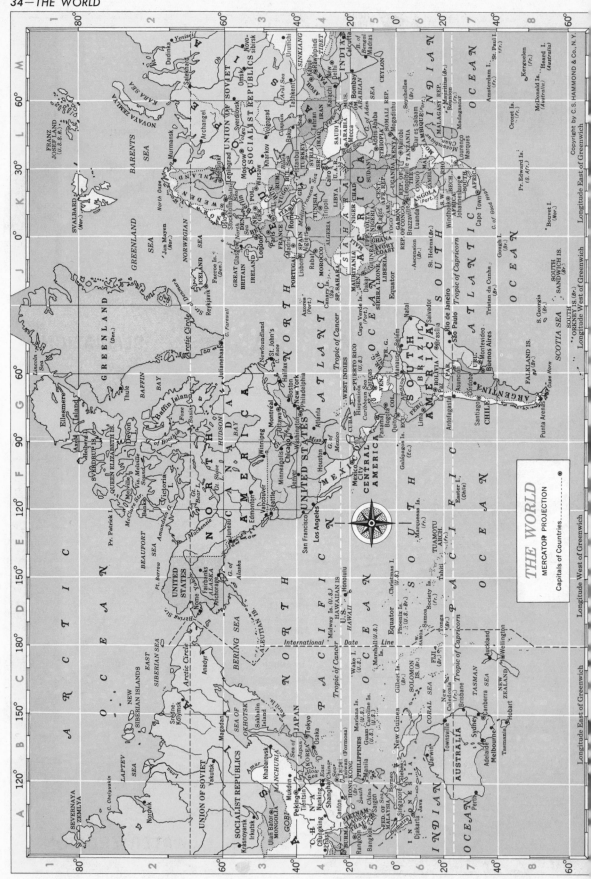

THE WORLD

MERCATOR PROJECTION

Capitals of Countries............●

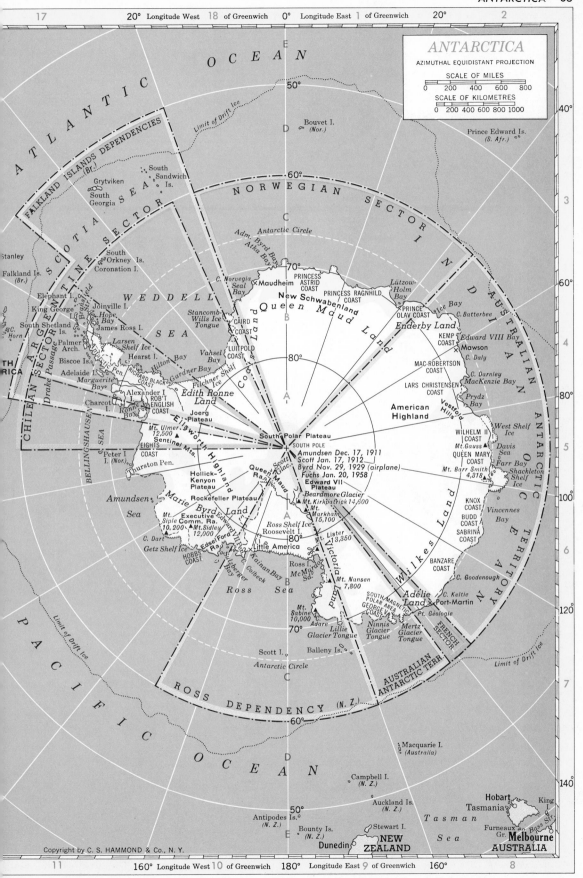

17 20° Longitude West 18 of Greenwich 0° Longitude East 1 of Greenwich 20° 2

ANTARCTICA
AZIMUTHAL EQUIDISTANT PROJECTION

SCALE OF MILES
0   200   400   600   800

SCALE OF KILOMETRES
0   200   400   600   800   1000

O   C   E   A   N

A T L A N T I C

50°

D   Bouvet I.
(Nor.)

Prince Edward Is.
(S. Afr.)

40°

Limit of Drift Ice

FALKLAND ISLANDS DEPENDENCIES (Br.)

South
Sandwich
Is.

Grytviken
South Georgia

60°

N   O   R   W   E   G   I   A   N   S   E   C   T   O   R

Antarctic Circle

Adm. Byrd Bay
Atka Bay

C

SCOTIA SEA

Stanley

Falkland Is.
(Br.)

South
Orkney Is.
Coronation I.

70°

60°

C. Norvegia
Seal
Bay   Maudheim

PRINCESS
ASTRID
COAST

Lützow-
Holm
Bay

Elephant I.
King George I.
Hope
Bay   Joinville I.
James Ross I.

WEDDELL

Stancomb-
Wills Ice
Tongue

New Schwabenland
Queen Maud Land

PRINCESS RAGNHILD
COAST

PRINCE
OLAV COAST   Ice Bay

C. Batterbee

Enderby Land

South Shetland
Is.

SEA

CAIRD
COAST

B

KEMP
COAST

Edward VIII Bay

Mawson

C. Horn

Palmer
Arch.

Larsen
Shelf Ice

Hearst I.

Vahsel
Bay

Gardner Bay

Filchner
Ice Shelf

LUITPOLD
COAST

C. Daly

MAC-ROBERTSON
COAST

C. Darnley
MacKenzie Bay

Biscoe Is.

Adelaide I.

Marguerite
Bay

RICHARD BLACK
COAST

Edith Ronne
Land

80°

LARS CHRISTENSEN
COAST

Prydz
Bay

Vestfold
Hills

80°

Charcot
I.

Alexander I   ROB'T
ENGLISH
COAST

Joerg
Plateau

American
Highland

West Shelf
Ice

Ronne
Bay

Mt. Ulmer
12,500

Sentinel Mts.

South Polar Plateau

WILHELM II
COAST

Mt.Gauss

Davis
Sea

BELLINGSHAUSEN
SEA

EIGHTS
COAST

Peter I.
I. (Nor.)

SOUTH POLE

Amundsen Dec. 17, 1911
Scott Jan. 17, 1912
Byrd Nov. 29, 1929 (airplane)
Fuchs Jan. 20, 1958

QUEEN MARY
COAST

Farr Bay
Shackleton
Shelf Ice

Mt. Barr Smith
4,318

Thurston Pen.

Hollick-
Kenyon
Plateau

Queen Maud
Ra.

Edward VII
Land

KNOX
COAST

Vincennes
Bay

Amundsen
Sea

Marie   Byrd   Land

Rockefeller Plateau

Beardmore Glacier
Mt. Kirkpatrick 14,600

BUDD
COAST

SABRINA
COAST

Mt.
Markham
15,100

Mt. Executive
Siple Comm. Ra.
10,200   Mt. Sidley
12,000

Ross Shelf Ice
Roosevelt I.

BANZARE
COAST

C. Dart

Edsel Ford Ra.

Little America

Mt. Lister
13,350

C. Goodenough

Getz Shelf Ice

HOBBS
COAST

Colbeck
Bay

Ross I.
McM'do Sd.

Mt. Nansen
7,800

C. Keltie

Adélie
Land   Port-Martin

Kainan Bay

70°

Ross   Sea

SOUTH MAGNETIC
POLAR AREA
GEORGE V
COAST

Pt. Géologie

Sulzberger
Bay

Mt.
Sabine
10,000

Adare   Lillie
Glacier Tongue

Ninnis
Glacier
Tongue

Mertz
Glacier
Tongue

FRENCH
SECTOR

Scott I.

Balleny Is.

Antarctic Circle

AUSTRALIAN
ANTARCTIC TERR.

Limit of Drift Ice

P A C I F I C

Limit of Drift Ice

R   O   S   S   D   E   P   E   N   D   E   N   C   Y   (N. Z.)

60°

O   C   E   A   N

Macquarie I.
(Australia)

140°

Campbell I.
(N. Z.)

Hobart

King
I.

Tasmania

Auckland Is.
(N. Z.)

Tasman

Furneaux
Gr.   Bass Str.

50°

Antipodes Is.
(N. Z.)

Bounty Is.
(N. Z.)

Stewart I.

Sea

Melbourne

Dunedin   NEW
ZEALAND

AUSTRALIA

11   160° Longitude West 10 of Greenwich   180°   Longitude East 9 of Greenwich   160°   8

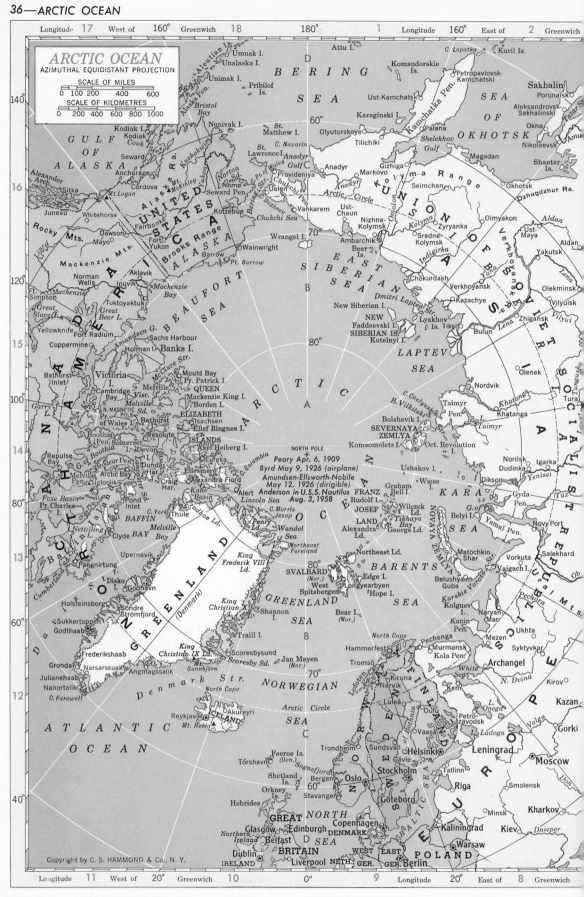

ARCTIC OCEAN
AZIMUTHAL EQUIDISTANT PROJECTION

SCALE OF MILES

0   100 200   400   600

SCALE OF KILOMETRES

0   200 400 600 800 1000

BERING SEA

Attu I.

Komandorskie Is.

C. Lopatka

Kuril Is.

Petropavlovsk-Kamchatski

SEA OF OKHOTSK

Sakhalin

Poronaisk

Aleksandrovsk-Sakhalinski

Okha

Nikolaevsk

Shantar Is.

Umnak I.
Unalaska I.
Unimak I.
Aleutian Is.
Pribilof Is.

Ust-Kamchatsk

Karaginski I.

Kamchatka Pen.

Palana

Shelekhov Gulf

Gizhiga

Magadan

Okhotsk

Dzhugdzhur Ra.

GULF OF ALASKA

Kodiak I.
Kodiak
Cook Inlet
Bristol Bay
Nunivak I.
St. Matthew I.
St. Lawrence I.

C. Navarin

Olyutorskoye

Tilichiki

60°

Kolyma Range

Oimyakon

Aldan

Ust-Maya

Yakutsk

Aldan

Seward
Anchorage
Cordova

Nome
Seward Pen.
Kotzebue
Pr. of Wales
Bering Str.
E. Dezhnev
Uelen

Gulf C
Provideniya
Anadyr
Markovo

Anadyr
Arctic Circle

Seimchan

Verkhoyansk Ra.

Olekminsk

Vilyuisk

Sitka
Juneau
Whitehorse

Mt. McKinley
Fairbanks
Fort Yukon
Yukon

Chukchi Pen.
Vankarem
Ust-Chaun

Nizhne-Kolymsk

Zyryanka

Srednekolymsk

Indigirka

Verkhoyansk

Kazachye

Bulun

Zhigansk

Lena

Vilyui

Rocky Mts.

Dawson
Mayo

Mt. Logan
Alaska Range

UNITED STATES
ALASKA
Brooks Range
Wainwright
Barrow
Pt. Barrow

Wrangel I.

Chukchi Sea

70°

Ambarchik
Bear Is.

Chokurdakh

Yana

Lena

Tiksi

Ft. Simpson
Norman Wells
Mackenzie
Great Slave L.
Yellowknife
Aklavik
Inuvik
Tuktoyaktuk
Mackenzie Bay

EASTERN SIBERIAN SEA

New Siberian I.

Dmitri Laptev Str.

Lyakhov Is.

NEW
FADDEEVSKI I.
SIBERIAN IS.
Kotelnyi I.

Nordvik

Olenek

AMERICA
NORTH
Great Bear L.
Coppermine
Port Radium
Holman I.
Sachs Harbour
Amundsen G.
BEAUFORT SEA

Banks I.

80°

LAPTEV SEA

Khatanga
L. Taimyr

Khatanga

Tura

Bathurst Inlet
Victoria
Cambridge Bay
Holman I.
Melville
Visc.
Mould Bay
Pr. Patrick I.
QUEEN
Mackenzie King I.
Borden I.

ARCTIC

C. Chelyuskin
B. Vilkitski
Taimyr Pen.

Bolshevik I.
SEVERNAYA
ZEMLYA
Oct. Revolution I.

Norilsk
Dudinka

Igarka

Yenisei

Garry
Pr. of Wales I.
Boothia
Pen.
Somerset I.
Devon
Bathurst
ELIZABETH
Isachsen
Ellef Ringnes I.
Axel Heiberg I.
ISLANDS

Komsomolets I.

Ushakov I.

Wiese I.

Dikson

KARA SEA

G. of Ob

Belyi I.

Yamal Pen.

Novy Port

N. MAGNETIC POLE
Resolute
Repulse Bay
Gulf of Boothia
Prince Regent
Arctic Bay
Igloolik
Dundas Har.
Craig Har.
Ellesmere I.
Alexandra Fiord
Eureka
C. Columbia
Alert

NORTH POLE
Peary Apr. 6, 1909
Byrd May 9, 1926 (airplane)
Amundsen-Ellsworth-Nobile
May 12, 1926 (dirigible)
Anderson in U.S.S. Nautilus
Aug. 3, 1958

FRANZ
Graham Bell I.
Rudolf I.
JOSEF
Wilczek Ld.
LAND
Tikhaya Bay
Alexandra Ld.
George Ld.

NOVAYA ZEMLYA

OCEAN

Gyda Pen.

Taz

Matochkin Shar

Salekhard

Vorkuta

Melville Pen.
Foxe Basin
Pr. Charles I.
Nettilling L.
BAFFIN
Pond Inlet
Bylot I.
Thule
Kane Basin
Smith Sd.
Etah
C. York
Peary Ld.
Lincoln Sea
C. Morris Jesup
Wandel Sea
Northeast Foreland

Northeast Ld.

BARENTS
SEA

Belushya Guba

Karskie Vorota Str.

Vaigach I.

Kolguev I.

Novaya Zemlya

Pechora

Narfyan-Mar

BAY
Melville Bay
Upernavik
Clyde
Pangnirtung
Cumberland Sd.
Disko I.
Godhavn
Holsteinsborg
Sukkertoppen
Godthaab

GREENLAND
(Denmark)

King Frederik VIII Ld.

King Christian X Ld.
Shannon I.
Traill I.

80°
SVALBARD
(Nor.)
West Spitsbergen
Edge I.
Hope I.
Longyearbyen

Bear I.
(Nor.)

GREENLAND
SEA

Kolguev I.
Kanin Pen.

Mezen

Belushya

Kolguev

Ukhta

Syktyvkar

Narssarssuaq
Frederikshaab
Grondal
Julianehaab
Nanortalik
C. Farewell

King Christian IX Ld.
Angmagssalik
Mt. Gunnbjørn
Scoresbysund
Scoresby Sd.
Jan Mayen (Nor.)

North Cape
Hammerfest
Tromsø
Lofoten
Kiruna
Narvik

Pechenga

Murmansk
Kola Pen.

North Cape

Kem

White Sea

N. Dvina

Archangel

Kirov

Kazan

ATLANTIC OCEAN

Denmark Str.
North Cape
Reykjavik
ICELAND
Mt. Hekla
Akureyri

NORWEGIAN SEA

Arctic Circle

70°

Luleå
G. of Bothnia
Oulu
Vaasa

Petrozavodsk

L. Onega
L. Ladoga

Volga

Gorki

EUROPE

Faeroe Is. (Den.)
Tórshavn

Sognefjord
Bergen
Stavanger
Shetland Is.
Orkney Is.
Hebrides

Trondheim
Sundsvall
Gävle
Oslo
Göteborg
Stockholm

60°

Helsinki
Tallinn
Riga

Leningrad

Moscow

Smolensk

40°

NORTH
SEA

GREAT
Glasgow
Edinburgh
Northern Ireland
Belfast
BRITAIN
Dublin
IRELAND
Liverpool

Copenhagen
DENMARK
WEST GER. EAST GER.
NETH.
Berlin
POLAND
Warsaw

Kaliningrad
Minsk
Kiev
Kharkov
Dnieper

Baltic Sea

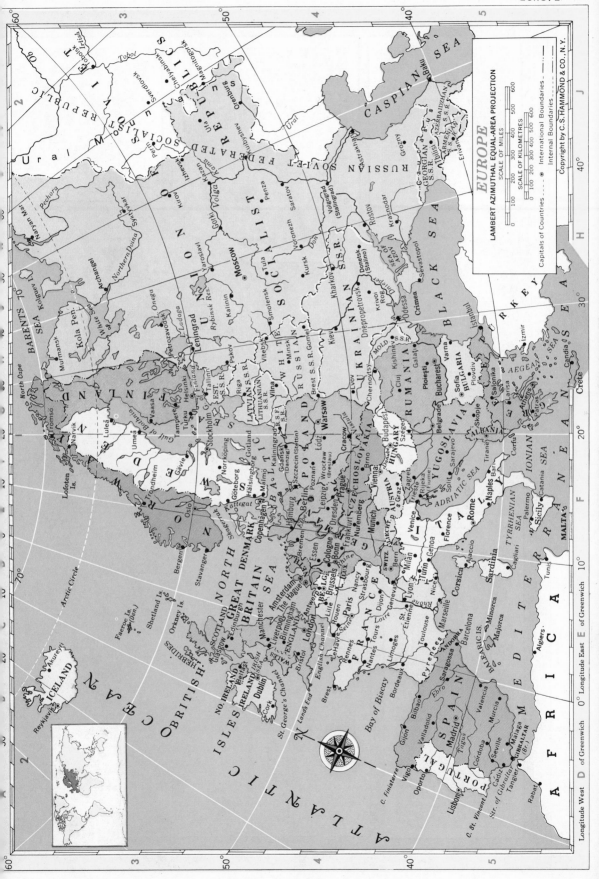

RUSSIAN SOVIET FEDERATED SOCIALIST REPUBLICS

CASPIAN SEA

BARENTS SEA

North Cape

ICELAND

Reykjavik
Akureyri

ATLANTIC OCEAN

BRITISH ISLES

NORTH SEA

GREAT BRITAIN
SCOTLAND
Glasgow
Edinburgh
ENGLAND
Manchester
Liverpool
Birmingham
London
Bristol
WALES

NO. IRELAND
Belfast
IRELAND
Dublin
Cork

NORWAY
Oslo
Bergen
Stavanger
Trondheim

SWEDEN
Stockholm
Göteborg

FINLAND
Helsinki

DENMARK
Copenhagen

POLAND
Warsaw

GERMANY
Berlin
Hamburg
Munich

CZECHOSLOVAKIA
Prague

AUSTRIA
Vienna

HUNGARY
Budapest

FRANCE
Paris
Lyon
Marseille
Bordeaux

SPAIN
Madrid
Barcelona

PORTUGAL
Lisbon

ITALY
Rome
Naples
Milan

YUGOSLAVIA
Belgrade

RUMANIA
Bucharest

BULGARIA
Sofia

ALBANIA
Tirana

GREECE
Athens

TURKEY
Istanbul

UKRAINIAN S.S.R.
Kiev

WHITE RUSSIAN S.S.R.
Minsk

LITHUANIAN S.S.R.
LATVIAN S.S.R.
Riga
EST. S.S.R.
Tallinn

MOSCOW
Leningrad

BLACK SEA

MEDITERRANEAN SEA

AFRICA
Algiers
Tunis
Rabat

Longitude West D of Greenwich 0° Longitude East E of Greenwich 40°

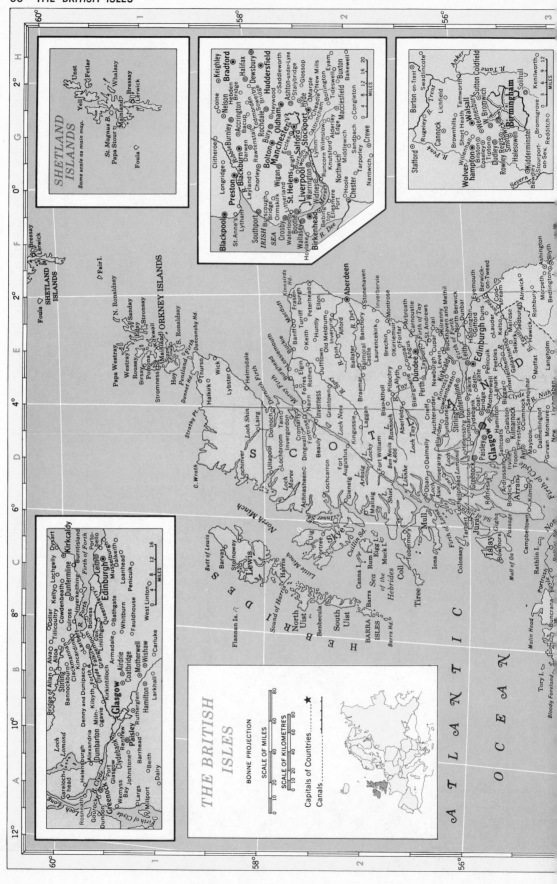

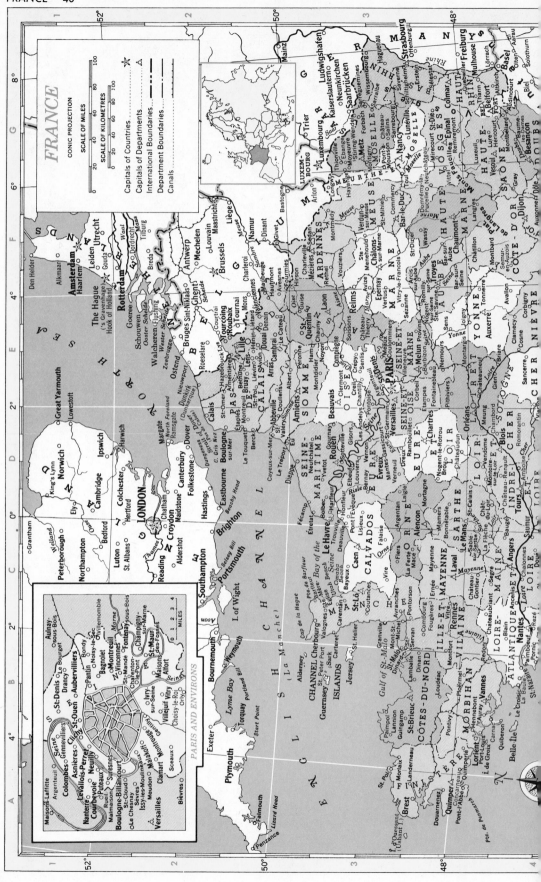

FRANCE

CONIC PROJECTION

SCALE OF MILES

SCALE OF KILOMETRES

Capitals of Countries .... ⊕
Capitals of Departments .... △
International Boundaries ....
Department Boundaries ....
Canals ....

PARIS AND ENVIRONS

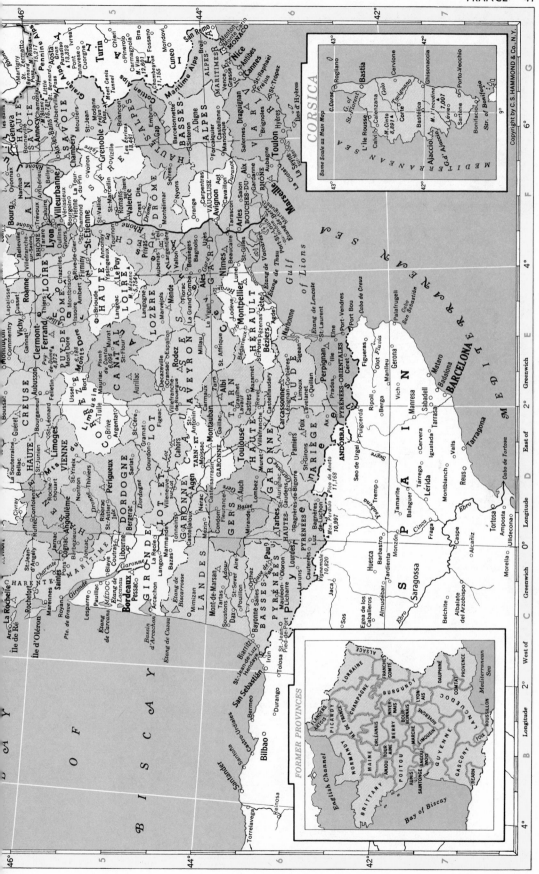

CORSICA

Same Scale as Main Map

M E D I T E R R A N E A N   S E A

Gulf of Lions

FORMER PROVINCES

English Channel

Bay of Biscay

Mediterranean Sea

GERMANY

CONIC PROJECTION

SCALE OF MILES
0 10 20   40   60

SCALE OF KILOMETRES
0 10 20   40   60

Capitals of Countries
State and District Capitals
Canals

Copyright by C.S. HAMMOND & Co., N.Y.

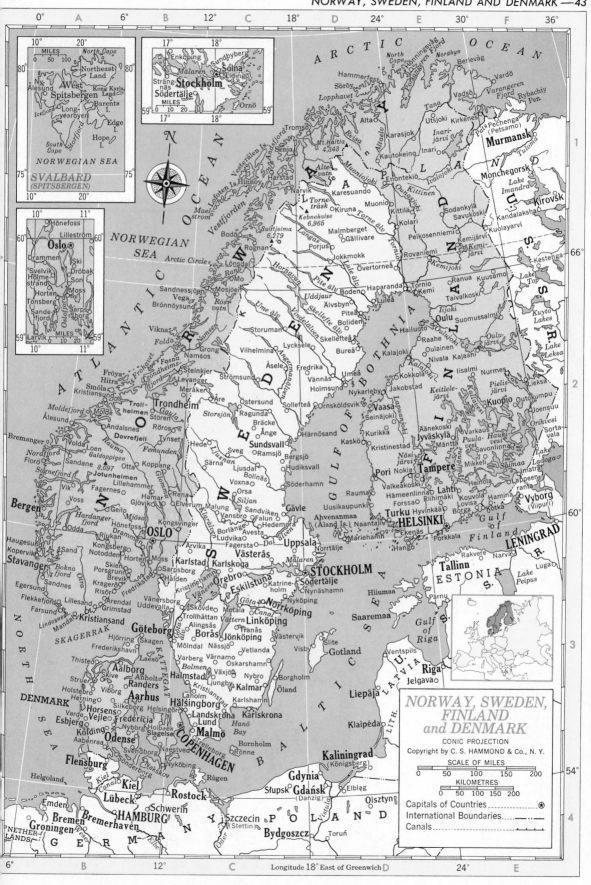

NORWAY, SWEDEN, FINLAND and DENMARK
CONIC PROJECTION
Copyright by C. S. Hammond & Co., N. Y.

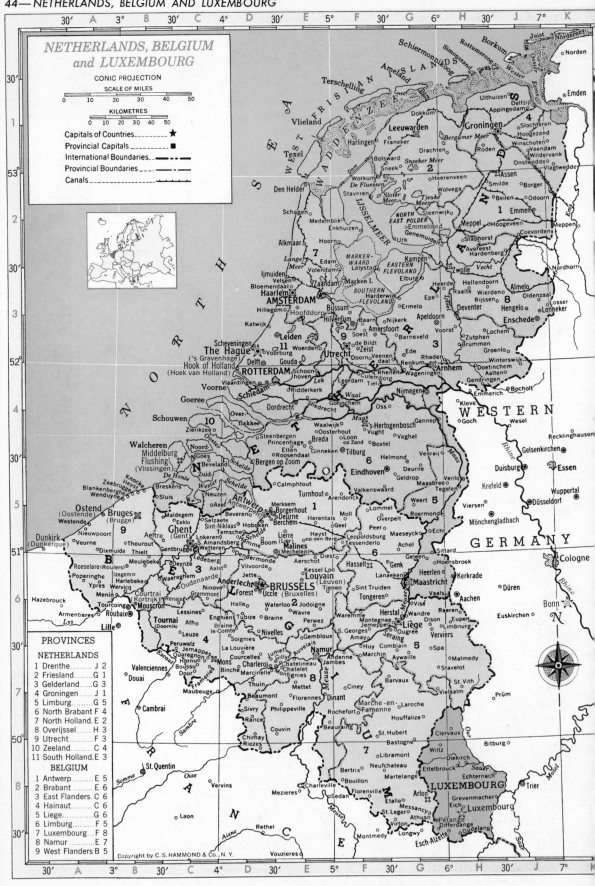

NETHERLANDS, BELGIUM and LUXEMBOURG

CONIC PROJECTION

SCALE OF MILES

0   10   20   30   40   50

KILOMETRES

0   10   20   30   40   50

Capitals of Countries..........★
Provincial Capitals..........■
International Boundaries......—·—·—
Provincial Boundaries......—···—
Canals............===

PROVINCES

NETHERLANDS

1 Drenthe......... J 2
2 Friesland........G 1
3 Gelderland......G 3
4 Groningen......J 1
5 Limburg.........G 5
6 North Brabant. F 4
7 North Holland. E 2
8 Overijssel......H 3
9 Utrecht.........F 3
10 Zeeland.........C 4
11 South Holland. E 3

BELGIUM

1 Antwerp.........E 5
2 Brabant.........E 6
3 East Flanders.. C 6
4 Hainaut.........C 6
5 Liege...........G 6
6 Limburg.........F 5
7 Luxembourg... F 8
8 Namur..........E 7
9 West Flanders B 5

Copyright by C. S. HAMMOND & Co., N.Y.

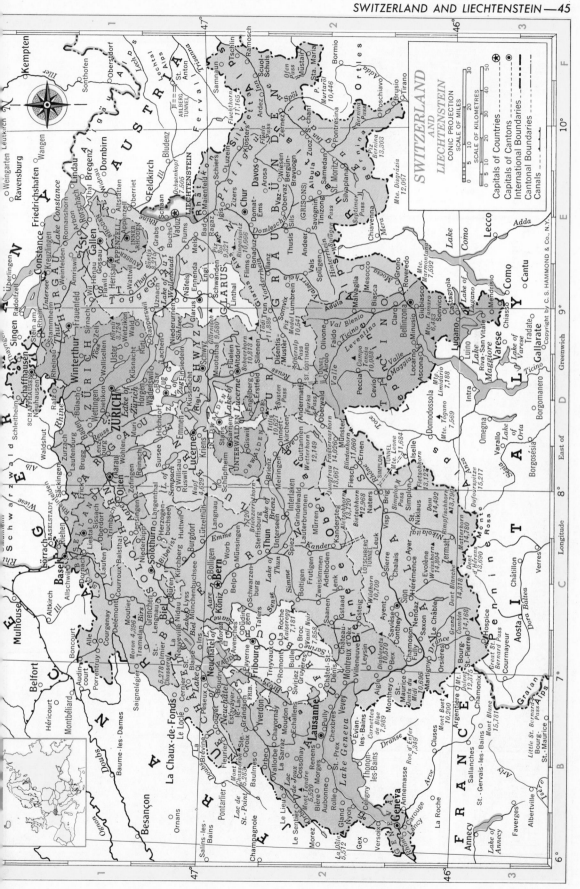

SWITZERLAND
AND
LIECHTENSTEIN
CONIC PROJECTION
SCALE OF MILES
SCALE OF KILOMETRES

⊛ Capitals of Countries
◉ Capitals of Cantons
— International Boundaries
—·—·— Cantonal Boundaries
Canals

Copyright by C.S. HAMMOND & Co., N.Y.

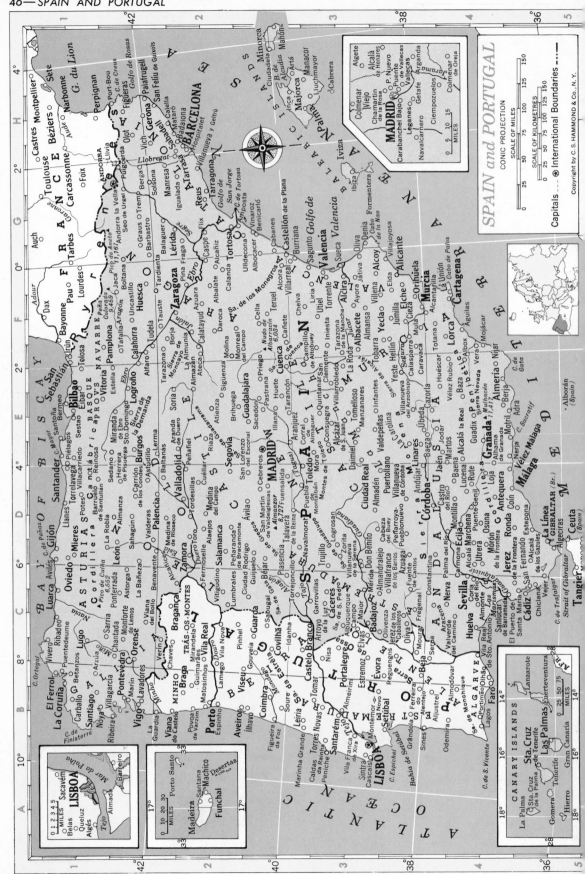

SPAIN and PORTUGAL

CONIC PROJECTION

SCALE OF MILES

0 25   50   75   100   125   150

SCALE OF KILOMETRES

0 25 50 75 100 125 150

Capitals----- ⊛ International Boundaries------

Copyright by C. S. HAMMOND & CO., N. Y.

ITALY

CONIC PROJECTION

SCALE OF MILES

0   20   40   60   80   100   120

SCALE OF KILOMETRES

0   20   40   60   80 100 120

Capitals of Countries ____ ⊛

Regional Capitals _____ ◉

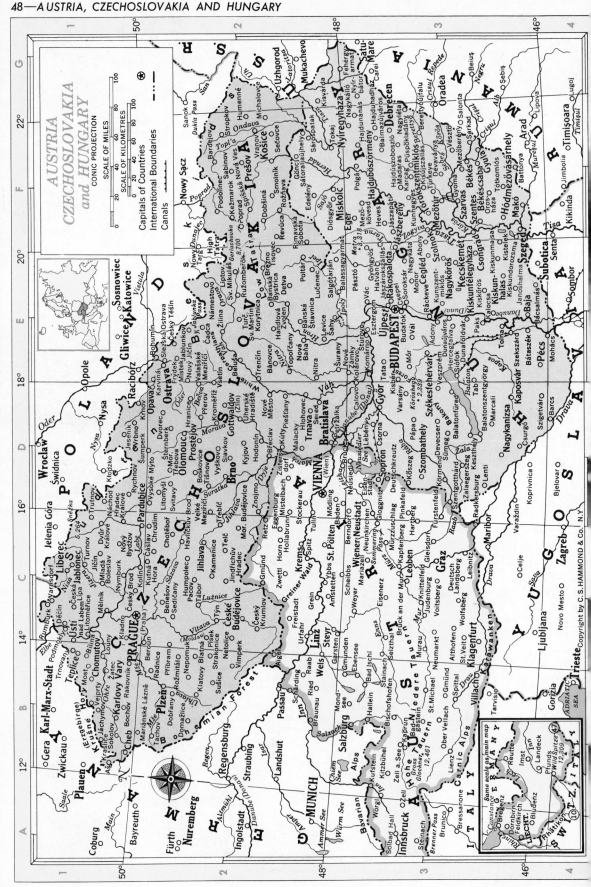

AUSTRIA
CZECHOSLOVAKIA
and HUNGARY

CONIC PROJECTION

SCALE OF MILES

SCALE OF KILOMETRES

Capitals of Countries
International Boundaries
Canals

Copyright by C. S. HAMMOND & Co., N.Y.

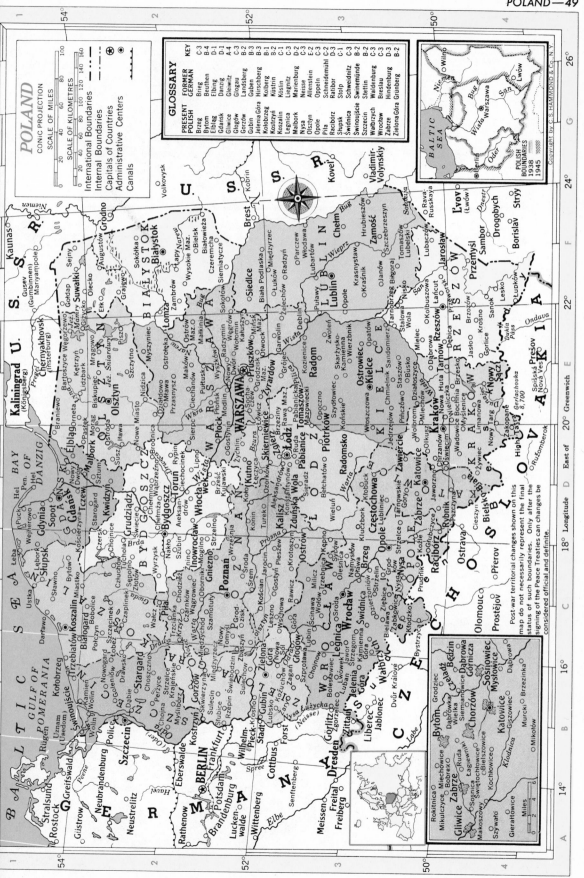

POLAND

CONIC PROJECTION

SCALE OF MILES

SCALE OF KILOMETRES

International Boundaries
Internal Boundaries
Capitals of Countries
Administrative Centers
Canals

GLOSSARY

PRESENT POLISH	FORMER GERMAN	KEY
Brzeg	Brieg	C-3
Bytom	Beuthen	B-4
Elbląg	Elbing	D-1
Gdańsk	Danzig	D-1
Gliwice	Gleiwitz	A-4
Głogów	Glogau	C-3
Gorzów	Landsberg	B-2
Gubin	Guben	B-3
Jelenia Góra	Hirschberg	B-3
Kołobrzeg	Kolberg	B-1
Kostrzyn	Küstrin	B-2
Koszalin	Köslin	C-1
Legnica	Liegnitz	C-3
Malbork	Marienburg	D-2
Nysa	Neisse	C-3
Olsztyn	Allenstein	E-2
Opole	Oppeln	C-3
Piła	Schneidemühl	C-2
Racibórz	Ratibor	D-3
Słupsk	Stolp	C-1
Świdnica	Schweidnitz	C-3
Świnoujście	Swinemünde	B-2
Szczecin	Stettin	B-2
Wałbrzych	Waldenburg	C-3
Wrocław	Breslau	C-3
Zabrze	Hindenburg	D-3
Zielona Góra	Grünberg	B-2

BALTIC SEA

POLISH BOUNDARIES 1938 1945

Copyright by C. S. HAMMOND & Co., N.Y.

Post-war territorial changes shown on this map do not necessarily represent the final status of such boundaries. Only after the signing of the Peace Treaties can changes be considered official and definite.

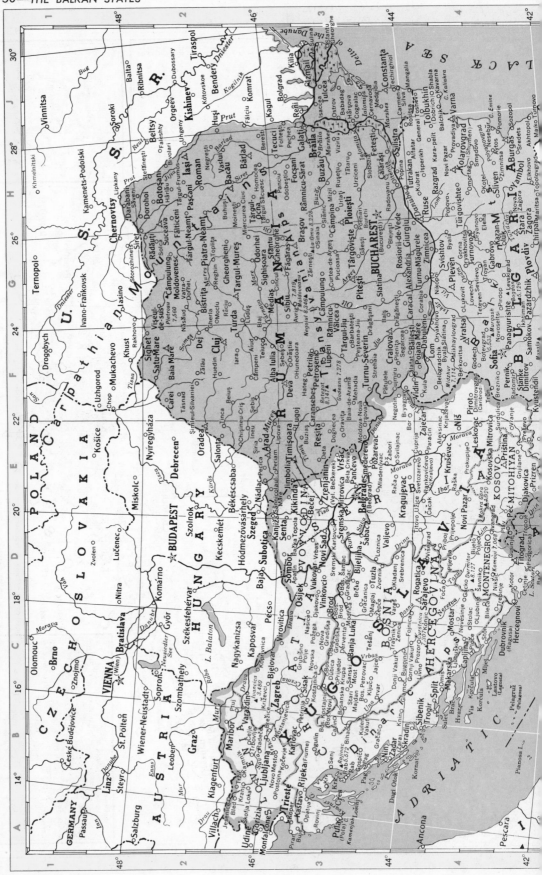

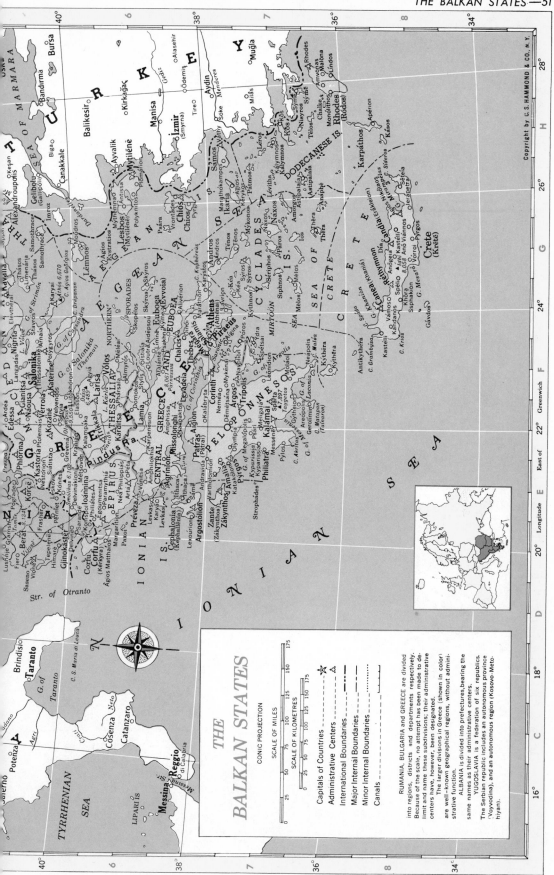

THE BALKAN STATES

CONIC PROJECTION

SCALE OF MILES

0 25 50 75 100 125 150 175

SCALE OF KILOMETRES

0 25 50 75 100 125 150 175

Capitals of Countries ⸺⸺⸺⸺

Administrative Centers ⸺⸺⸺

International Boundaries ⸺ — ⸺ — ⸺

Major Internal Boundaries ⸺ ⸺ ⸺

Minor Internal Boundaries ············

Canals ············

RUMANIA, BULGARIA and GREECE are divided into regions, districts and departments respectively. Because of the scale, no attempt has been made to de-limit and name these subdivisions; their administrative centers have, however, been designated.

The larger divisions in Greece (shown in color) are well-known geographical regions, without admini-strative function.

ALBANIA is divided into prefectures, bearing the same names as their administrative centers.

YUGOSLAVIA is a federation of six republics. The Serbian republic includes an autonomous province (Voyvodina), and an autonomous region (Kosovo-Meto-hiyan).

UNION OF SOVIET SOCIALIST REPUBLICS
European Part
CONIC PROJECTION

SCALE OF MILES
0 50 100 200 300

SCALE OF KILOMETRES
0 50 100 200 300

National Capitals .... ★
Capitals of Union Republics .... ☆
Administrative Centers .... ⊙
International boundaries ....
Union Republic boundaries ....
A.S.S.R., Oblast, Kray boundaries ....
Autonomous Oblast boundaries ....
Canals ....

The government of the United States does not recognize
the incorporation of Estonia, Latvia and Lithuania into the
Soviet Union.
Post-war territorial changes shown on this map do not
necessarily represent the final status of such boundaries.
Only after the signing of peace treaties can changes be
considered official and definite.

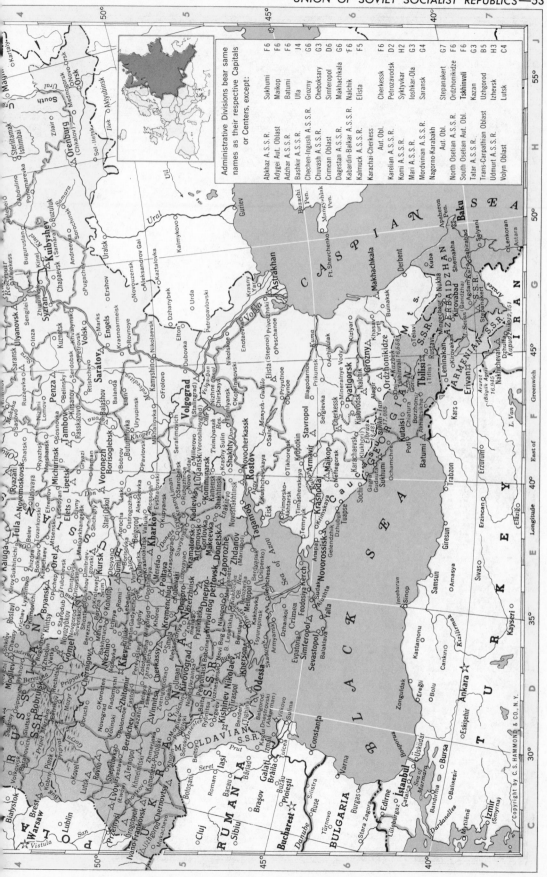

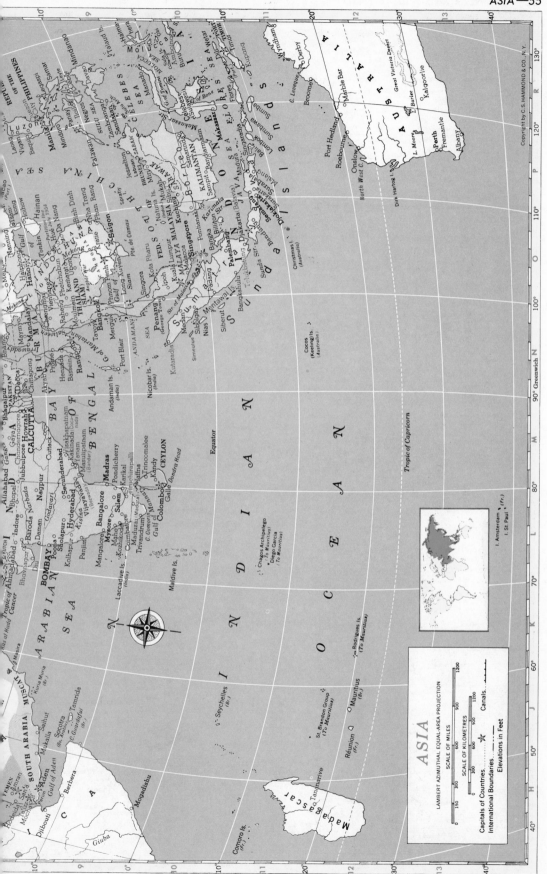

ASIA

LAMBERT AZIMUTHAL EQUAL-AREA PROJECTION

SCALE OF MILES

0   150   300   600   900   1200

SCALE OF KILOMETRES

0   300   600   900   1200

Capitals of Countries . . . . ★

International Boundaries . . . .

Canals . . . .

Elevations in Feet

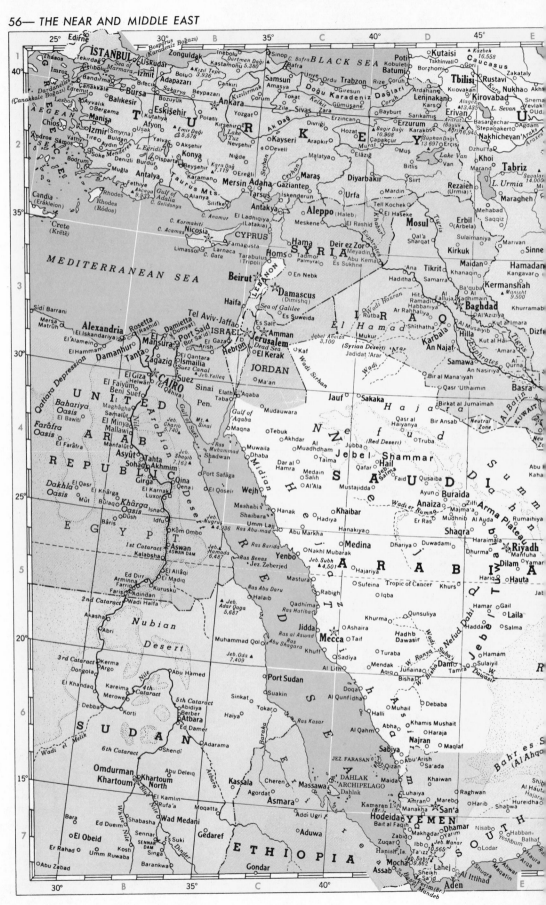

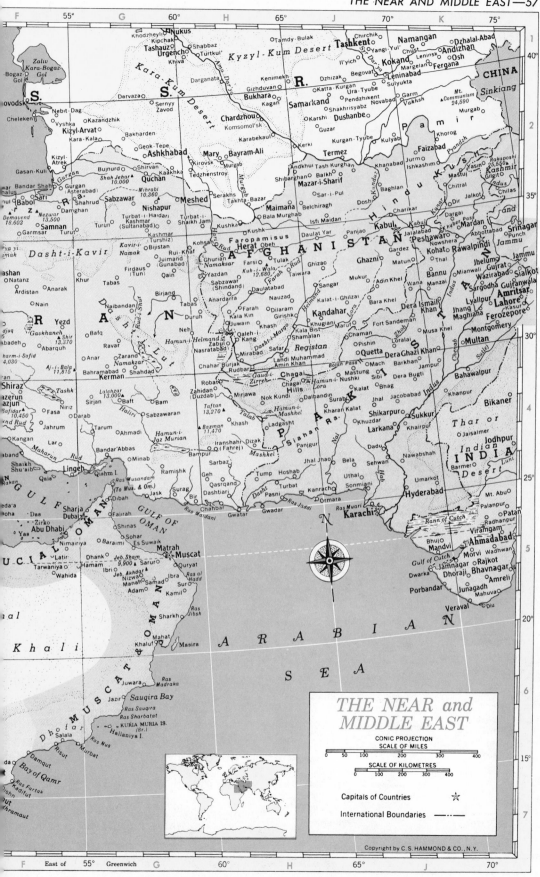

THE NEAR and MIDDLE EAST

CONIC PROJECTION

SCALE OF MILES

| 0 | 50 | 100 | 200 | 300 | 400 |

SCALE OF KILOMETRES

| 0 | 100 | 200 | 300 | 400 |

Capitals of Countries .... ☆

International Boundaries .... — ·· — ·· —

Copyright by C. S. HAMMOND & CO., N.Y.

ISRAEL and JORDAN
CYLINDRICAL PROJECTION
Copyright by C.S. HAMMOND & CO., N.Y.
SCALE OF MILES
0   5   10   15   20   25   30
SCALE OF KILOMETRES
0   5   10   15   20   25   30

Capitals of Countries .... ★
District and Provincial Capitals ...... ⊙
International Boundaries ....
District and Provincial Boundaries ....
Demilitarized Zone Boundaries ....
Neutral Zone Boundaries ....

MEDITERRANEAN SEA

SYRIA

LEBANON

JORDAN

UNITED ARAB REPUBLIC EGYPT

NEUTRAL ZONE

GAZA STRIP
(U.A.R. Administration)

NORTHERN GALILEE

HAIFA

CENTRAL

SAMARIA

JERUSALEM

HEBRON

SOUTHERN

AJLUN

EL ASIMA

35° Longitude East of Greenwich 30'

MILES
0   10   20   30

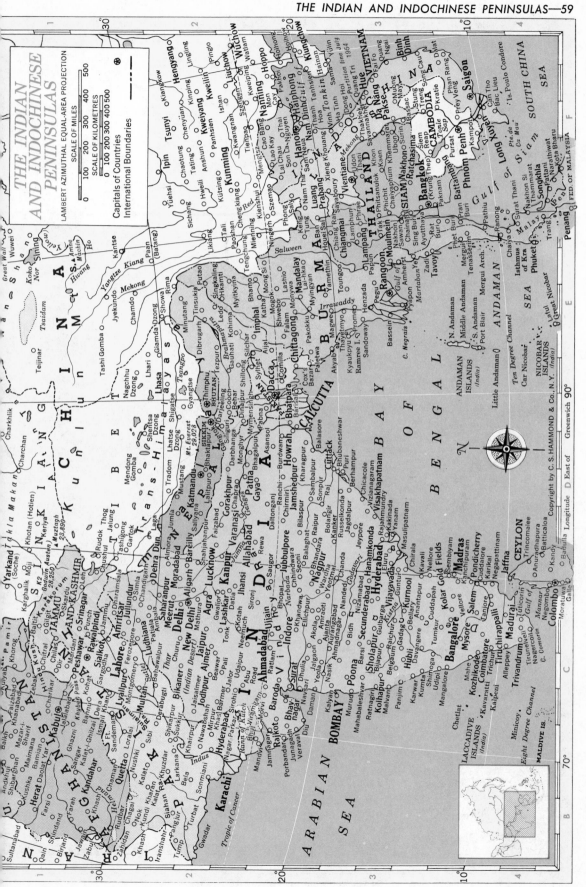

EASTERN CHINA,
JAPAN & KOREA

CONIC PROJECTION

SCALE OF MILES

SCALE OF KILOMETRES

Capitals of Countries .... ☆   International Boundaries ......
Provincial Capitals .... ◉   Provincial Boundaries ......
Canals ....   Walls ......

©C. S. HAMMOND & Co., Maplewood, N. J.

*Wuhan municipality consists of
Hankow, Hanyang and Wuchang
†Lüta municipality includes
Port Arthur and Dairen

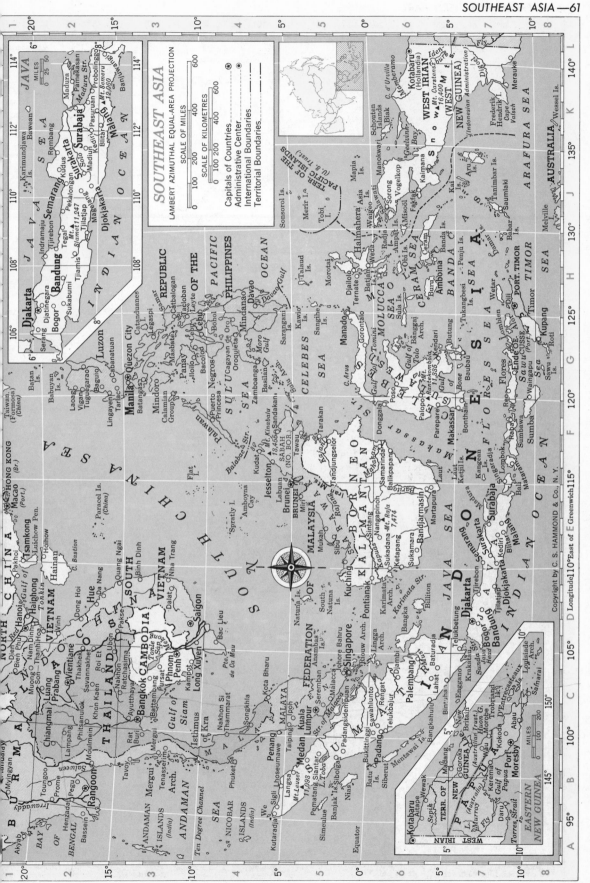

SOUTHEAST ASIA
LAMBERT AZIMUTHAL EQUAL-AREA PROJECTION

SCALE OF MILES

0   100   200   400   600

SCALE OF KILOMETRES

0   100 200   400   600

Capitals of Countries .... ⊛
Administrative Center .... ⊛
International Boundaries ....
Territorial Boundaries ....

JAVA

MILES
0 25 50

J A V A   S E A

Djakarta   Bandung

I N D I A N   O C E A N

Surabaja   Semarang   Surakarta   Djokjakarta

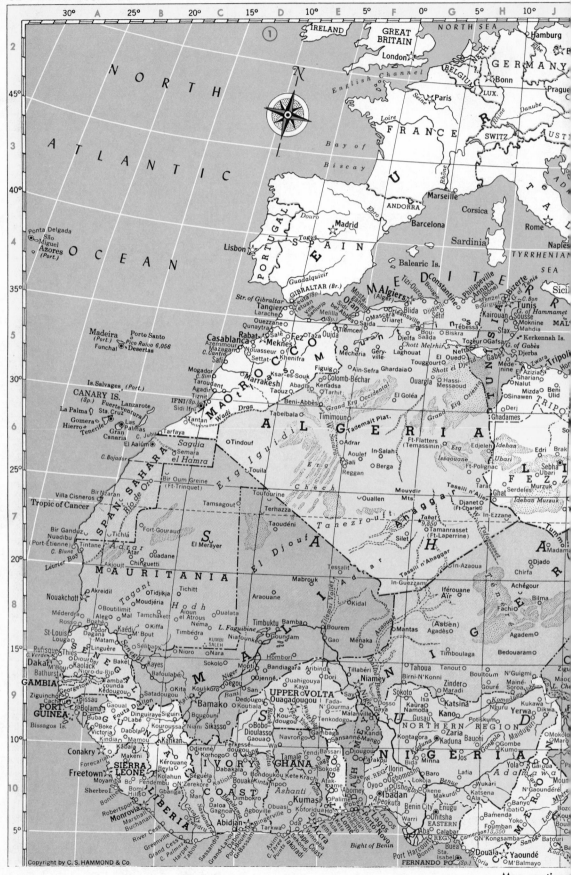

Map continued

AFRICA
Northern Part

LAMBERT AZIMUTHAL EQUAL-AREA PROJECTION

SCALE OF MILES
0   100   200   400   600

SCALE OF KILOMETRES
0 100 200   400   600

Capitals of Countries ⎯⎯⎯⎯⎯⎯ ☆
Other Capitals ⎯⎯⎯⎯⎯⎯⎯⎯ ◉
International Boundaries ⎯·⎯·⎯
Internal Boundaries ⎯ ⎯ ⎯
Canals ⎯⎯⎯⎯ Wells ⎯⎯⎯ ○

Countries, cities and geographic features:

Warsaw, U.S.S.R., Kiev, Kharkov, Odessa, Rostov, RUMANIA, Bucharest, Danube, BULGARIA, Sofia, Belgrade, İstanbul, Ankara, BLACK SEA, Sea of Azov, Dnieper, Bug, CASPIAN SEA, U.S.S.R.

GREECE, AEGEAN SEA, Athens, Crete, TURKEY, CYPRUS, SYRIA, Mosul, Baghdad, Tigris, Euphrates, IRAQ, IRAN, Tehran

Beirut, LEBANON, Damascus, Tel Aviv-Jaffa, ISRAEL, Jerusalem, JORDAN, MEDITERRANEAN SEA

Shahat (Cyrene), Derna, Tobruk, El Bardi, Salûm, Sidi Barrani, Mekili, Soluk, Ajedabia, Jarabub (Jaghbub), Aujila, Jalo, Jeb. elten, CYRENAICA, LIBYA, Tazerbo, El Geziro Oasis, Buzeima, Rebiana, El Jauf, Kufra Oasis, Bishiara, Jebel Uweinat 6,255, Sarra

Alexandria (El Iskandariya), El Alamein, Damietta (Dumyât), Port Said, Suez Canal, Ismailia, Suez, CAIRO (El Qâhira), El Faiyûm, Beni Suef, Sinai Pen., Gulf of Aqaba, Qattara Depression, Siwa, Siwa Oasis, El Minya, Manfalut, El Qasr, Qasr Farâfra, Farâfra Oasis, Asyût, Akhmîm, Sohâg, Kharga, Kharga Oasis, El Quseir, UNITED ARAB REPUBLIC, EGYPT, Idfu, Aswân Dam 1st Cat., Aswân, Luxor, Qena, Ras Bânâs

NEUTRAL ZONE, KUWAIT, Neutral Zone, Persian Gulf, Dhahran, BAHREIN, QATAR, TRUCIAL OMAN, SAUDI, Medina, Riyadh, ARABIA, Tropic of Cancer, Mecca, R. Abu Shagara, Ras Abu Dara, Ras Elba, Halaib, Dungunab, Muhammad Qol, Port Sudan, Suakin, Sinkat, Tokar, Trinkitat, Haiya Jct., Berber, DAHLAK ARCH, Farasan Is., San'a, YEMEN, SOUTH ARABIA

RED SEA, Arabian Desert, Nile, Farâs, Arminna, 2nd Cat., Wadi Halfa, Abri, Selima Oasis, Nubian Desert, NORTHERN PROV., Laqiya Umra, 3rd Cat., Kerma, Dongola, 4th Cat., Karima, NURI, Merowe, Ed Debba, 6th Cat., Ed Damer, Atbara, Shendi, MEROE, NAQA, Omdurman, Khartoum, Khartoum North, Kassala, Keren, Agordat, Massawa, Asmara, Aduwa, Aksum, Makale, Assab, Danakil

Ouanga-Kébir, Fada, Ennedi, Arada, Biltine, Abécher, Geneina, El Fasher, Kebkabia, Okutum, Umm Keddada, Sodiri, Ed Dueim, Bara, Wad Medani, Gedaref, Sennar, Singa, Ras Dashan 15,157, Gondar, Debra Tabor, DARFUR, Mogororo, Nyala, Ed Da'ein, Babanusa, El Muglad, En Nahud, El Obeid, Rashad, Renk, Kosti, BLUE NILE, Roseires L. Tana, Debra Markos, Magdala, Dessye, KORDOFAN, SUDAN, ETHIOPIA, Am-Timan, Birao, Buram, Kadugli, Talodi, Kaka, Famaka, Asosa, Addis Alam, Gore, Jimma, Haddama, Asselle, Dabat, Abbai, Debra Sina, Débé

Ouanda-Djalé, Ouadda, Mouka, Kafia Kingi, Raga, Deim Zubeir, Wau, Tonj, Shambe, Bor, Pibor Post, Malakal, Kodok (Fashoda), Dembidollo, Gambela, Soddu, Goba, Ginir, Imi, BAHR EL GHAZAL, Sudd, Nasir, Akobo, Maji, Gardula, Yirga-Alam, UPPER NILE, Ndélé, Yalinga, Bria, Bambari, Bangassou, Rafai, Zémio, Djéma, Tambura, AFRICAN REPUBLIC, -de-Possel, Bambari, Mobaye, Bomi, Banzyville, Gemena, Uele, Bondo, Niangara, Dungu, Poko, Faradje, Yei, Nimule, Nagishot, Juba, Mongalla, Maridi, EQUATORIA, L. Rudolf, L. Stefanie, Dawa, Moyale, Negelli, Dolo, Lugh, Baidoa, Bur Acaba, El Bur, Obbia

Gulf of Aden, Aden, Tadjoura, Djibouti, FR. SOMALILAND, Zeila, Bulhar, Berbera, Bender Kassim, Alula, C. Guardafui, Ras Hafun, Hafun (Dante), Bender Beila, Candala, Hordio, Erigavo, Ankhor, Burao, Gardo, Eil, Garad, Hargeisa, Las Anod, Dagabur, Harrar, Dire Dawa, Jijiga, Borama, Gerlogubi, Wardere, Gorrahei, Callafo, Webi Shebeli, Mudugh, Galkayu, SOMALI REP., Obbia, Marek, Eil Bur, Bulo Burti, Hoduro, Isha Baidoa, Belet Uen, Webi, Ghinir, Goba, Canale, Dolo

Map continued

GULF OF GUINEA

Equator

SOUTH

ATLANTIC

OCEAN

° Ascension
(St. Helena)

St. Helena °
(Br.)

Tropic of Capricorn

AFRICA
Southern Part

LAMBERT AZIMUTHAL EQUAL-AREA PROJECTION

SCALE OF MILES

| 0 | 100 | 200 | 400 | 600 |

SCALE OF KILOMETRES

| 0 | 100 | 200 | 400 | 600 |

Capitals of Countries .... ☆
Other Capitals .... ◉
International Boundaries ..... ─ ─ ─
Internal Boundaries .... ───
Canals .... Wells ....○

N

Longitude West of Greenwich   Longitude East of Greenwich

Bight of Biafra
Kribi ○ Ebolowa Campo Dja Mol
Bata ○ Bitam
Santo António ○ Eloboy RIO ○ Oyem Souanké Oues
Príncipe MUNI ○ Mitzic
SÃO TOMÉ E PRÍNCIPE (Sp.) Makokou○ Mékamb
(Port.) São Tomé Corisco Kelle
São Tomé ✕ Libreville Booué Kelle
GABON
Annobón ○ Kango Ogooué
(Fernando Po) Lambaréné Fr-Roi
C. Lopez Lastoursville Koula-Moutou
Port-Gentil Mouila Franceville
Ombouè ○ Gambon
Francville
Sette-Cama ○ Tchibanga Djambalâo Pa
Nyanga Loudima ○
Mayumba Dolisie Brazzaville
CONGO
Pointe-Noire Tshela Ol
CABINDA Landana ○ ○ Luozi
Cabinda ○ Matadi
Banana São Ma
Santo António Salvador
do Zaire Da
Ambrizete ○ Bembe
CON
Ambriz ○
Luanda ☆ LUANDA Cu
Gabe
Porto Amboim ○ Cu
Novo Redondo ○ ANGOLA
CUANZA-SUL
Lobito ○
Benguela Nova
Dombe Grande ○
C. de Sta. Maria BENGUELA
Sá da Bandeira ◉ Art
Moçâmedes ○ Ovi
(Mossâmedes) HUÍ
Porto Alexandre ○ Vila de
Tigres Bay Vila de Av
Cunene
SO
C. Frio Ov
Etosh
Otj
Walvis B SO
Walvis Bay Om
(C. of Good Hope) Ka
Hollam's Bird I. •
Lüderi
Ora
Alexa

19°
Kasteel Wolseley ○ Ceres ○
Mts.
Malmesbury ○ Hermon ○ Hex River Mts.
Abbotsdale ○ De Doorns ○
Kalbaskraal ○ Botha
Wellington Worcester
Berg Breede Nuy ○
Kliphheuvel ○ Brandvlei ○ Langvlei ○
Paarl
Durban- ○ Klapmuts
ville ○ Groot-Drakenstein
Robben I. Kraaifontein ○ ○ Franschhoek
Table Bay Bellville ○
Cape Town ☆ Stellenbosch Zonderend
Woodstock ○ Maitland Villiersdorp ○ Mts.
Wynberg 5,212 ▲ Genadendal ○ Greyton
Table Mt. Sneeuwkop 34°
(3,550) Somerset Zonderend
Muizenberg W. Strand ○ Grabouw
Cape Seal I. ○ Gordon's Houhoek ○ Caledon ○ ○ Krige
Slangkop Pt. Vishoek Bay Botrivier ○
Simonstown False Bay Bot
Peninsula Hawston ○
Cape of Good Hope Sandown Hermanus
Cape Pt. Bay Mosselrivier
C. Maclear C. Hangklip Walker Bay

SOUTH

ATLANTIC SCALE OF MILES

OCEAN | 0 | 5 | 10 | 20 | 30 |

34°

Longitude East of Greenwich 19°

| A | 25° | B | 20° | C | 15° | D | 10° | E | 5° | F | 0° | G | 5° | H | 10° | J |

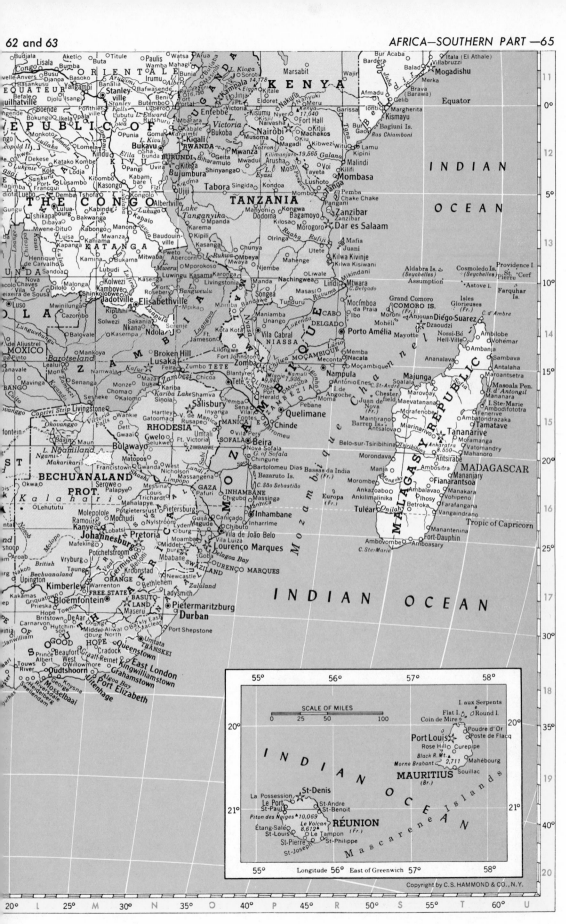

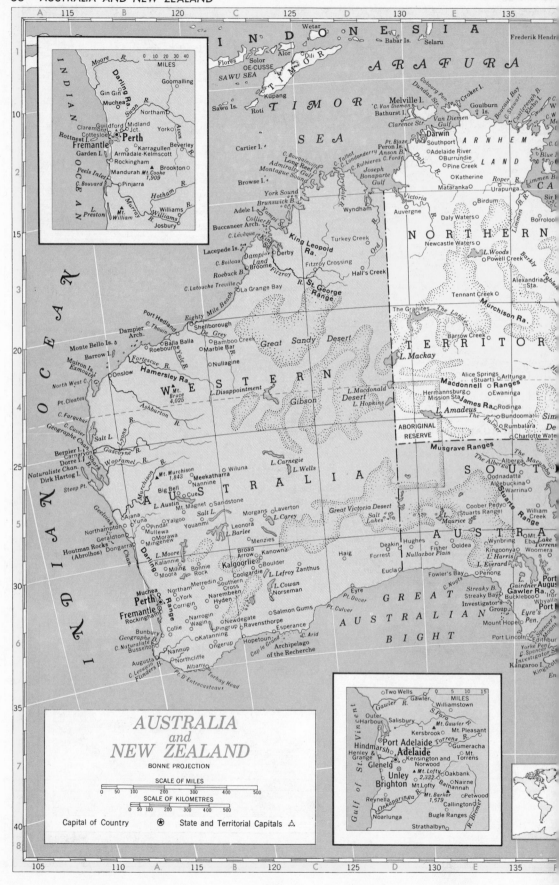

AUSTRALIA
and
NEW ZEALAND

BONNE PROJECTION

SCALE OF MILES

0 50 100   200   300   400   500

SCALE OF KILOMETRES

0 50 100 200 300 400 500

Capital of Country ⊛ State and Territorial Capitals ⌂

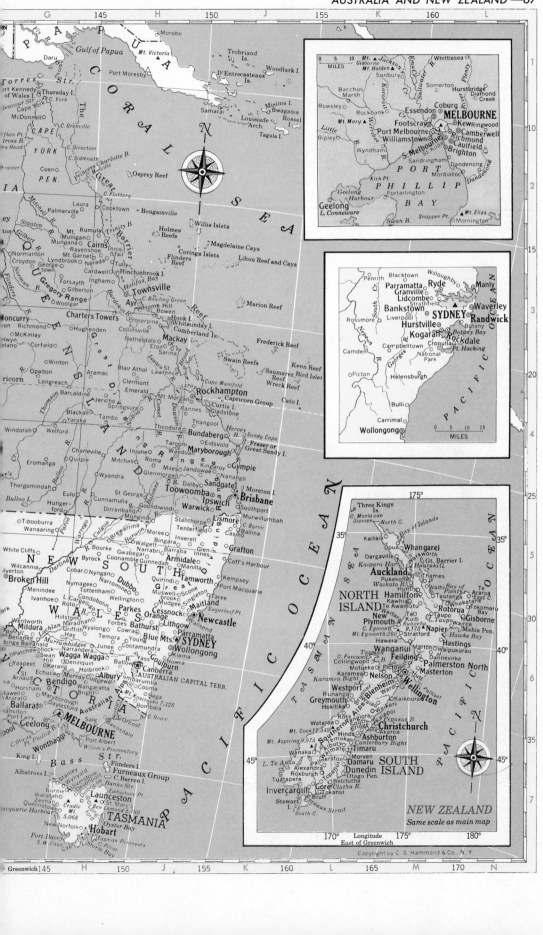

MELBOURNE inset:

MILES 0 5 10

Whittlesea
Mt. Jackson · Gisborne
Mt. Holden · Sunbury
Somerton · Hurstbridge · Diamond Creek
Rowsley · Bacchus Marsh · Rockbank
Coburg
Mt. Mary · Essendon
Ringwood
MELBOURNE · Kew
Footscray · Camberwell
Mt. Mary · Port Melbourne · Richmond
Little · Williamstown · S. Melbourne · Caulfield
Ripley · Wyndham · St. Kilda · Brighton · Dandenong
Sandringham · Mordialloc
Kirk Pt. · PORT
Geelong · Portarlington · PHILLIP · Dandenong
Harbour
Geelong · BAY
L. Conneware · Snapper Pt. · Mt. Eliza
Swan B. · Mornington

SYDNEY inset:

Willoughby
Penrith · Blacktown
Parramatta · Ryde · Manly
Granville · Lidcombe
Strathfield · Waverley
Bankstown
Rossmore · Liverpool · Hurstville · SYDNEY · Randwick
Botany
Kogarah · Botany Bay
Rockdale
Camden · Campbelltown · Cronulla · Pt. Hacking
Georges R.
Helensburgh · National Park
Picton
Bulli
Carrimal
Wollongong
MILES 0 5 10 15

PACIFIC OCEAN

NEW ZEALAND inset:

Three Kings Is.
C. Maria van Diemen · North C.
Kaitaia · Bay of Islands
Whangarei
Dargaville · Opua · Warkworth
Kaipara Har. · Gt. Barrier I.
Hauraki G.
Auckland
Pukekohe · Thames
New · Waikato R. · Waihi · Bay of Plenty
Kawhia · Hamilton · Te Aroha · Tauranga
NORTH · Te Awamutu · Whakatane
ISLAND · Te Kuiti · Rotorua · Tokomaru Bay
New · Taupo
Plymouth · C. Egmont · L. Taupo · Gisborne
Mt. Egmont 8,260 · Ruapehu · Napier
Stratford · 9,175 · Hawke Bay
Hawera · Wanganui · Waipukurau
Wanganui · Feilding · Dannevirke
C. Farewell · Collingwood · Palmerston North
Motueka · Masterton
Karamea · Picton · Palliser
Westport · Nelson · Hutt · Wellington
Karamea Bight · Blenheim
Runanga · Wairau
Greymouth · Kaikoura
Hokitika · Waipara
Ross · Rangiora · Pegasus B.
Wataroa · Southern Alps · Waikari · Akaroa
Mt. Cook 12,349 · Christchurch
Mt. Aspiring 9,975 · Hinds · Canterbury Bight
Temuka · Ashburton
L. Te Anau · Albury · Waimate · Timaru
Palmerston · Morven
Alexandra · Oamaru · SOUTH
Tuatapere · Roxburgh · Otago Pen. · ISLAND
Topapa · Dunedin
Invercargill · Gore · Balclutha
Stewart I. · Bluff · Clutha R.
Foveaux Strait · Tokanui
South C.

NEW ZEALAND
Same scale as main map

Longitude East of Greenwich
170° 175° 180°

Copyright by C. S. Hammond & Co., N.Y.

Main map labels:

PAPUA · Morobe
Gulf of Papua · Mt. Victoria · Trobriand Is.
Daru · Port Moresby · Woodlark I.
Torres Str. · D'Entrecasteaux Is.
Thursday I. · C. York · Samarai · Misima I.
Pt. Kennedy · Cape of Wales I. · Bwagaoia · Rossel I.
Seaflower Str. · Louisiade Arch. · Tagula I.
McDonnell
CAPE · C. Direction
YORK · C. Sidmouth · CORAL SEA
PEN. · Coen · Osprey Reef
Princess Charlotte B.
C. Melville
The · Holmes Reefs
C. Flattery · Willis Islets
Laura · Cooktown · Bougainville
Palmerville · Magdelaine Cays
Mungana · Mt. Garnet · Cairns · Trinity · Coringa Islets · Lihou Reef and Cays
Normanton · Ravenshoe · Flinders Reef
Croydon · Lyndbrook · Nerada · Tully · Hinchbrook I.
Forsayth · Gilberton · Ingham · Halifax Bay
George-town · Cardwell · Townsville · Marion Reef
Gilbert · Ayr · Home Hill · Bowen
Charters Towers · C. Bowling Green Reef
Hughenden · Collinsville · Hook I. · Whitsunday I.
Richmond · Netherdale · Cumberland Is.
McKinlay · Mackay · Frederick Reef
Corfield · Eton · Sarina
Winton · Aramac · Swain Reefs
Opalton · Clermont · Kenn Reef
Longreach · Emerald · Saumarez Bird Islet Reef · Wreck Reef
Barcaldine · Mt. Morgan · Cato I.
Jericho · Springsure · Rockhampton
Blackall · Tambo · Theodore · Capricorn Group
Windorah · Welford · Curtis I. · Gladstone
Charleville · Injune · Bundaberg
Eromanga · Quilpie · Mitchell · Roma · Eidsvold · Fraser or Great Sandy I.
Thargomindah · Wyandra · Kingaroy · Maryborough
Bullo L. · Eulo · Cunnamulla · Jandowae · Gympie
Hungerford · St. George · Dalby · Sandgate
Tibooburra · Goondiwindi · Toowoomba · Moreton I.
Wanaaring · Dirranbandi · Ipswich · Brisbane
White Cliffs · Moree · Warwick · Southport
Wilcannia · Bourke · Stanthorpe · Lismore · Murwillumbah
Broken Hill · Byrock · Tenterfield · Casino · C. Byron · Ballina
Menindee · Cobar · Nyngan · Inverell · Glen Innes · Grafton
Ivanhoe · Narromine · Armidale · Coff's Harbour
NEW SOUTH WALES · Quirindi · Tamworth · Manilla · Kempsey
Tottenham · Muswellbrook · Port Macquarie
Hillston · Condobolin · Wellington · Singleton · Taree
Parkes · Orange · Mudgee · Maitland · Sugarloaf Pt.
Naradhan · Forbes · Bathurst · Cessnock · Newcastle
Griffith · Cowra · Young · Lithgow · Wallsend
Temora · Cootamundra · Blue Mts. · SYDNEY
Junee · Wollongong · Kiama
Wagga Wagga · Yass · Goulburn
Narrandera · Canberra · Batlow
Deniliquin · Gundagai · AUSTRALIAN CAPITAL TERR.
Swan Hill · Kerang · Cudgewa · Cooma · C. Howe
Mildura · Holbrook · Albury · Jindabyne · Bombala
VICTORIA · Corowa · Bright · Mt. Kosciusko 7,328
Horsham · Maryborough · Benalla · Bega
Ballarat · Daylesford · Australia · C. Howe
Geelong · MELBOURNE · Sale · Bairnsdale
Wonthaggi · Port Albert · Wilson's Promontory
King I. · BASS STR. · Flinders I.
Albatross I. · Furneaux Group
Stanley · Wynyard · C. Barren I. · Banks Str.
Burnie · Ulverstone · Eddystone Pt.
Waratah · Zeehan · Launceston · St. Mary's
Queenstown · Cradle Mt. 5,068 · Ben Lomond 5,160
Macquarie Harbour · TASMANIA
Port Davey · New Norfolk · Hobart
S. W. Cape · Tasman Peninsula
Oyster Bay · C. Pillar · Storm Bay

QUEENSLAND
Great Dividing Range
Gregory Range
Thomson R.
Barcoo R.
Warrego R.
Darling R.
Murrumbidgee R.
Murray R.
Lachlan R.
PACIFIC OCEAN
TASMAN SEA

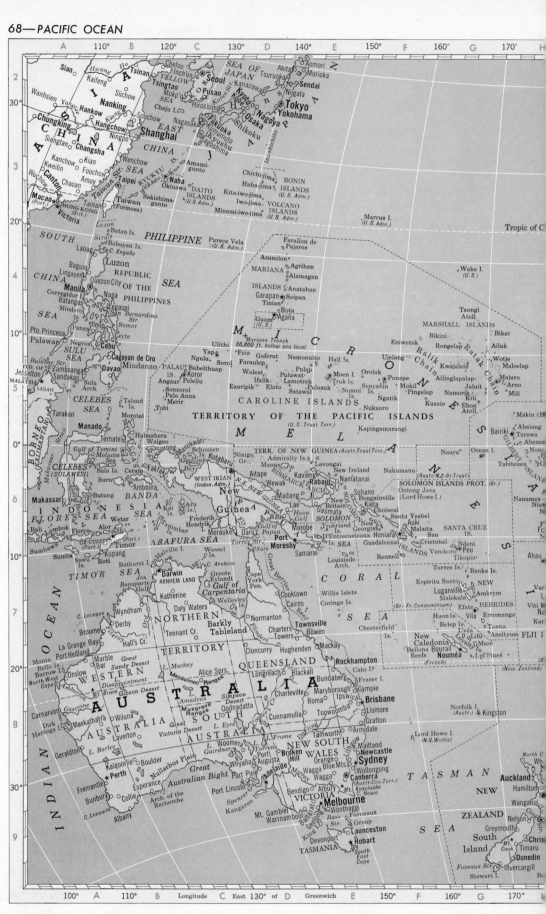

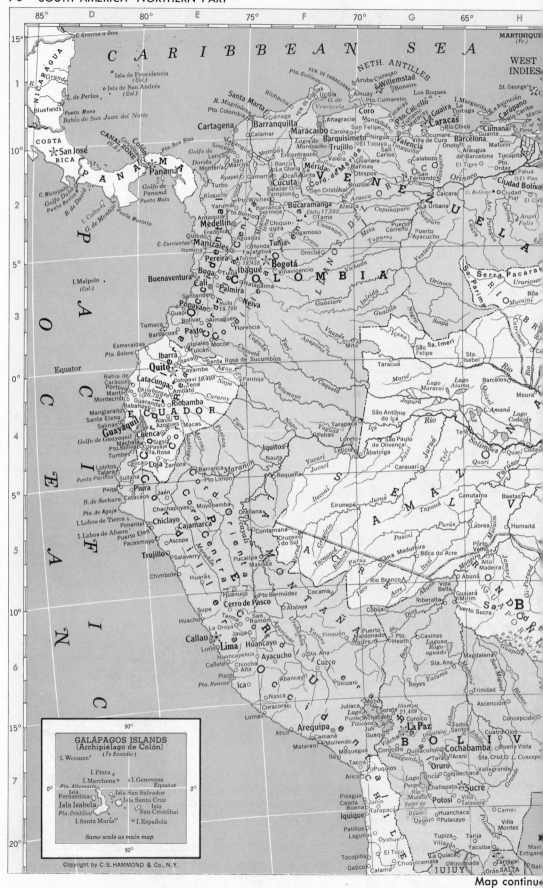

Map continued

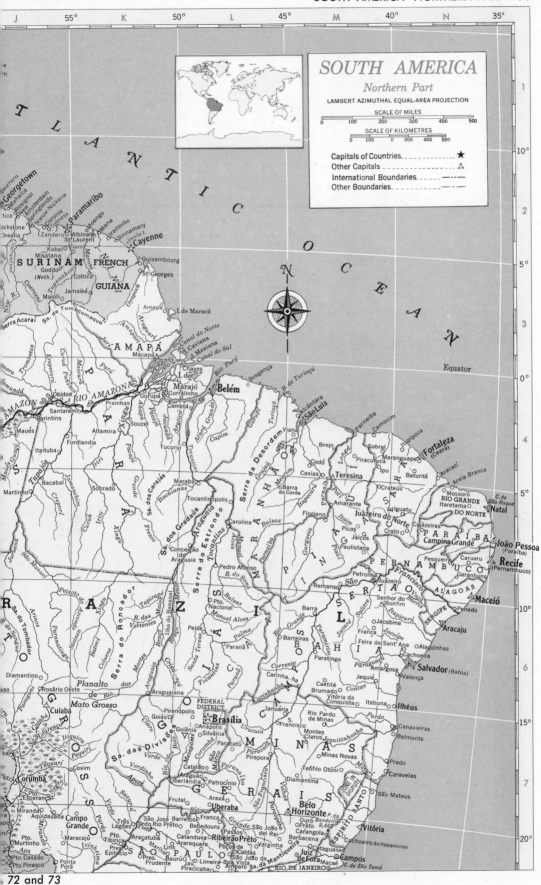

SOUTH AMERICA
Northern Part
LAMBERT AZIMUTHAL EQUAL-AREA PROJECTION

SCALE OF MILES
0   100   200   300   400   500

SCALE OF KILOMETRES
0   100   0   300   400   500

Capitals of Countries..............★
Other Capitals..................⌂
International Boundaries......___ ___
Other Boundaries..............___ · ___

Map continued

PACIFIC OCEAN

Tropic of Capricorn

I. de San Félix • I.San Ambrosio
(Chile)   (Chile)

IS. JUAN FERNÁNDEZ
(Chile)
I. Más a Tierra
I. Más Afuera   I. Santa Clara

Mejillones
Antofagasta
Caleta Coloso
Aguas Blancas
Taltal

San Antonio
de los Cobres
Puna
de S.
Arizaro
Llullaillaco
22,145

Embarcación   El Chorro
Lib. Gen.
San Martín   Rivadavia
JUJUY   Perico
Salta   Las L.
El
Quebrachal

Potrerillos
Chañaral
Pueblo Hundido
Caldera
Copiapó
Juan Godoy
Huasco
Cabo Bascuñan
Vallenar

Antofagasta
de la Sierra
Ojos
del
Salado
Puquios
Tres
Puentes
Tinogasta

Alemania
Rosario
de la Frontera
Atacama
San Carlos
Concepción
Andalgala

Campo
Gallo

Tucumán
Río
Hondo
Tintina

SANTIAGO
DEL
ESTERO

Cruz Grande   El Toto
La Serena
Coquimbo
Tongoy

Rivadavia
Jachal

Chilecito
La
Rioja
Patquia

Famatina

Catamarca   Añatuy
Deán
Funes
Grandes

Mar Chiquita

Rafaela

Ovalle
Illapel

San Juan

Villa Dolores

Córdoba
Francisco
CÓRDOBA

Sant

Los Vilos
Viña del Mar
Valparaíso
Santiago
Rancagua
Pichilemu
San Fernando
Curepto
Constitución
Cauquenes
Quirihue
Talcahuano
Concepción
Arauco
Lebu
Cañete
Traiguén
Temuco
Nueva Imperial
Valdivia
Corral
La Unión
Osorno

SAN JUAN

Aconcagua
22,834

Mendoza
Godoy Cruz
S. Carlos
Maipú 17,388

SAN
San Luis

Alta Gracia
Villa María

Bell Ville

Río Cuarto   Ros
Mercedes

Uspallata Pass

LUIS
Venado Tuerto
Laboulaye   Rufin

MENDOZA
San Rafael
Soitué
Gral. Alvear
Ing. Luiggi

Lincol

B

Pehu
Trenc
Lauqu

Talca
Linares
Parral

Telén
Victorica
Sta. Rosa

Lago
Llancanelo
Gen. Pico
Gen. Acha
Dobla

BUF

LA PAMPA

Cereales

Los
Ángeles
Mulchén
Curacautín

Chillán
Lota

Colorado   Bernasconi

Cor. Pring

Bahía B

Curaco

Algarrobo
Colorado

Pl. Huincul
Gen.
Roca

Chelforó

NEUQUÉN

Zapala
Villarrica
Riñihue
Rinco
Junín de los Andes

Picun Leufú
Neuquén
El Cuy

Negro

Patag
C. Berme

RÍO   NEGRO
Nahuel Huapi
San Carlos de Bariloche

Sierra
Colorada
Valcheta
San Antonio
Oeste
Viedma

Golfo San Matías
Pta. Norte
PEN. VALDE
Salina Gran
Pta. Delgada

Puerto Varas
Maullín
Calbuco
Pto. Montt   Maquinchao
Ancud   Norquinco
Castro   Esquel
Isla de Chiloé
Cabo Quilan

Canal de Chacao

Leleque
Gastre

Telsen

Puerto
Madryn
Trelew
Gaiman
Rawson

Las
Plumas

CHUBUT

Camarones   B. Camarones
C. Dos Bahías

ARCHIPIÉLAGO
de los
CHONOS

G. del Corcovado

Sarmiento
L. Colhue Huapi

Comodoro Rivadavia
Golfo San Jorge
Colonia Las Heras

Pto.
Aysen

PEN. DE TAITAO
C. Tres Montes
G. de Penas

L. Buenos Aires
Deseado
Cabo Tres Puntas
Puerto Deseado

I. Campana
I. Wellington

L. San
Martín

L. Cardiel

San Julián
Chico

SANTA
CRUZ

I. Madre de Dios
I. Hanover

L. Viedma

Santa Cruz

L. Argentino

Bahía Grande

FA
Jaso

El Turbio
Río Gallegos

West F
Wedd

Estrecho Nelson
ARCHIPIÉLAGO
REINA ADELAIDA
Strait of Magellan

Pto. Natales
Cabo Vírgenes
Strait of Magellan
Springhill
Pto. Porvenir

B. Otway
I. Desolación
B. Sta. Inés

Punta Arenas
Río Grande

TIERRA DEL FUEGO

San Diego
Estrecho Le M
Sta

I. Clarence
I. Stewart
I. Londonderry

Ushuaia
I. Navarino
B. Nassau
I. Wollaston
Cape Horn

I. Hermite   Is. Diego Ramírez

DRAKE   PAS

SOUTH AMERICA
Southern Part

LAMBERT AZIMUTHAL EQUAL-AREA PROJECTION

SCALE OF MILES
0 100 200 300 400 500

SCALE OF KILOMETRES
0 100 200 300 400 500

Capitals of Countries .... ★
Other Capitals .... △
International Boundaries ___ · ___
Other Boundaries ___ · · ___

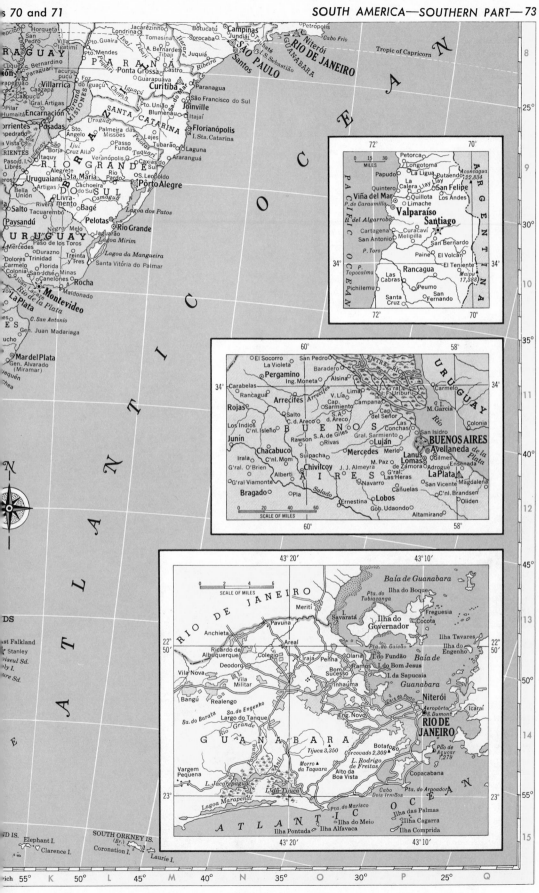

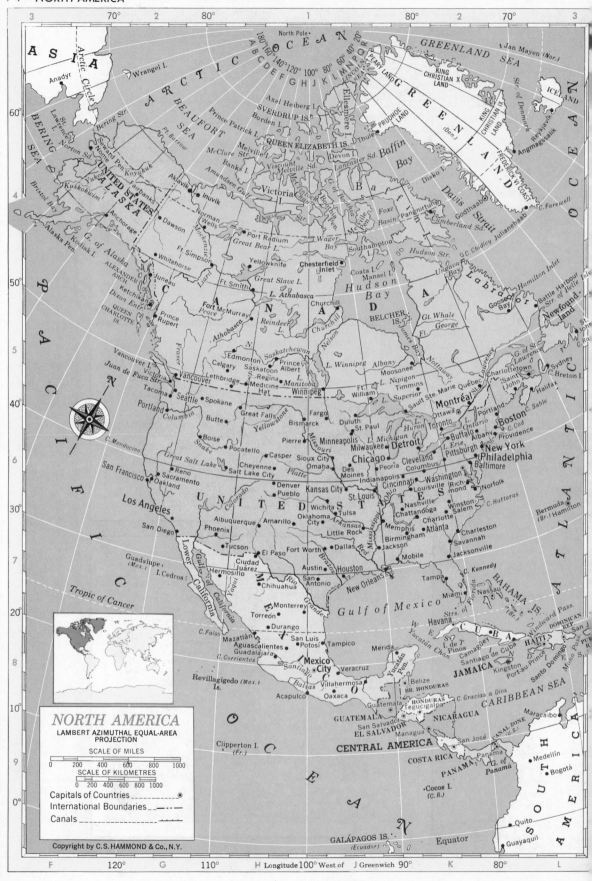

NORTH AMERICA

LAMBERT AZIMUTHAL EQUAL-AREA
PROJECTION

SCALE OF MILES

0 200 400 600 800 1000

SCALE OF KILOMETRES

0 200 400 600 800 1000

Capitals of Countries .... ⊙
International Boundaries ___.___.___
Canals _____

Copyright by C.S. HAMMOND & Co., N.Y.

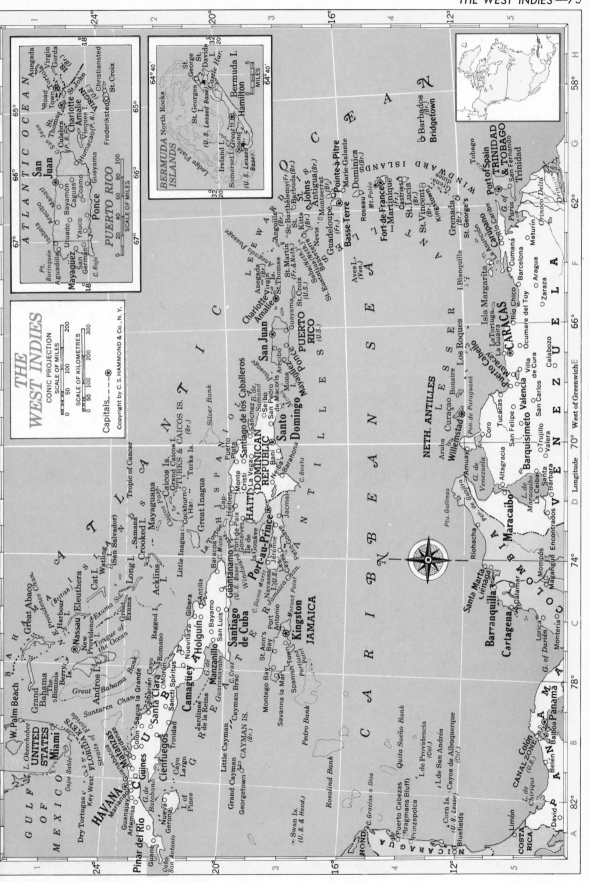

THE WEST INDIES

CONIC PROJECTION

SCALE OF MILES
0   50   100   200

SCALE OF KILOMETRES
0   50   100   200   300

Capitals - - - ⊛

Copyright by C. S. HAMMOND & Co., N.Y.

PUERTO RICO

ATLANTIC OCEAN

San Juan
Mayagüez
Ponce

SCALE OF MILES
0   20   40   60   80   100

BERMUDA ISLANDS

North Rocks

Ledge Flats

St. Georges
St. David I.
(U. S. Leased Base) Castle Har.
Bermuda I.
Hamilton

Ireland I.
Somerset I. Great Sd.
(U. S. Leased Base)
64°40'
5
MILES

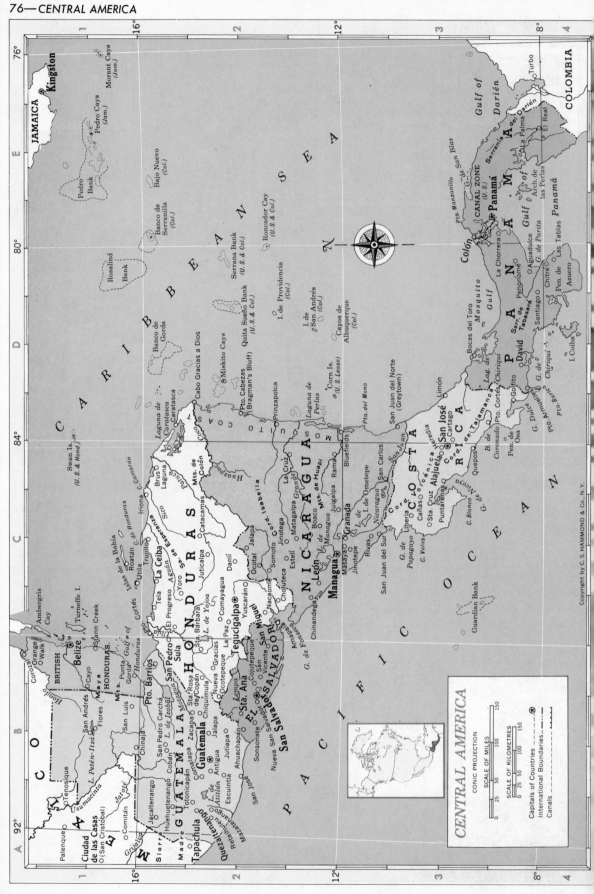

CENTRAL AMERICA

CONIC PROJECTION

SCALE OF MILES
0   25   50   100   150

SCALE OF KILOMETRES
0 25 50   100   150

Capitals of Countries ----------⊛
International Boundaries -------
Canals -------------------

Copyright by C. S. HAMMOND & Co., N.Y.

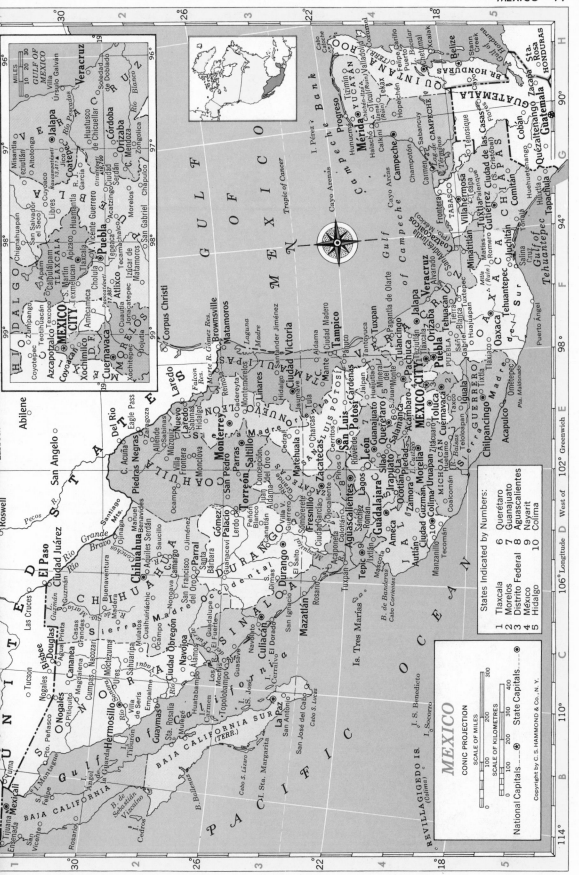

MEXICO
CONIC PROJECTION
SCALE OF MILES
0   100   200   300
SCALE OF KILOMETRES
0   100   200   300   400
National Capitals ⊙   State Capitals ⊙
Copyright by C. S. HAMMOND & CO., N. Y.

States Indicated by Numbers:
1 Tlaxcala   6 Querétaro
2 Morelos   7 Guanajuato
3 Distrito Federal 8 Aguascalientes
4 México   9 Nayarit
5 Hidalgo   10 Colima

GULF OF MEXICO
MILES
0 10 20 30

REVILLAGIGEDO IS.
(Colima)

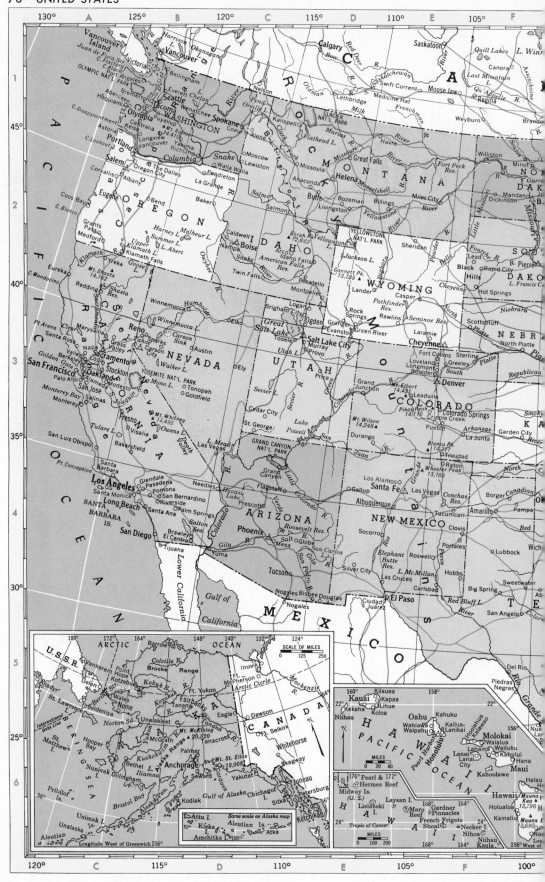

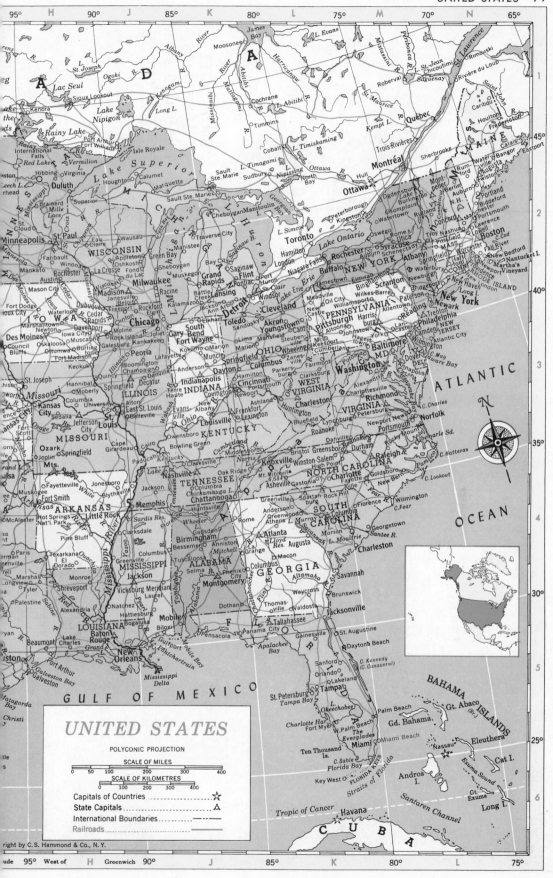

UNITED STATES

POLYCONIC PROJECTION

SCALE OF MILES

| 0 | 50 | 100 | 200 | 400 |

SCALE OF KILOMETRES

| 0 | 100 | 200 | 300 | 400 |

Capitals of Countries .... ☆
State Capitals .... △
International Boundaries .... ———
Railroads

right by C.S. Hammond & Co., N.Y.

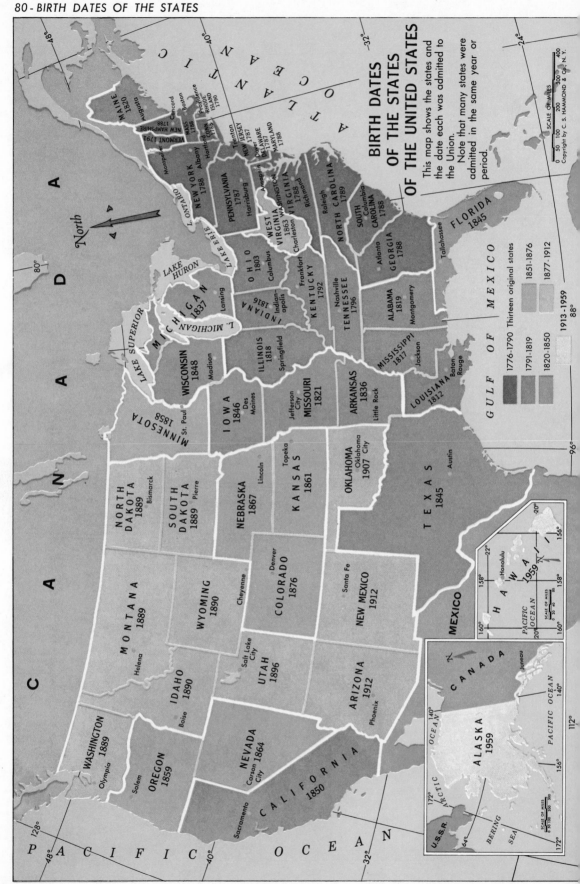

BIRTH DATES OF THE STATES OF THE UNITED STATES

This map shows the states and the date each was admitted to the Union.
Note that many states were admitted in the same year or period.

SCALE OF MILES
0 50 100 200 300 400
Copyright by C. S. HAMMOND & Co., N.Y.

1776-1790 Thirteen original states

1791-1819   1851-1876

1820-1850   1877-1912

1913-1959

MAINE 1820 — Augusta — Concord — Boston
NEW HAMPSHIRE 1788 — RHODE ISLAND 1790
VERMONT 1791 — MASS. 1788 — CONN. 1788
Montpelier — Providence — Hartford
NEW YORK 1788 — Albany — Trenton
NEW JERSEY 1787 — DELAWARE 1787
PENNSYLVANIA 1787 — Harrisburg
MARYLAND 1788 — Dover — Annapolis
WEST VIRGINIA 1863 — VIRGINIA 1788 — Washington — Richmond
OHIO 1803 — Columbus
NORTH CAROLINA 1789 — Raleigh
Frankfort — Charleston
SOUTH CAROLINA 1788 — Columbia
KENTUCKY 1792
GEORGIA 1788 — Atlanta
MICHIGAN 1837 — Lansing
INDIANA 1816 — Indianapolis
TENNESSEE 1796 — Nashville
ALABAMA 1819 — Montgomery
FLORIDA 1845 — Tallahassee
WISCONSIN 1848 — Madison
ILLINOIS 1818 — Springfield
MISSISSIPPI 1817 — Jackson
MINNESOTA 1858 — St. Paul
IOWA 1846 — Des Moines
MISSOURI 1821 — Jefferson City
ARKANSAS 1836 — Little Rock
LOUISIANA 1812 — Baton Rouge
NORTH DAKOTA 1889 — Bismarck
SOUTH DAKOTA 1889 — Pierre
NEBRASKA 1867 — Lincoln
KANSAS 1861 — Topeka
OKLAHOMA 1907 — Oklahoma City
TEXAS 1845 — Austin
MONTANA 1889 — Helena
WYOMING 1890 — Cheyenne
COLORADO 1876 — Denver
NEW MEXICO 1912 — Santa Fe
IDAHO 1890 — Boise
UTAH 1896 — Salt Lake City
ARIZONA 1912 — Phoenix
WASHINGTON 1889 — Olympia
OREGON 1859 — Salem
NEVADA 1864 — Carson City
CALIFORNIA 1850 — Sacramento

North

LAKE SUPERIOR — LAKE HURON — LAKE MICHIGAN — LAKE ONTARIO — LAKE ERIE

CANADA

ATLANTIC OCEAN

GULF OF MEXICO

MEXICO

PACIFIC OCEAN

HAWAII 1959 — Honolulu — PACIFIC OCEAN
SCALE OF MILES

ALASKA 1959 — Juneau
CANADA — PACIFIC OCEAN — U.S.S.R. — BERING SEA — ARCTIC OCEAN
SCALE OF MILES

FACTS ABOUT THE
STATES AND TERRITORIES
OF THE
UNITED STATES

State or Territory	Admitted to the Union	Settled at	Date	State Nickname	State Flower
Alabama	Dec. 14, 1819	Mobile	1702	Cotton State	Golden Rod
Alaska	Jan. 3, 1959	Sitka	1801	The Great Land	Forget-me-not
Arizona	Feb. 14, 1912	Tucson	1580	Baby State	Saguaro Cactus
Arkansas	June 15, 1836	Arkansas Post	1685	Wonder State	Apple Blossom
California	Sept. 9, 1850	San Diego	1769	Golden State	Golden Poppy
Colorado	Aug. 1, 1876	Near Denver	1858	Centennial State	Columbine
Connecticut	†Jan. 9, 1788	Windsor	1635	Nutmeg State	Mountain Laurel
Delaware	†Dec. 7, 1787	Cape Henlopen	1627	Diamond State	Peach Blossom
District of Columbia	** 1790-1791		1790		American Beauty Rose
Florida	Mar. 3, 1845	St. Augustine	1565	Peninsula State	Orange Blossom
Georgia	†Jan. 2, 1788	Savannah	1733	Cracker State	Cherokee Rose
Guam	‡Dec. 10, 1898	Agana	....		
Hawaii	Aug. 21, 1959		....	Aloha State	Red Hibiscus
Idaho	July 3, 1890	Coeur d'Alene	1842	Gem State	Syringa
Illinois	Dec. 3, 1818	Kaskaskia	1720	Sucker State	Violet
Indiana	Dec. 11, 1816	Vincennes	1730	Hoosier	Zinnia
Iowa	Dec. 28, 1846	Burlington	1788	Hawkeye State	Wild Rose
Kansas	Jan. 29, 1861		1831	Sunflower State	Sunflower
Kentucky	June 1, 1792	Harrodsburg	1774	Blue Grass State	Goldenrod
Louisiana	April 30, 1812	Iberville	1699	Pelican State	Magnolia
Maine	Mar. 15, 1820	Bristol	1624	Pine Tree State	Pine Cone
Maryland	†April 28, 1788	St. Mary's	1634	Free State	Blackeyed Susan
Massachusetts	†Feb. 6, 1788	Plymouth	1620	Bay State	Mayflower
Michigan	Jan. 26, 1837	Near Detroit	1650	Wolverine State	Apple Blossom
Minnesota	May 11, 1858	St. Peter's River	1805	North Star State	Lady Slipper
Mississippi	Dec. 10, 1817	Natchez	1716	Magnolia State	Magnolia
Missouri	Aug. 10, 1821	St. Louis	1764	Show Me State	Hawthorn
Montana	Nov. 8, 1889		1809	Treasure State	Bitter Root
Nebraska	Mar. 1, 1867	Bellevue	1847	Tree Planter's State	Goldenrod
Nevada	Oct. 31, 1864	Genoa	1850	Battle Born State	Sage Brush
New Hampshire	†June 21, 1788	Dover and Portsmouth	1623	Granite State	Purple Lilac
New Jersey	†Dec. 18, 1787	Bergen	1617	Garden State	Violet
New Mexico	Jan. 6, 1912	Santa Fe	1605	Sunshine State	Yucca
New York	†July 26, 1788	Manhattan Island	1614	Empire State	Rose
North Carolina	†Nov. 21, 1789	Albemarle	1650	Tar Heel State	Dogwood
North Dakota	Nov. 2, 1889	Pembina	1780	Sioux State	Wild Prairie Rose
Ohio	Mar. 1, 1803	Marietta	1788	Buckeye State	Scarlet Carnation
Oklahoma	Nov. 16, 1907		1889	Sooner State	Mistletoe
Oregon	Feb. 14, 1859	Astoria	1810	Beaver State	Oregon Grape
Pennsylvania	†Dec. 12, 1787	Delaware River	1682	Keystone State	Mountain Laurel
Puerto Rico	‡Dec. 10, 1898	Caparra	1510		
Rhode Island	†May 29, 1790	Providence	1636	Little Rhody	Violet
South Carolina	†May 23, 1788	Port Royal	1670	Palmetto State	Yellow Jessamine
South Dakota	Nov. 2, 1889	Sioux Falls	1856	Coyote State	The Pasque
Tennessee	June 1, 1796	Ft. Loudon	1757	Volunteer State	Iris
Texas	Dec. 29, 1845	Matagorda Bay	1686	Lone Star State	Bluebonnet
Utah	Jan. 4, 1896	Salt Lake City	1847	Beehive State	Sego Lily
Vermont	Mar. 4, 1791	Ft. Dummer	1764	Green Mountain State	Red Clover
Virgin Islands	***Mar. 31, 1917		....		
Virginia	†June 26, 1788	Jamestown	1607	Old Dominion State	American Dogwood
Washington	Nov. 11, 1889	Astoria	1811	Evergreen State	Rhododedron
West Virginia	June 20, 1863	Wheeling	1774	Mountain State	Rhododedron
Wisconsin	May 29, 1848	Green Bay	1670	Badger State	Violet
Wyoming	July 10, 1890	Ft. Laramie	1834	Equality State	Indian Paintbrush

† Ratified the Constitution. ‡ Treaty of Peace with Spain. Puerto Rico became an Associated Free State in 1952. ** Established under Acts of Congress.

*** Date of purchase from Denmark. Philippines became independent in 1946.

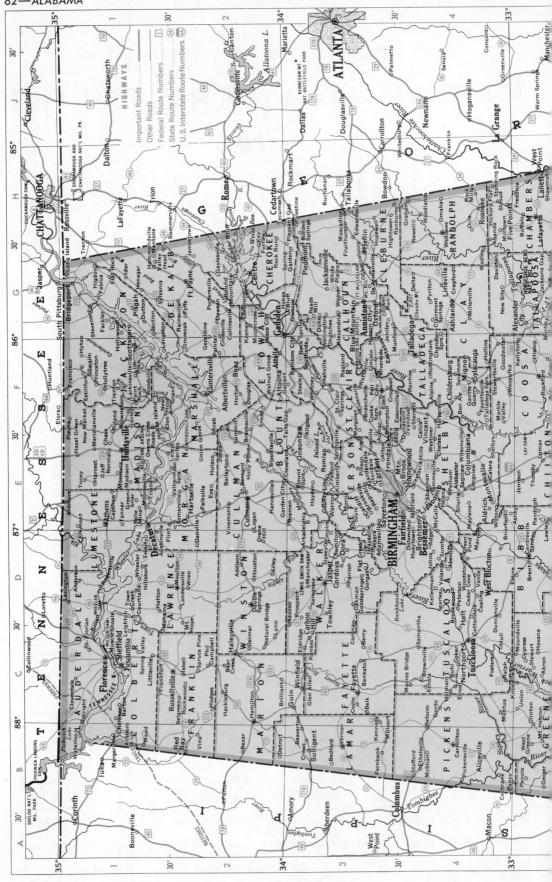

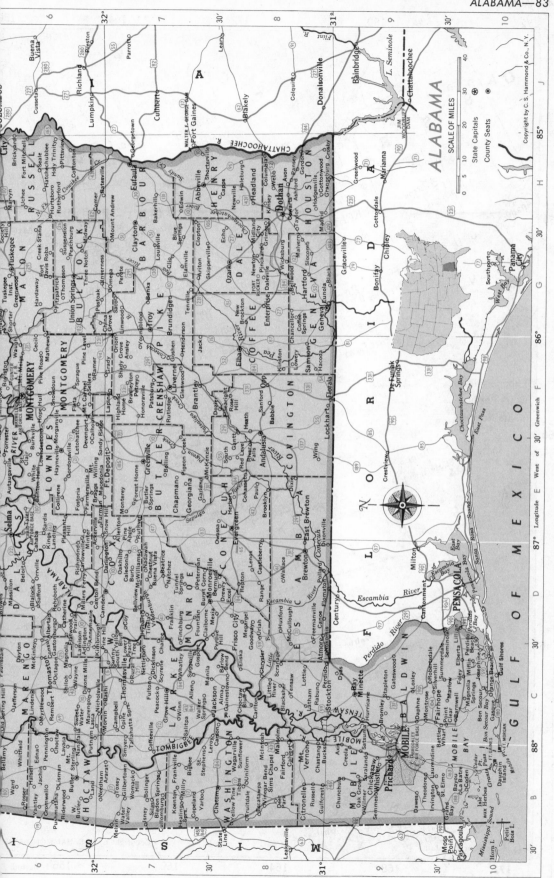

ALABAMA

SCALE OF MILES

State Capitals
County Seats

Copyright by C. S. Hammond & Co., N. Y.

GULF OF MEXICO

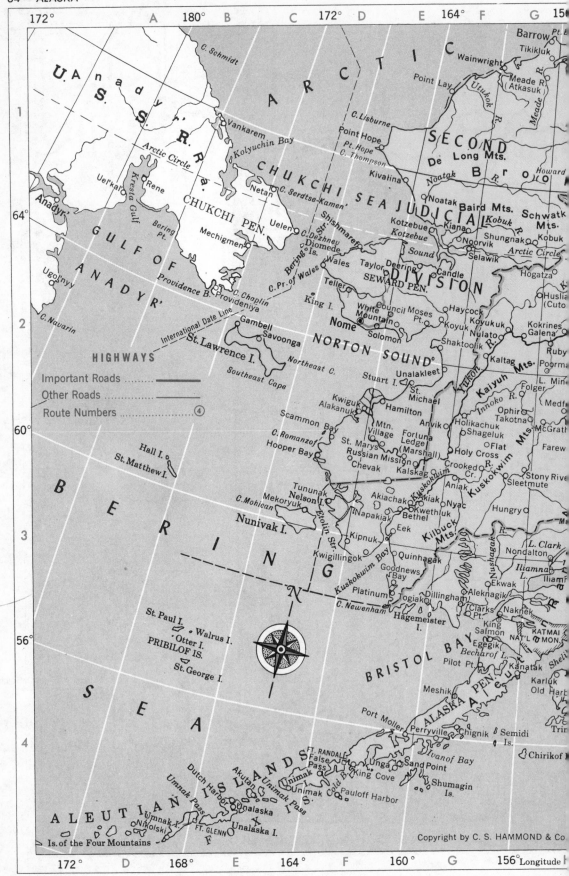

ARCTIC

U.A S. S. R.
n a d y r'

Anadyr'

Anadyr' Ra.

Arctic Circle

Uerkal   Kresta Gulf   Rene

CHUKCHI PEN.

GULF OF ANADYR'

Ugol'nyy

Bering Pt.

Mechigmen

C. Navarin

C. Schmidt

Vankarem

Kolyuchin Bay

Netan

C. Serdtse-Kamen

Uelen

CHUKCHI SEA

C. Lisburne

Point Lay

Wainwright

Barrow   Pt. B

Tikikluk

Meade R. (Atkasuk)

Meade R.

SECOND

De Long Mts.

Point Hope
Pt. Hope
C. Thompson

Kivalina

Noatak   Baird Mts.   Schwatk Mts.

Brook

Howard

Kotzebue   Kiana   Kobuk R.   Shungnak   Kobuk

Noorvik

JUDICIAL

Shishmaref

C.Dezhnev
Diomede Is.

Wales

Bering Str.

C. Pr. of Wales

Taylor   Deering   Candle   Selawik   Arctic Circle

Kotzebue Sound

DIVISION

Hogatza

Huslia (Cuto

King I.

Teller

White Mountain

Council Moses Pt.

Haycock   Koyuk   Koyukuk   Nulato

Kokrines   Galena

Solomon

Nome

SEWARD PEN.

Shaktoolik

Kaltag

Kaiyuh Mts.

Ruby
Poorma

L. Min

Unalakleet

Stuart I.

St. Michael

Yukon R.

Folger

Medf

HIGHWAYS

Important Roads ....

Other Roads ....

Route Numbers .... ④

NORTON SOUND

Kwiguk
Alakanuk

Hamilton

Anvik   Holikachuk

Innoko R.   Ophir   Takotna

McGrath

Flat   Farew

International Date Line

St. Lawrence I.

Gambell
Savoonga

Northeast C.

Southeast Cape

Scammon Bay

C. Romanzof

Hooper Bay

Mtn. Village

St. Marys

Russian Mission

Chevak

Fortuna Ledge (Marshall)

Shageluk

Holy Cross

Kalskag   Crooked Cr.

Kuskokwim R.

Stony Rive

Sleetmute

B E R I N G

Hall I.

St. Matthew I.

C.Mohican

Tununak

Mekoryuk

Nelson I.

Akiachak

Napakiak

Eek

Kuskokwim

Kwigak   Nyac

Kwethluk

Bethel

Aniak

Hungry

Kilbuck

L. Clark

Nondalton

Iliamna
L.
Iliam

Nunivak I.

Etolin Str.

Kipnuk

Kwigillingok

Kuskokwim Bay

Goodnews Bay

Quinhagak

N

St. Paul I.   Walrus I.

Otter I.

PRIBILOF IS.

St. George I.

Platinum

C. Newenham

Togiak

Dillingham

Hagemeister I.

Aleknagik

Ekwak

Clarks Pt.

Naknek

King Salmon

KATMAI NAT'L MON.

Becharof L.

Egegik

S E A

BRISTOL BAY

Pilot Pt.

Kanatak   Shelf

Karluk   Old Harb

Meshik

ALASKA PEN

Port Moller

Perryville   Chignik   Semidi Is.

Ivanof Bay

Chirikof

Trin

A L E U T I A N   I S L A N D S

FT. RANDALL
False Pass

Unimak

Unimak Pass

Cold B.   King Cove   Sand Point   Shumagin Is.

Pauloff Harbor

Umnak Pass

Dutch Harbor

Akutan   Unimak Pass

Unalaska

Umnak I.   Nikolski   Unalaska I.

Is. of the Four Mountains   FT. GLENNO

Copyright by C. S. HAMMOND & Co.

O C E A N

BEAUFORT SEA

kett Bay
rrison Bay

Flaxman I.
Camden Bay
Kaktovik
(Barter I.)
Demarcation Pt.
British
Mt. Michelson
9,239▲

Richards I.
Tuktoyaktuk
Mackenzie
Bay
Reindeer
Depot
Inuvik

R a n g e
Sagavanirktok R.
Canning R.
Davidson Mts.
Sheenjek R.
Porcupine R.

Arctic Village
Big
Lake
Chandalar
Venetie
ttles Field
Beaver
Ft. Yukon

Mackenzie
Mts.
Aklavik
Ft. McPherson
Arctic
Red River
Mackenzie R.
Peel R.

Stevens
Village
JUDICIAL
Livengood
Circle
Central
Circle
Sprs.
Coal
Cr.
Eagle
Yukon R.

C A N A D A

Mackenzie Mts.

Dawson
Mayo

H
rt
ELLIOTT
HWY.
7
STEESE
HWY.
LADD A.F.B.
College
Fairbanks
EIELSON A.F.B.
VISION
Minto
Nenana
North Pole
Clear
Suntrana
aly Fork
na
Delta
Jct.
McKinley Park
MT. McKINLEY
NAT'L PARK
Cantwell
Highest Summit
Point in U.S.
Curry
R A N G E
RICHARDSON HWY.
Tanana R.
Chicken
Boundary
TAYLOR
HWY.
3
Tanacross
Tok
2
Tetlin
Northway
Nabesna

Pelly R.

Fort Selkirk

Talkeetna
Talkeetna
Mts.
Jones-
ville
rage
Spenard
Whittier
Pr.
William
Sd.
ENAI
ewardd
EN
4
Hope
Montague I.
Middleton I.
C. Cleare
THIRD JUDICIAL
DIVISION
Cape
Yakataga
Icy Bay
Katalla
Yakutat Bay
Yakutat

Stikine R.

Watson Lake
Lower Post
97

Teslin
60°

DENALI HWY.
8
Paxson
Slana
Gulkana
Mt. Sanford
16,208
Copper
Center
Chitina
Glenallen
Copper
McCarthy
Mt. Bona
16,421▲
Mt. Bear
14,850▲
Mt. St. Elias
18,008▲
Mt.
Vancouver
Wrangell
Mts.
Kluane
L.
Mt. Logan
19,850▲
Haines
Junction
Whitehorse
Carcross
Atlin
Skagway
Haines
Port Chilkoot
Chilkoot
Lynn
Canal
Taku R.

ALASKA HIGHWAY
Kluane
HAINES
HWY.
Chilkat
Pass
St. Elias Mts.
Chilkat
GLACIER
BAY
NAT'L MON.
Gustavus
Dry Bay
Mt. Fairweather
15,300

COAST

Telegraph
Creek

G U L F   O F   A L A S K A

FIRST
JUDICIAL
DIVISION
ALEXANDER
ARCH.
Cross Sd.
Pelican
Chichagof I.
Hoonah
Admiralty
I.
Angoon
Sitka
SITKA NAT'L MON.
Baranof I.
Kake
Port
Alexander

Juneau
Douglas

Petersburg
Wrangell
MTS.

Hyder
Ketchikan
Klawock
Craig
Hydaburg
Metlakatla
C. Muzon
Dixon Entr.
Hecate Str.

56°

B E R I N G   S E A
THIRD JUDICIAL
DIVISION
A L E U T I A N   I S L A N D S
Attu
u I.
Shemya I.
Semichi
Is.
Buldir
I.
Kiska I.
RAT IS.
Amchitka I.
Semisopochnoi
Tanaga I.
Adak I.
Kanaga
I.
ANDREANOF IS.
Atka I.
Atka
Amlia I.
Amukta
Pass
Seguam
I.
P A C I F I C   O C E A N
Same scale as main map
52°

QUEEN
CHARLOTTE
IS.

ALASKA
POLYCONIC PROJECTION

SCALE OF MILES
0 50 100 150 200 250

SCALE OF KILOMETRES
0 50 100 150 200 250

State Capital⊛
Judicial Division
Headquarters◉

68°

1

64°

2

60°

3

56°

4

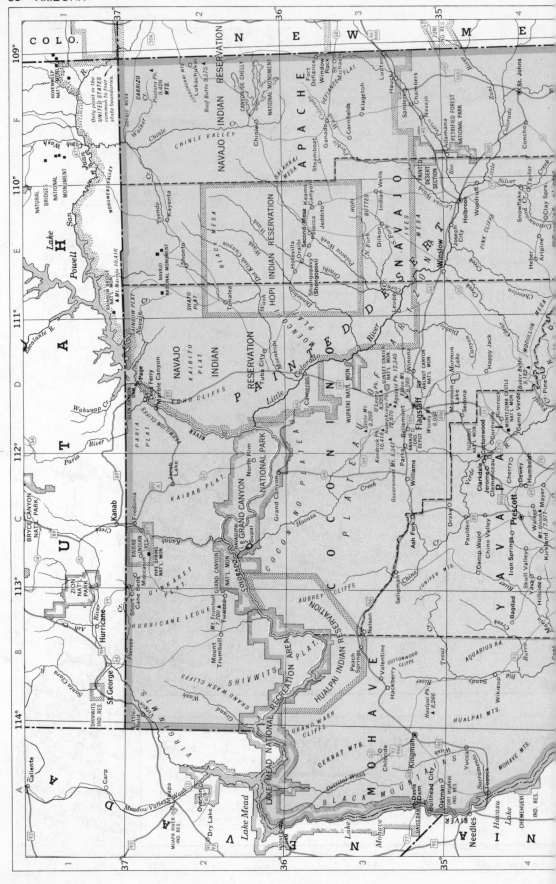

ARIZONA

SCALE OF MILES

HIGHWAYS

Important Roads
Other Roads
Federal Route Numbers
State Route Numbers
U.S. Interstate Route Numbers

State Capitals
County Seats

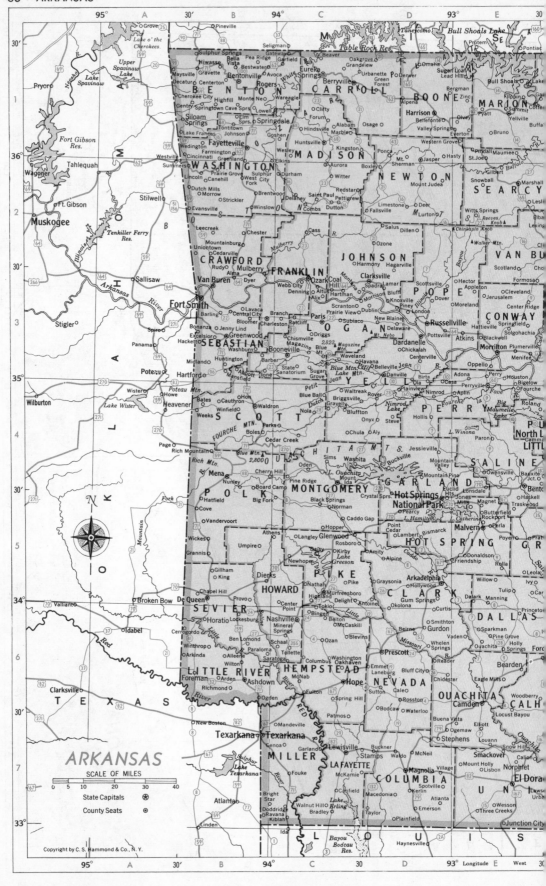

ARKANSAS

SCALE OF MILES

0 5 10   20   30   40

State Capitals ⊛
County Seats ◉

Copyright by C. S. Hammond & Co., N.Y.

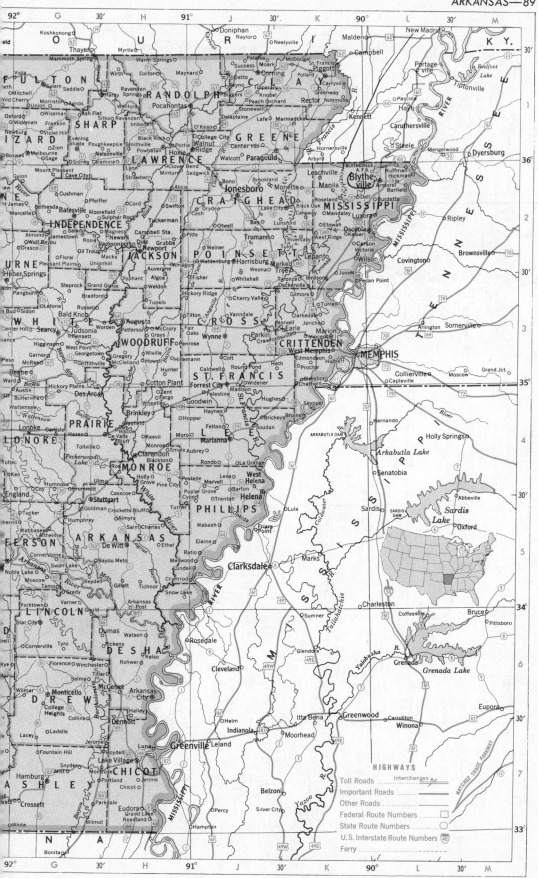

HIGHWAYS

Toll Roads .... Interchanges *
Important Roads ....
Other Roads ....
Federal Route Numbers..........
State Route Numbers ....
U.S. Interstate Route Numbers
Ferry ....

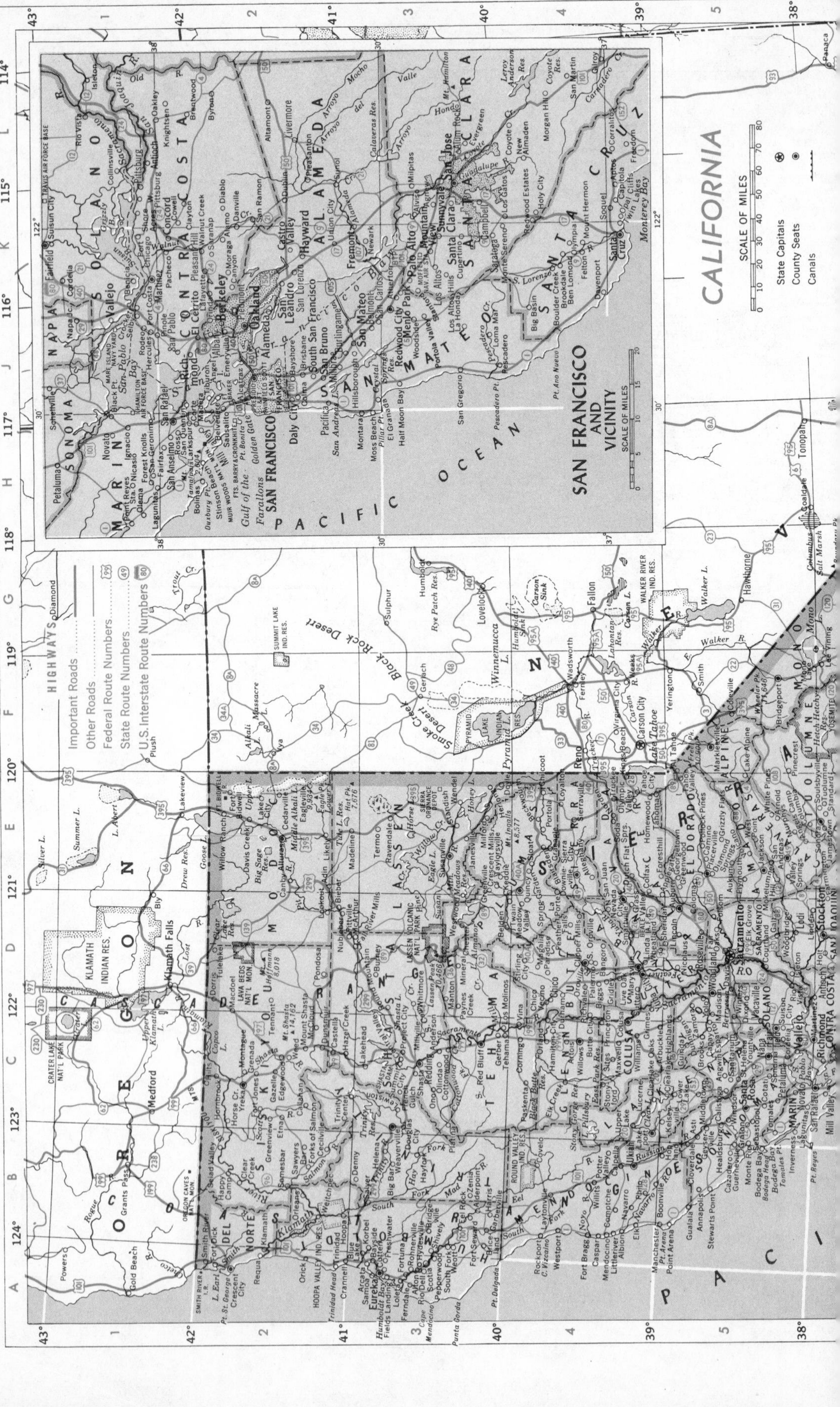

CALIFORNIA

SCALE OF MILES

0 10 20 30 40 50 60 70 80

State Capitals
County Seats
Canals

SAN FRANCISCO AND VICINITY

SCALE OF MILES

0 5 10 15 20

PACIFIC OCEAN

HIGHWAYS

Important Roads
Other Roads
Federal Route Numbers
State Route Numbers
U.S. Interstate Route Numbers

OREGON

NEVADA

PACIFIC

SACRAMENTO
AND
VICINITY

SCALE OF MILES

LOS ANGELES
AND VICINITY

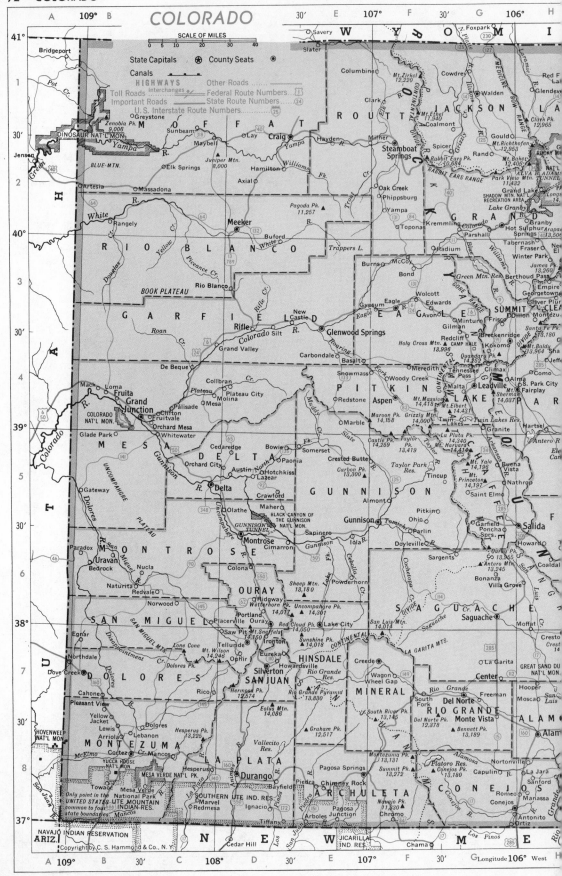

COLORADO

SCALE OF MILES

State Capitals ⊛ County Seats ⊙

Canals

HIGHWAYS   Other Roads ....
Toll Roads Interchanges   Federal Route Numbers... 73
Important Roads   State Route Numbers.... 24
U.S. Interstate Route Numbers........... 25

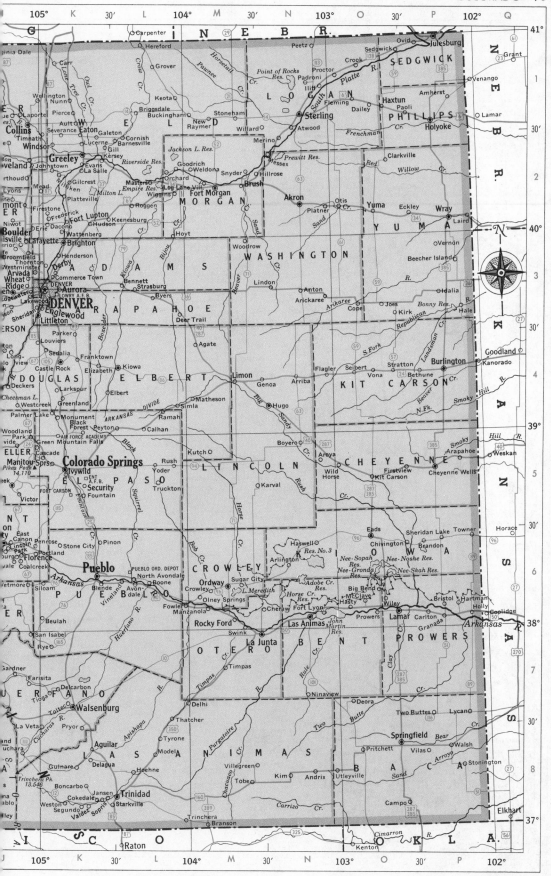

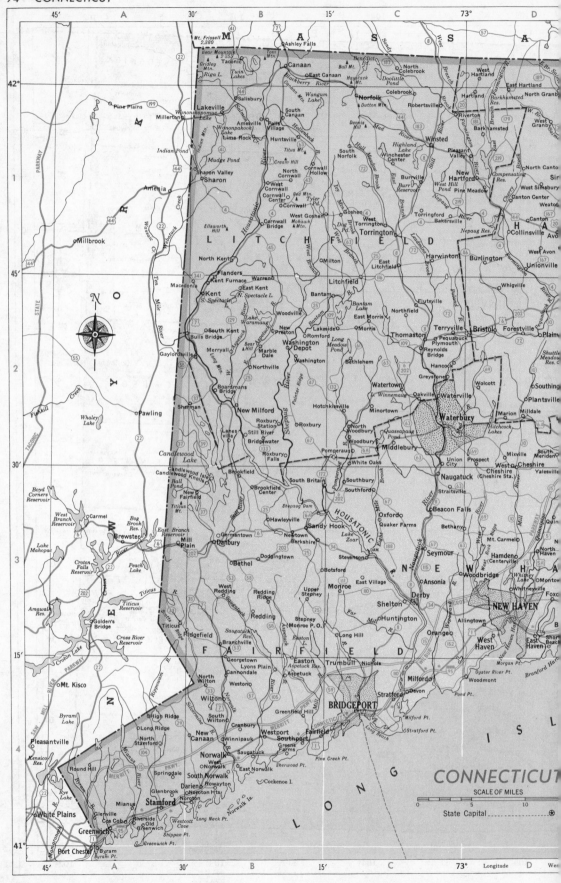

CONNECTICUT

SCALE OF MILES

0   5   10

State Capital .... ⊕

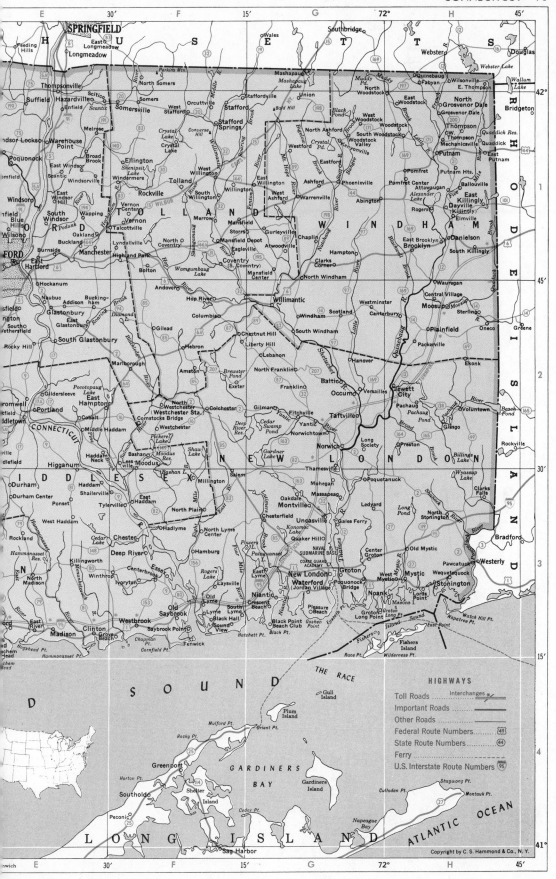

HIGHWAYS

Toll Roads .... Interchanges *
Important Roads ....
Other Roads ....
Federal Route Numbers.......... 449
State Route Numbers............ 44
Ferry ....
U.S. Interstate Route Numbers. 95

FLORIDA

SCALE OF MILES

State Capitals
County Seats
Canals

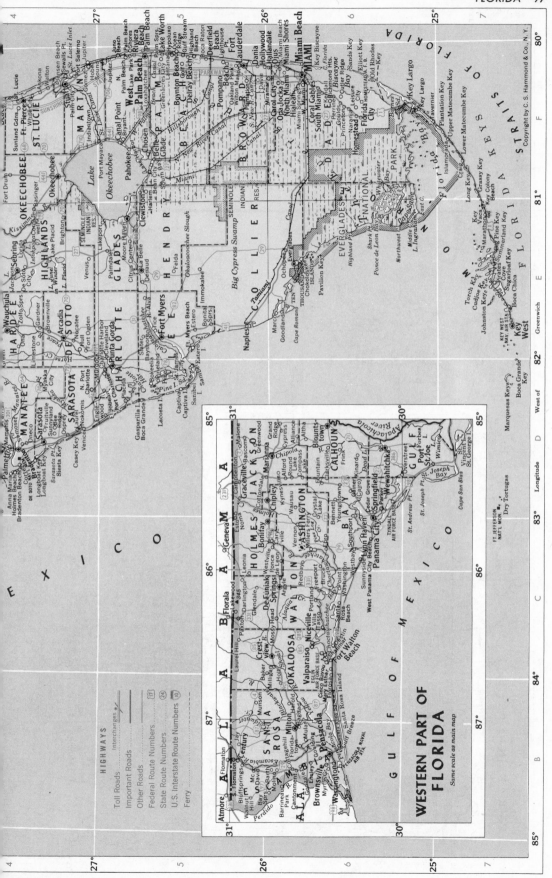

STRAITS OF FLORIDA

FLORIDA KEYS

GULF OF MEXICO

WESTERN PART OF FLORIDA

Same scale as main map

HIGHWAYS

Toll Roads — Interchanges
Important Roads
Other Roads
Federal Route Numbers
State Route Numbers
U.S. Interstate Route Numbers
Ferry

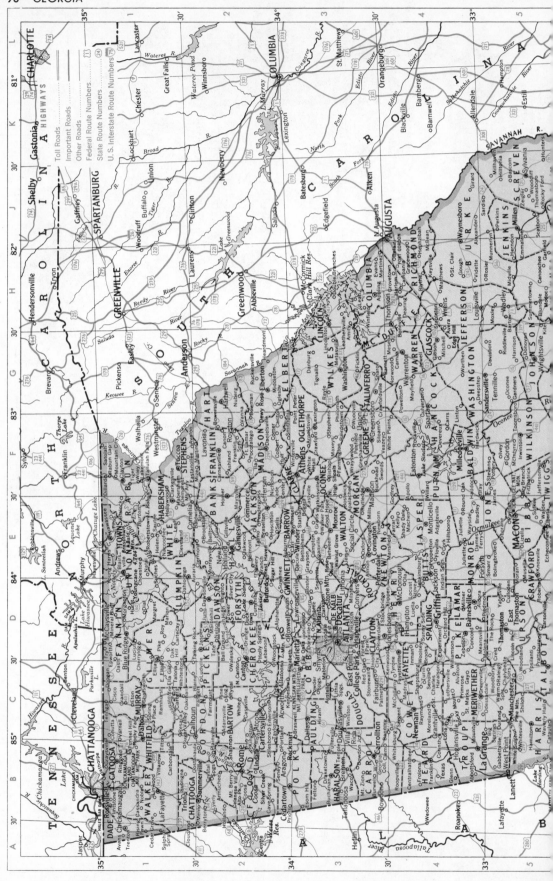

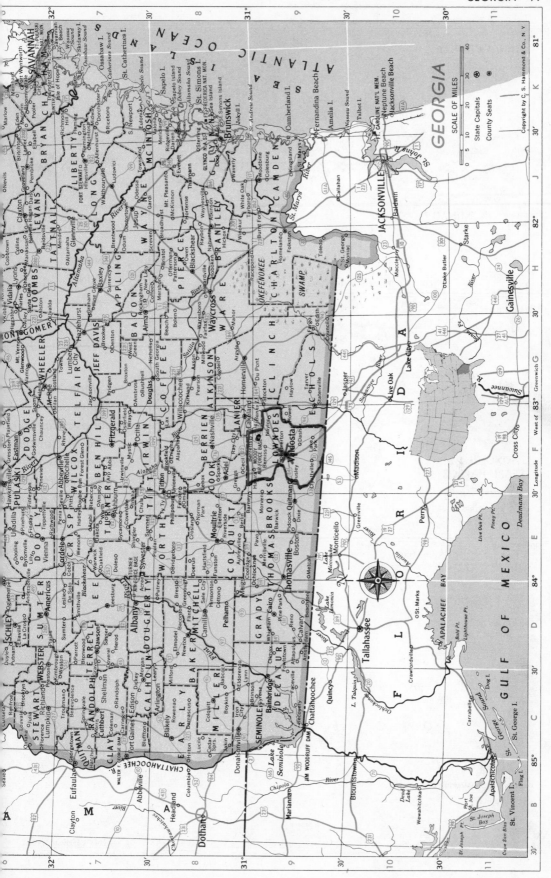

GEORGIA

SCALE OF MILES

0   5   10   20   30   40

⊛ State Capitals

◉ County Seats

Copyright by C. S. Hammond & Co., N.Y.

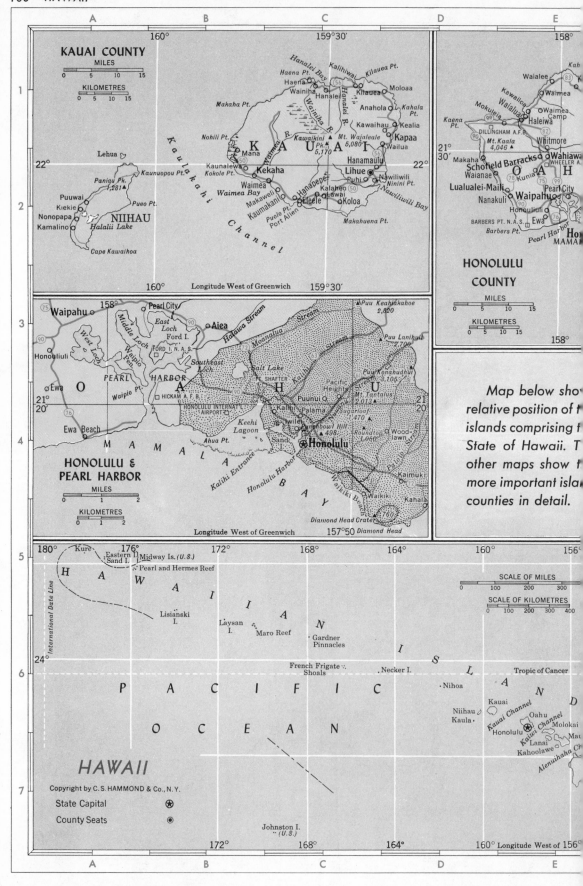

KAUAI COUNTY

MILES

0   5   10   15

KILOMETRES

0   5   10   15

160°   159°30'

Hanalei Bay
Kalihiwai   Kilauea Pt.
Haena Pt.   Haena   Kilauea   Moloaa
Wainiha   Hanalei
Makaha Pt.   Anahola
Wainiha R.   Kahala Pt.
Kawaihau   Kealia
Nohili Pt.   Kawaikini   Kapaa
Pk.   Mt. Waialeale   Wailua
Lehua   Mana   5,170   5,080
K A U A I   Hanamaulu
Paniau Pk.   Kaunalewa   Lihue
1,281   Kekaha   Kokole Pt.   Puhi   Nawiliwili
Puuwai   Waimea   Kalaheo   Lawai   Ninini Pt.
Kiekie   Pueo Pt.   Makaweli   Koloa   Nawiliwili Bay
Nonopapa   Waimea Bay   Makakani   Eleele
Kamalino   NIIHAU   Kaumakani   Puolo Pt.   Makahuena Pt.
Halalii Lake   Port Allen

Kaulakahi Channel

Cape Kawaihoa

22°   22°

160°   Longitude West of Greenwich   159°30'

HONOLULU & PEARL HARBOR

MILES

0   1   2

KILOMETRES

0   1   2

Waipahu   158°   Pearl City
West Loch   Middle Loch   East Loch
Honouliuli   Waipio Pen.   Ford I.   Aiea   Halawa Stream
O   PEARL   Ford I.N.A.S.   Moanalua Stream
Ewa   Waipio Pt.   HARBOR   Southeast   Salt Lake
21°   Loch   Ft. Shafter
20'   HICKAM A.F.B.   Kalihi
Ewa Beach   HONOLULU INTERNAT'L   Puunui
AIRPORT   Kalihi   Pacific
M A M A L A   Keehi   Palama   Heights
Lagoon   Kewalo   Punchbowl Hill
Ahua Pt.   Sand I.   498
Honolulu   Roundtop
Kalihi Entrance   Honolulu Harbor   B A Y   Waikiki Beach
Waikiki
Diamond Head Crater   Diamond Head

Puu Keahiakahoe
2,820
Puu Lanihuli
2,700
O A H U
Puu Konahuanui
3,105
Mt. Tantalus
2,013
Sugarloaf
1,470
Wood-
lawn
Kaimuki
Palolo Stream
Kahala   760

21°
20'

Longitude West of Greenwich   157°50'

HONOLULU COUNTY

MILES

0   5   10   15

KILOMETRES

0   5   10   15

158°

Kah
Waialee
Kawailoa   Waimea
Mokuleia   Waialua   Waimea
Kaena   Haleiwa   Camp
Pt.   DILLINGHAM A.F.B.   Mt. Kaala   Whitmore
4,046   82
Makaha   Schofield Barracks   Wahiawa
Waianae   Kunia   WHEELER A.
Lualualei-Maili   Pearl
Nanakuli   Waipahu   City
Honouliuli   99
BARBERS PT. N.A.S.   Ewa   Ho
Barbers Pt.   Pearl Harbor   MAMA

21°
30'

158°

Map below sho
relative position of
islands comprising
State of Hawaii. T
other maps show t
more important isla
counties in detail.

180°   176°   172°   168°   164°   160°   156°
Kure   Eastern I.   Midway Is. (U.S.)
Sand I.   Pearl and Hermes Reef
H   A   W   A   I   I   A   N   SCALE OF MILES
0   100   200   300
SCALE OF KILOMETRES
0   100   200   300   400
Lisianski I.
Laysan I.   Maro Reef   Gardner Pinnacles
24°   French Frigate   Necker I.   I   S   L   A   N   D   Tropic of Cancer
Shoals   Nihoa
Niihau   Kauai
Kaula   Oahu
P   A   C   I   F   I   C   Honolulu   Molokai
Lanai   Mau
Kahoolawe
O   C   E   A   N   Alenuihaha Ch

HAWAII

Copyright by C.S. HAMMOND & Co., N.Y.

State Capital   ⊛

County Seats   ◉

International Date Line

172°   168°   164°   160°   Longitude West of   156°

Johnston I.
(U.S.)

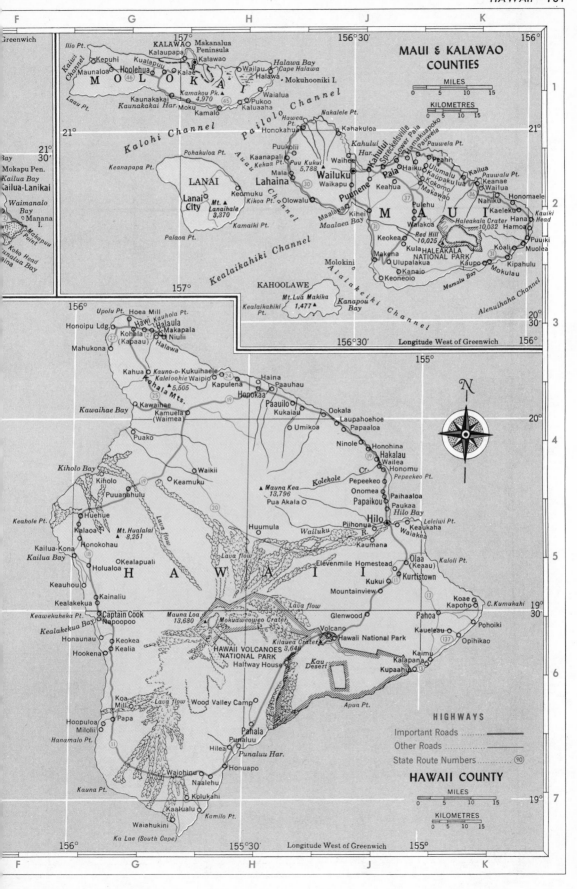

MAUI & KALAWAO
COUNTIES

MILES
0   5   10   15

KILOMETRES
0   5   10   15

Greenwich

F   G   H   J   K

157°   Makanalua
KALAWAO   Peninsula
Ilio Pt. Kalaupapa Kalawao
Kepuhi Kualapuu Kalae Makanalua
Maunaloa Hoolehua (46) KALOHI
Kaiwi M O L O K A I Waialu Halawa Bay
Channel Kamakou Pk. Cape Halawa
Laau Pt. 4,970 (45) Mokuhooniki I.
Kaunakakai Moku Pukoo Waialua
Kaunakakai Har. Kamalo Kaluaaha

Kalohi Channel Pailolo Channel Hawea Pt. Nakalele Pt.
Honokahua Kahakuloa
Pohakuloa Pt. Puukolii
Keanapapa Pt. Kaanapali Puu Kukui Kahului Spreckelsville Pauwela Pt.
LANAI Kekaa 5,788 Waihee Har. Lower Paia Pauwela
Mala Wailuku Haiku Peahi
Lanai Mt. Keomuku Lahaina Waikapu Pala Ulumalu Kailua
City Lanaihale Kikoa Pt. Olowalu Puunene Kaupakulua Pauwalu
3,370 Channel Maalaea Keahua Kokomo Keanae Wailua
Kamaiki Pt. Kihei M A U I Makawao Nahiku
Palaoa Pt. Maalaea Bay Pulehu Haleakala Crater Honomaele
Kaelepulu 10,032 Kauiki Head
Keokea Haleakala Hamoa
KAHOOLAWE Kula 10,025 Koali
Molokini HALEAKALA Muolea
Kealaikahiki Mt. Lua Makika Makena NATIONAL PARK Kipahulu
Pt. 1,477 Ulupalakua Kaupo Mokulau
Kanapou Kanaio Mamala Bay
Bay Keoneoio Alenuihaha Channel

Mokapu Pen.
Kailua Bay
Kailua-Lanikai
Waimanalo Manana I.
Bay Makapuu
Point
Koko Head
Hualalai Bay

21°30'

21°

20°30'

157° 156°30' Longitude West of Greenwich 156°

156° 155° Longitude West of Greenwich

Important Roads ....
Other Roads ....
State Route Numbers 90

HAWAII COUNTY

MILES
0   5   10   15

KILOMETRES
0   5   10   15

N

Upolu Pt. Hoea Mill
Honoipu Ldg. Hawi Kauhola Pt.
Kohala Halaula Makapala
(Kapaau) Niulii
Mahukona (27) Halawa

Kahua Kauno-o-Kukuihaele Haina
Kaleloohie Waipio Paauhau
Kawaihae Kohala Mts. Kapulena
5,505 Honokaa Umikoa
Kawaihae Bay Kamuela Paauilo Ookala
(Waimea) Kukaiau Laupahoehoe
Puako (19) Papaaloa
Ninole Honohina
Kiholo Bay Waikii Hakalau
Kiholo Keamuku (19) Wailea
Puuanahulu Kolekole Honomu
Mauna Kea Pepeekeo Pepeekeo Pt.
Keahole Pt. 13,796 Onomea
Huehue Pua Akala Papaikou Paihaaloa
Kalaoa (20) Paukaa
Honokohau Mt. Hualalai Hilo Hilo Bay
8,251 Huumula Wailuku Piihonua Leleiwi Pt.
Kailua-Kona Keaukaha
Kailua Bay OKealapuali Waiakea
Holualoa Kaumana
Keauhou H A W A I I Lava flow Olaa Kaloli Pt.
Elevenmile Homestead (Keaau)
Kealakekua Kainaliu Kukui (11) Kurtistown
Kealakekua Bay Mountainview (13) Koae
Keawekaheka Pt. Lava flow Kapoho C. Kumukahi
Captain Cook Mauna Loa Glenwood Pahoa
Napoopoo 13,680 Mokuweoweo Crater Kaueleau Pohoiki
Honaunau Keokea Volcano (137) Opihikao
Hookena Kealia Kilauea Crater Hawaii National Park Kaimu
HAWAII VOLCANOES 3,646 Kalapana
NATIONAL PARK Kupaahu
Koa- Halfway House Kau
Mill Desert Apua Pt.
Hoopuloa Lava flow Wood Valley Camp
Milolii Papa
Hanamalo Pt. (11) Pahala
Hilea Punaluu
Honuapo Punaluu Har.
Waiohinu
Naalehu
Kauna Pt. Kolukahi
Kaalualu Kamilo Pt.
Waiahukini
Ka Lae (South Cape)

20°

19°30'

19°

20°30'

F   G   H   J   K

1

2

3

4

5

6

7

156° 155°30' Longitude West of Greenwich 155°

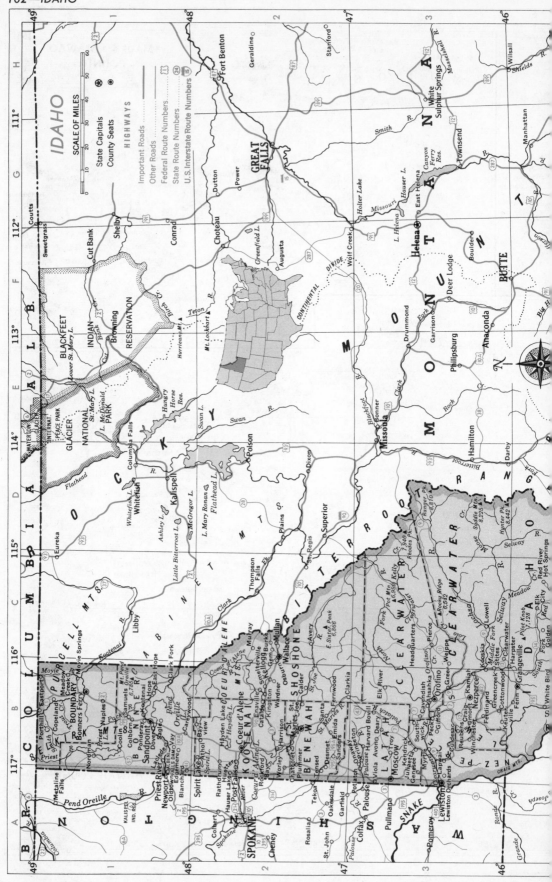

IDAHO

SCALE OF MILES
0 10 20 30 40 50 60

State Capitals ⊛
County Seats ⊙

HIGHWAYS
Important Roads
Other Roads
Federal Route Numbers
State Route Numbers
U.S. Interstate Route Numbers

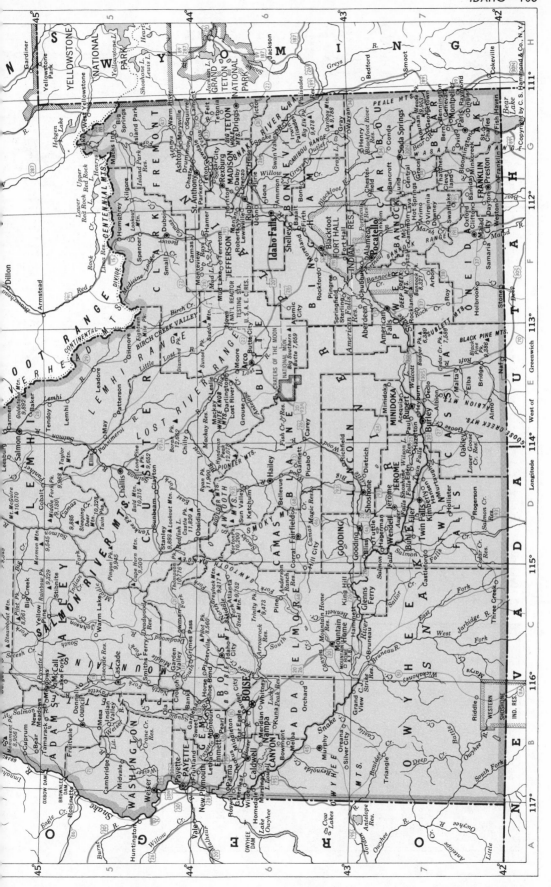

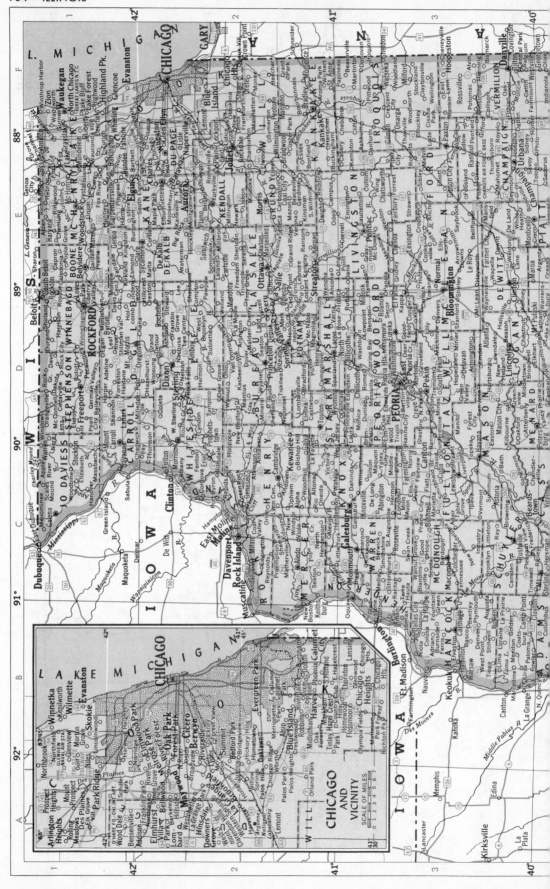

CHICAGO
AND
VICINITY

SCALE OF MILES
0 1 2 3 4 5

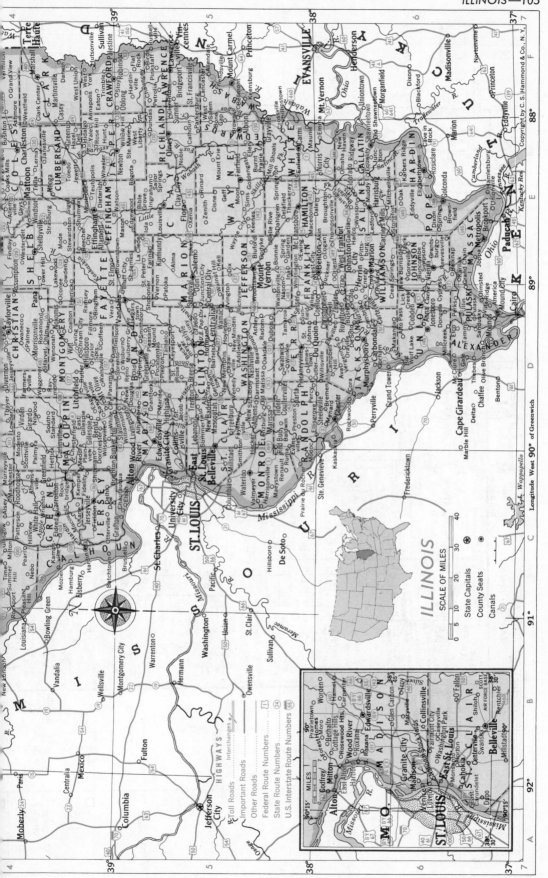

ILLINOIS

SCALE OF MILES

0 5 10 20 30 40

⊛ State Capitals
⊙ County Seats
Canals

HIGHWAYS

Toll Roads
Interchanges
Important Roads
Other Roads
Federal Route Numbers ⟨24⟩
State Route Numbers ⟨55⟩
U.S. Interstate Route Numbers

Copyright by C. S. Hammond & Co., N. Y.

Longitude West 90° of Greenwich

ST. LOUIS

MADISON

ST. CLAIR

MISSOURI

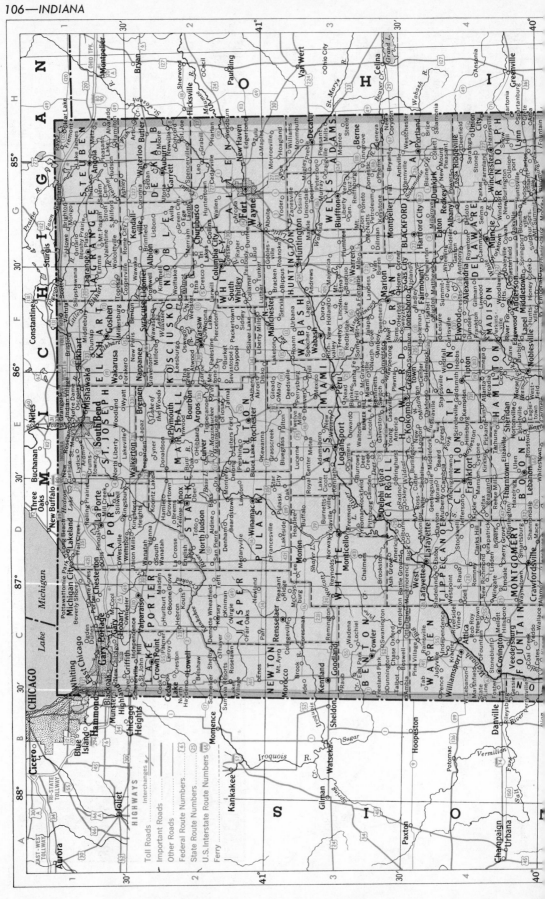

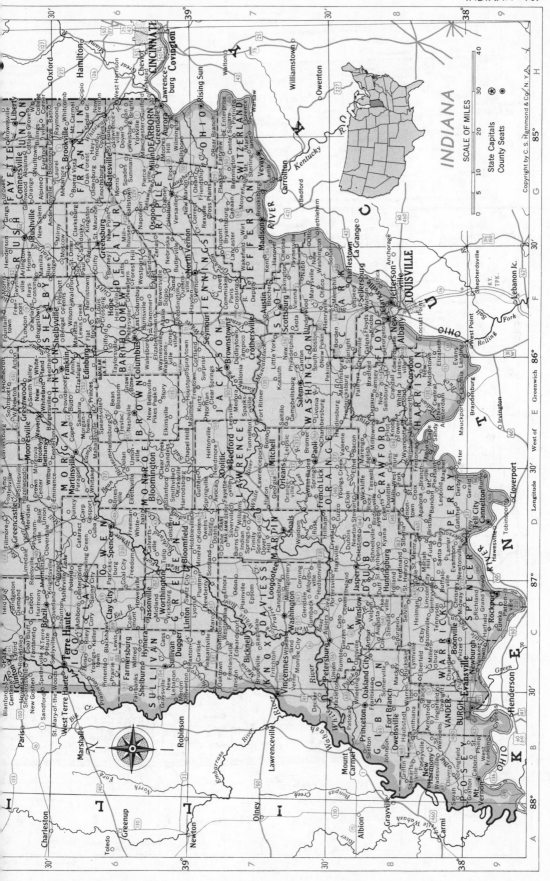

INDIANA

SCALE OF MILES

State Capitals ⊛
County Seats ⊗

Copyright by C. S. Hammond & Co., N.Y.

IOWA

SCALE OF MILES

0 5 10   20   30   40

State Capitals ⊛
County Seats ⊙

HIGHWAYS

Important Roads ....
Other Roads ....
Federal Route Numbers ...... ⬡
State Route Numbers .... ◯
U.S. Interstate Route Numbers ...... 🛡

Copyright by C. S. HAMMOND & Co., N.Y.

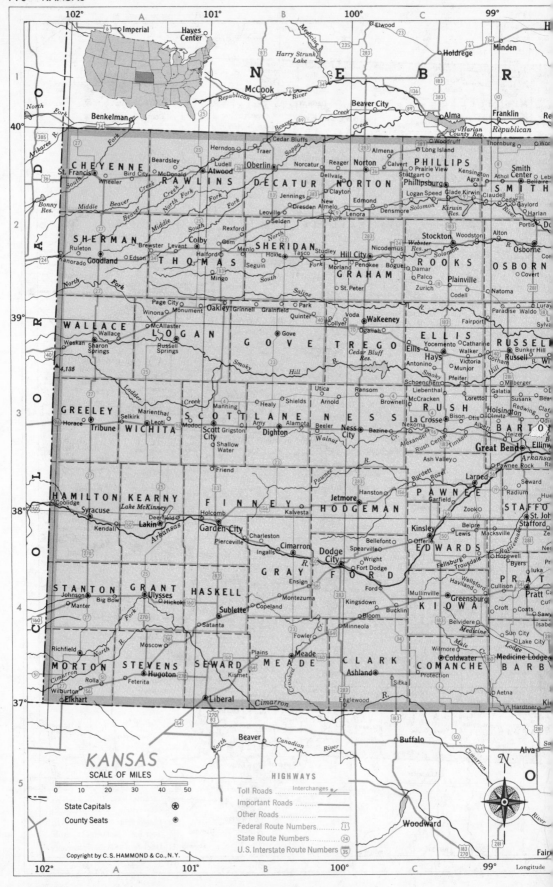

KANSAS
SCALE OF MILES

0 10 20 30 40 50

State Capitals
County Seats

HIGHWAYS

Toll Roads .... Interchanges
Important Roads ....
Other Roads ....
Federal Route Numbers 11
State Route Numbers 24
U.S. Interstate Route Numbers 35

Copyright by C. S. HAMMOND & Co., N.Y.

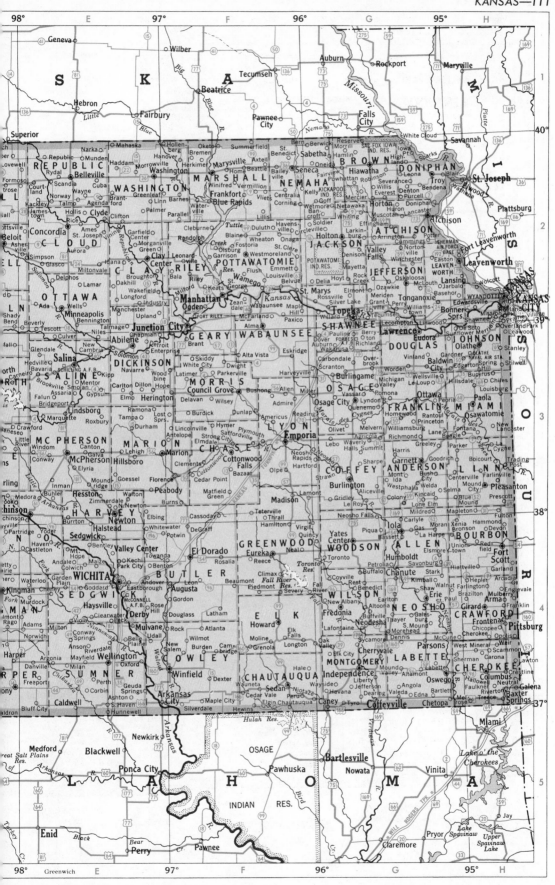

WESTERN PART
OF
KENTUCKY
Same scale as main map.

KENTUCKY

SCALE OF MILES

0 5 10 20 30 40

State Capitals ⊛
County Seats ⊙

HIGHWAYS

Toll Roads .... interchanges *
Important Roads ....
Other Roads ....
Federal Route Numbers .... [21]
State Route Numbers .... [24]
U.S. Interstate Route Numbers [64]

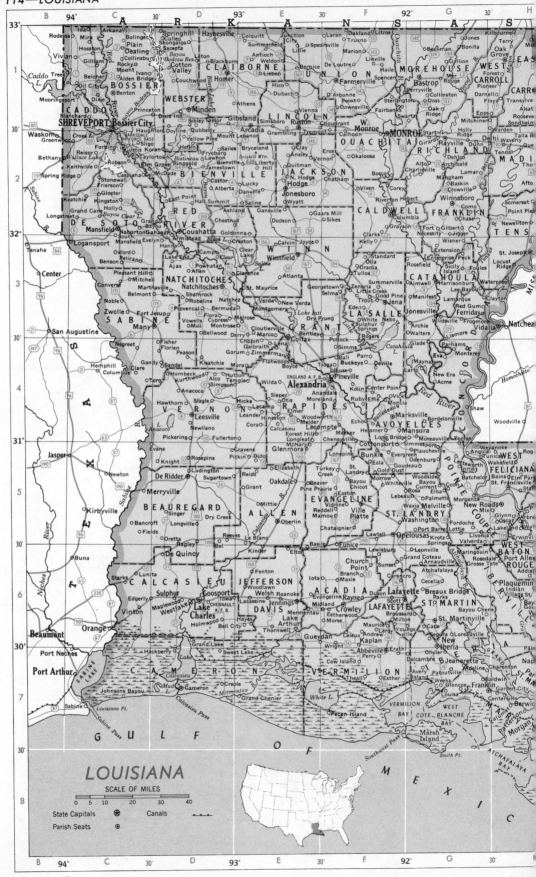

LOUISIANA

SCALE OF MILES

0   5   10   20   30   40

State Capitals   ⊗   Canals

Parish Seats   ⊙

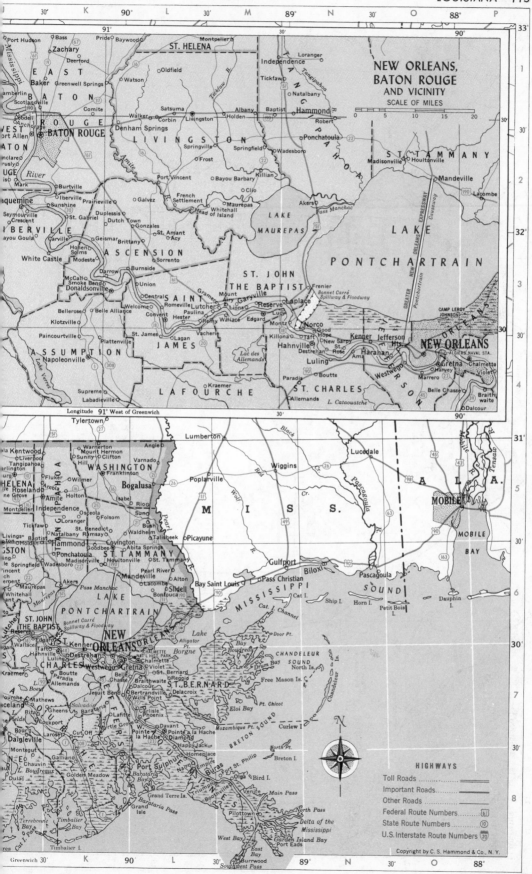

NEW ORLEANS,
BATON ROUGE
AND VICINITY
SCALE OF MILES

HIGHWAYS

Toll Roads
Important Roads
Other Roads
Federal Route Numbers
State Route Numbers
U.S. Interstate Route Numbers

Copyright by C. S. Hammond & Co., N. Y.

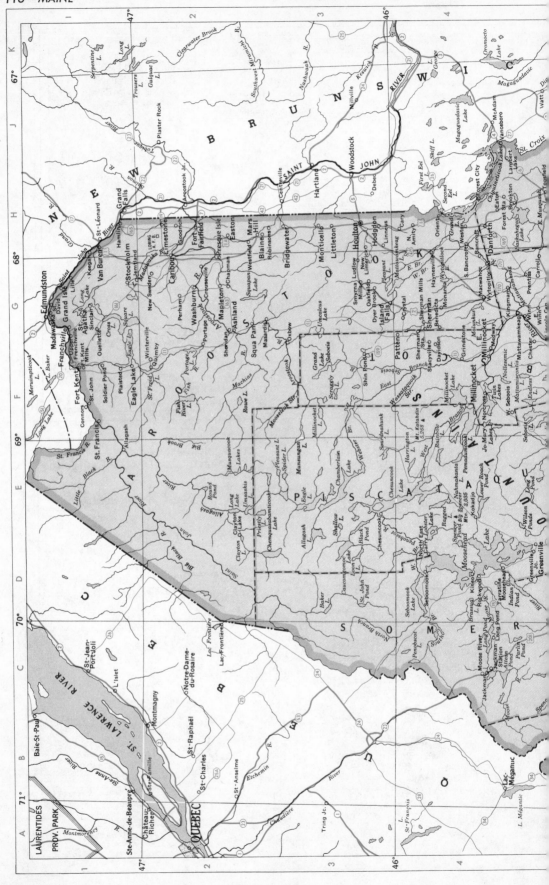

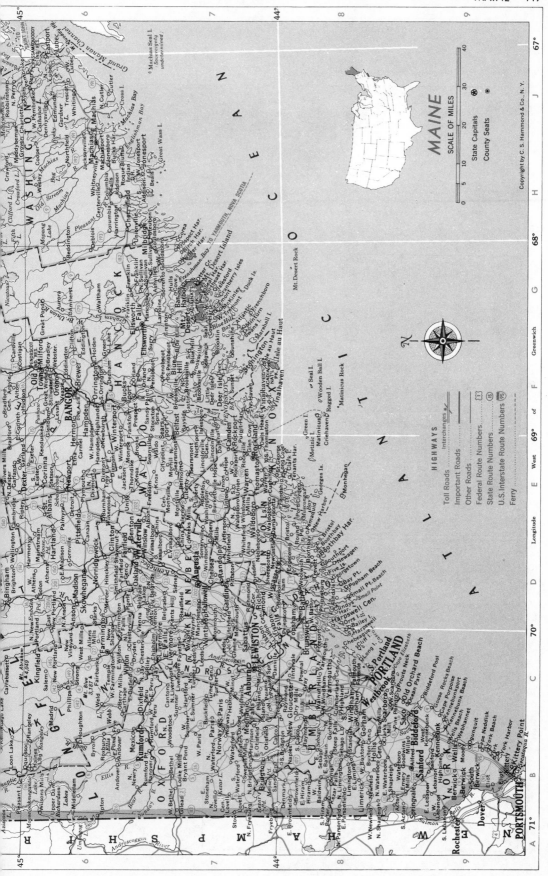

MAINE

SCALE OF MILES

State Capitals ⊛
County Seats ⊙

Copyright by C. S. Hammond & Co., N. Y.

HIGHWAYS

Toll Roads
Important Roads
Other Roads
Interchanges
Federal Route Numbers
State Route Numbers
U.S. Interstate Route Numbers
Ferry

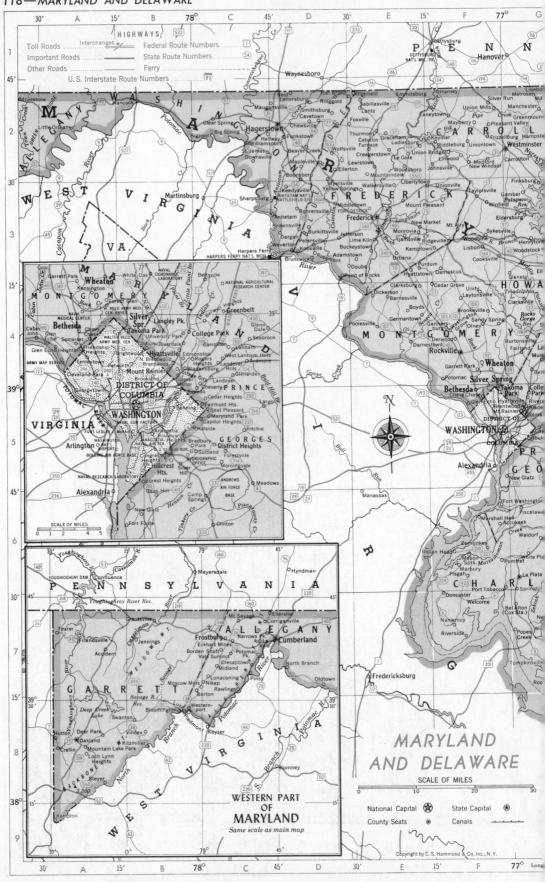

MARYLAND
AND DELAWARE

SCALE OF MILES

National Capital ★ State Capital ⊛
County Seats ⊙ Canals

WESTERN PART
OF
MARYLAND
Same scale as main map

Copyright by C. S. Hammond & Co. Inc., N.Y.

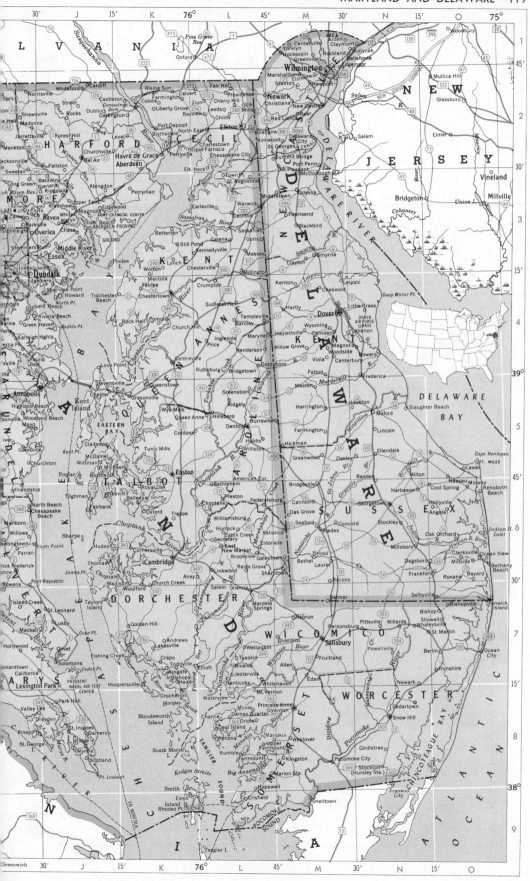

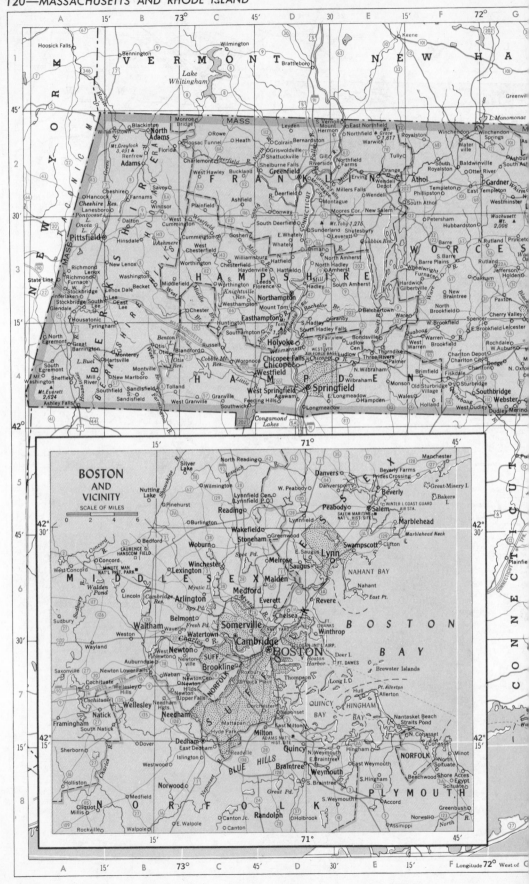

BOSTON
AND
VICINITY

SCALE OF MILES

0   2   4   6

MASSACHUSETTS
AND RHODE ISLAND

SCALE OF MILES

0   10   20

State Capitals ⊛   Canals
County Seats & Courthouses ⊙

HIGHWAYS

Toll Roads .... Interchanges
Important Roads ....
Other Roads ....
Federal Route Numbers ....
State Route Numbers ....
U.S. Interstate Route Numbers 95
Ferry ....

Copyright by C. S. Hammond & Co., N.Y.

MICHIGAN

SCALE OF MILES

0   10   20   30   40   50

⊛ State Capitals
◉ County Seats
— Canals

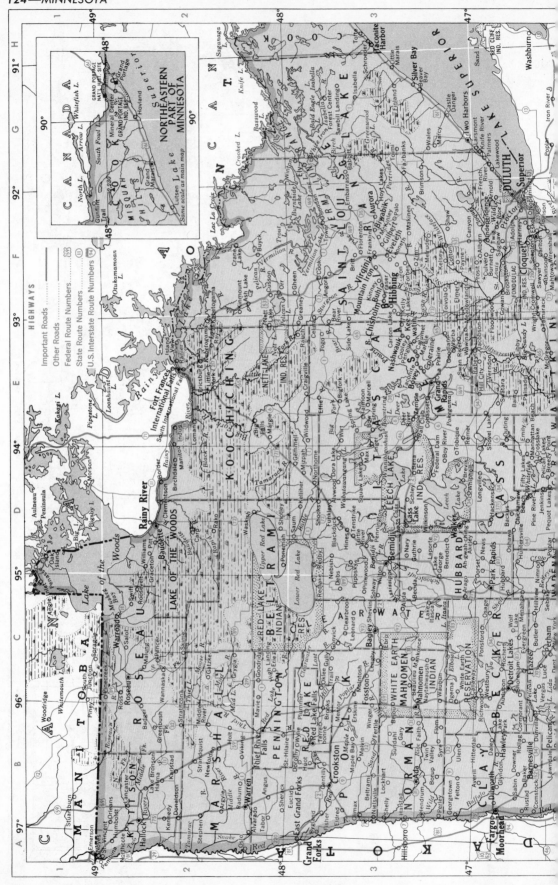

NORTHEASTERN PART OF MINNESOTA
Some scale as main map

HIGHWAYS

Important Roads
Other Roads
Federal Route Numbers .... (59)
State Route Numbers .... (11)
U.S. Interstate Route Numbers ... (94)

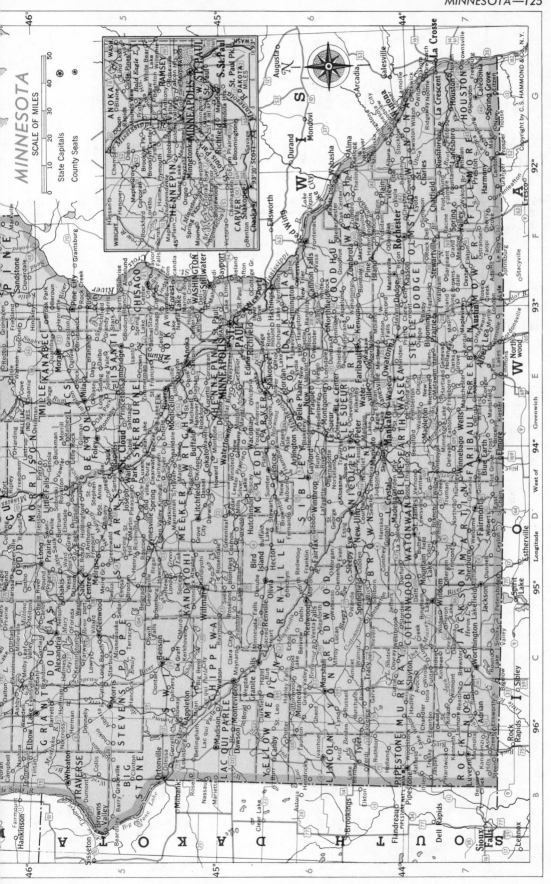

MINNESOTA

SCALE OF MILES

0   10   20   30   40   50

⊛ State Capitals
● County Seats

Copyright by C.S. HAMMOND & Co., N.Y.

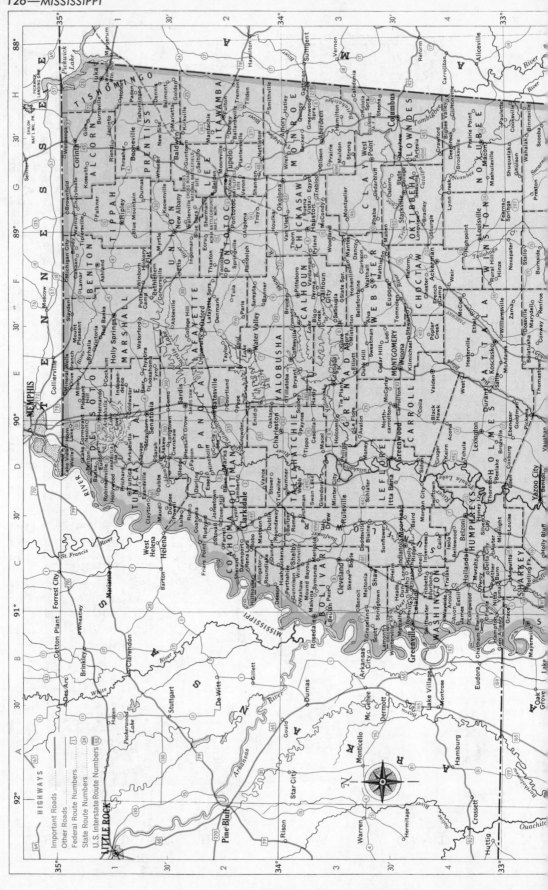

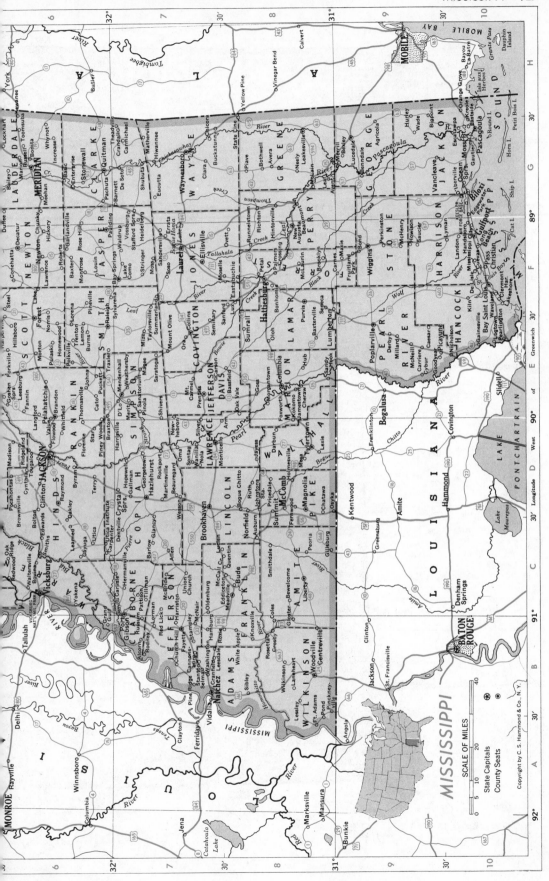

MISSISSIPPI

SCALE OF MILES

State Capitals ⊛
County Seats ◉

0 5 10 20 40

Copyright by C. S. Hammond & Co., N.Y.

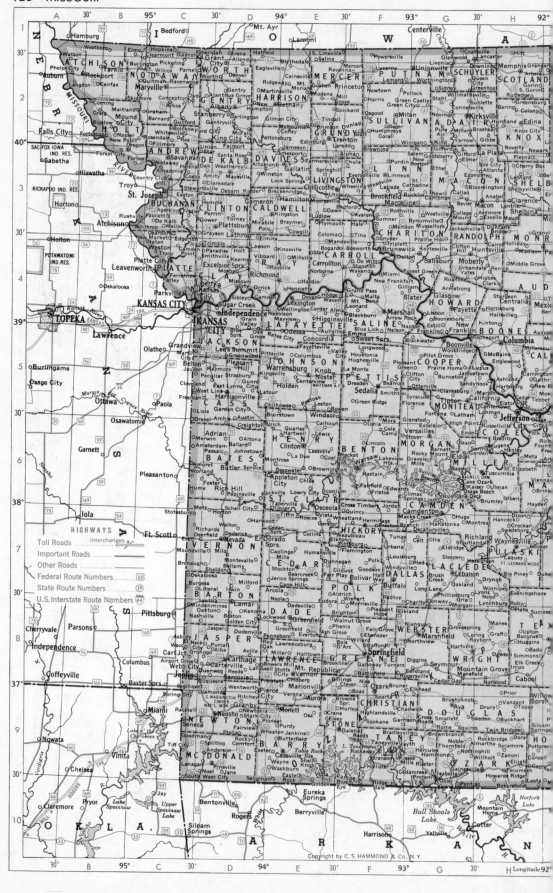

ST. LOUIS
AND
VICINITY
SCALE OF MILES
0 5 10 15
KANSAS CITY
AND
VICINITY
SCALE OF MILES
0 5 10 15
MISSOURI
SCALE OF MILES
0 10 20 30 40
State Capitals
County Seats
LINCOLN
ST. CHARLES
ST. LOUIS
FRANKLIN
JEFFERSON
PLATTE
CLAY
RAY
JACKSON
KANSAS
ILLINOIS
KENTUCKY
TENN.
WASHINGTON
ST. FRANCOIS
STE. GENEVIEVE
PERRY
MADISON
CAPE GIRARDEAU
BOLLINGER
REYNOLDS
WAYNE
CARTER
BUTLER
RIPLEY
STODDARD
SCOTT
MISSISSIPPI
NEW MADRID
PEMISCOT
DUNKLIN
WARREN
PIKE
MISSISSIPPI
Missouri R.
Kansas
River
OHIO
Tennessee R.
St. Louis
Kansas City
Cape Girardeau
Paducah
Cairo

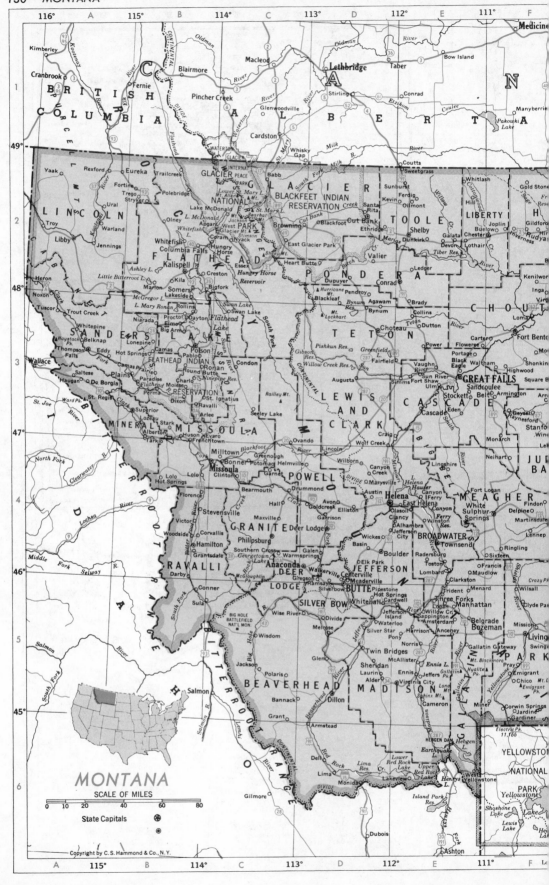

MONTANA

SCALE OF MILES

0 10 20   40   60   80

State Capitals ⊕

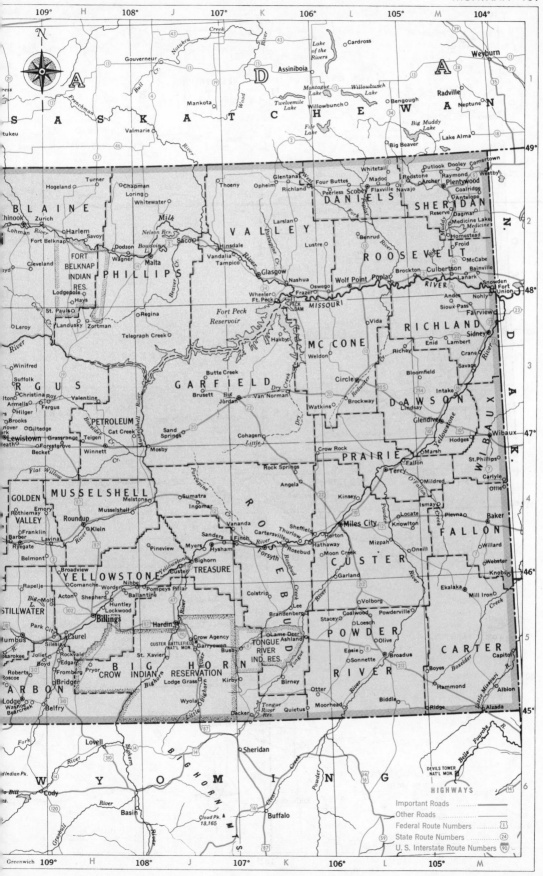

HIGHWAYS

Important Roads	
Other Roads	
Federal Route Numbers	
State Route Numbers	
U. S. Interstate Route Numbers	

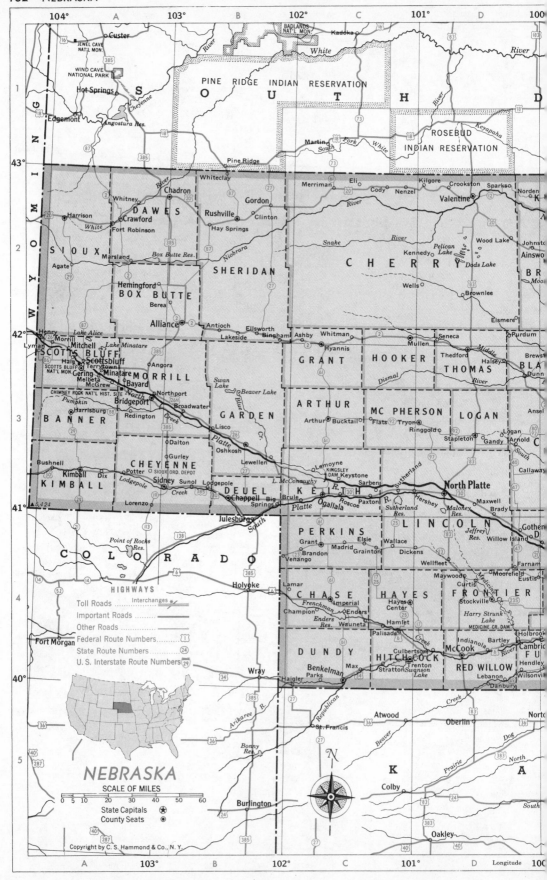

HIGHWAYS

Toll Roads .... Interchanges
Important Roads ....
Other Roads ....
Federal Route Numbers ....
State Route Numbers ....
U.S. Interstate Route Numbers

NEBRASKA

SCALE OF MILES

0 5 10   20   30   40   50   60

State Capitals ⊛
County Seats ◉

Copyright by C. S. Hammond & Co., N.Y.

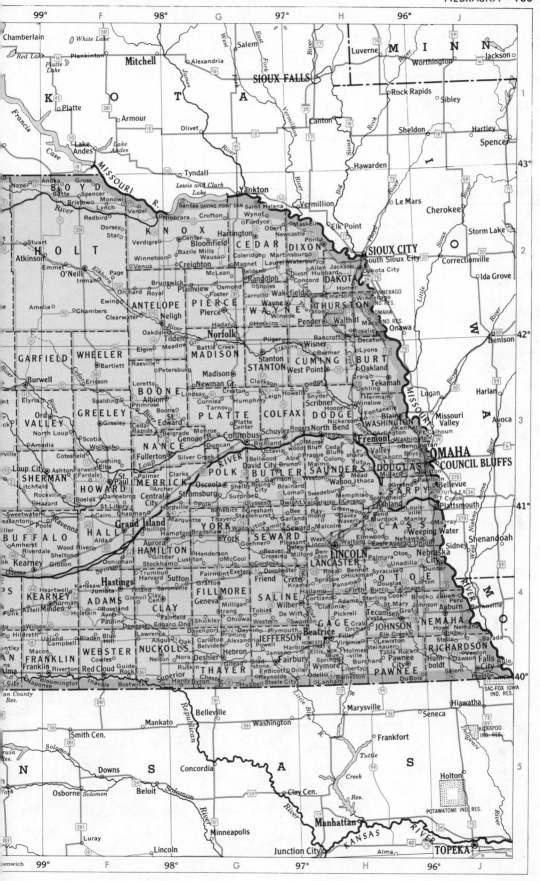

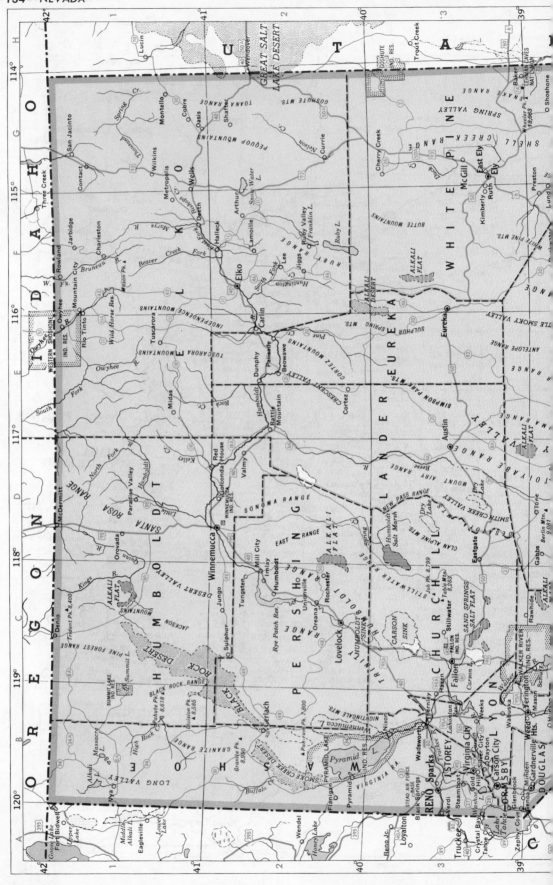

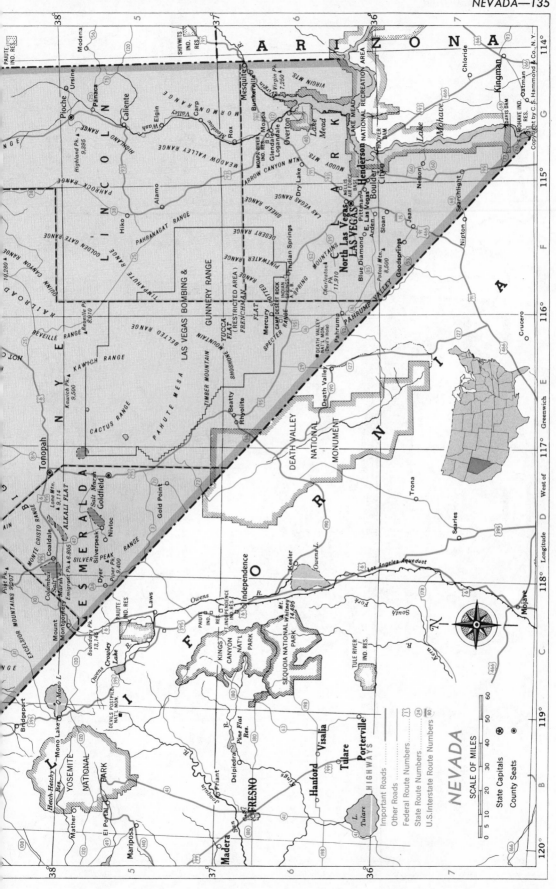

ARIZONA

NEVADA

SCALE OF MILES

0 5 10 20 30 40 50 60

HIGHWAYS

Important Roads ....
Other Roads ....
Federal Route Numbers (24)
State Route Numbers (24)
U.S. Interstate Route Numbers 80

State Capitals ⊛
County Seats ⊙

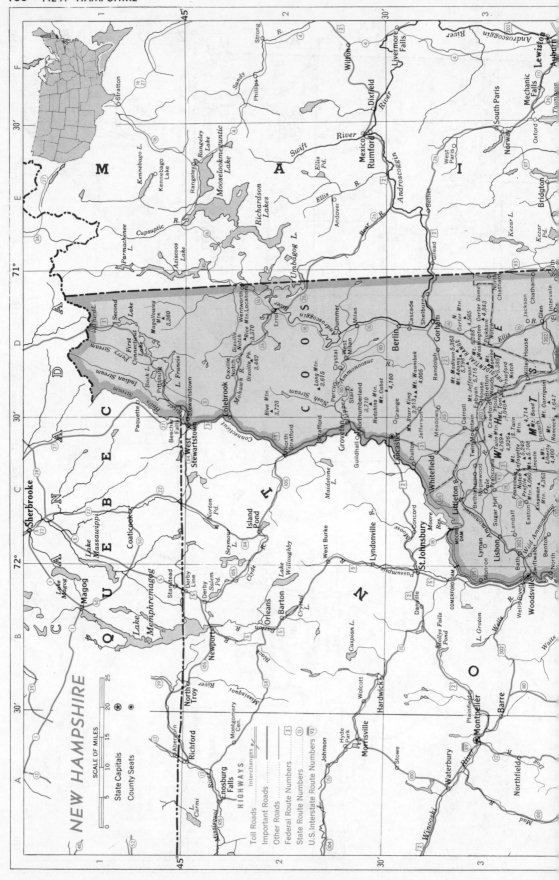

NEW HAMPSHIRE

SCALE OF MILES

0 5 10 15 20 25

State Capitals ⊛

County Seats ⦿

HIGHWAYS

Toll Roads............Interchanges *

Important Roads.........................

Other Roads.............................

Federal Route Numbers..............③

State Route Numbers...................⑪

U.S. Interstate Route Numbers......⑬

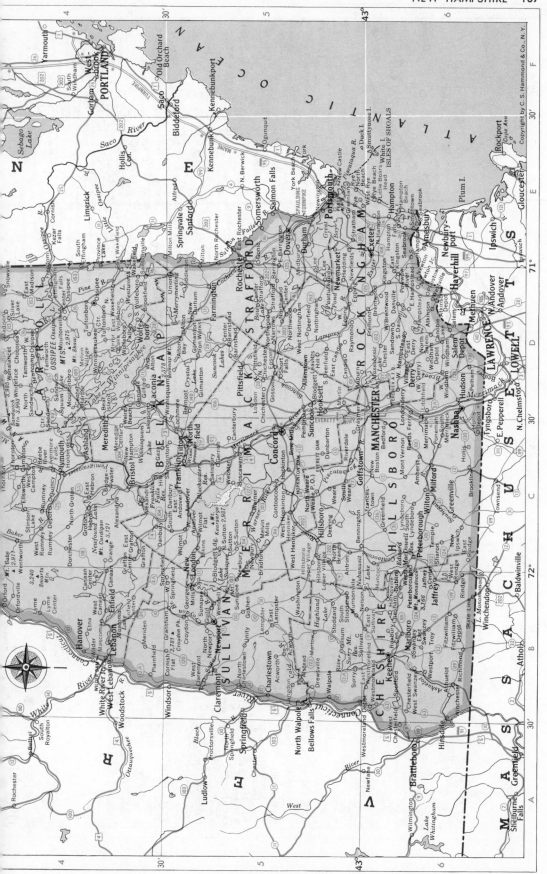

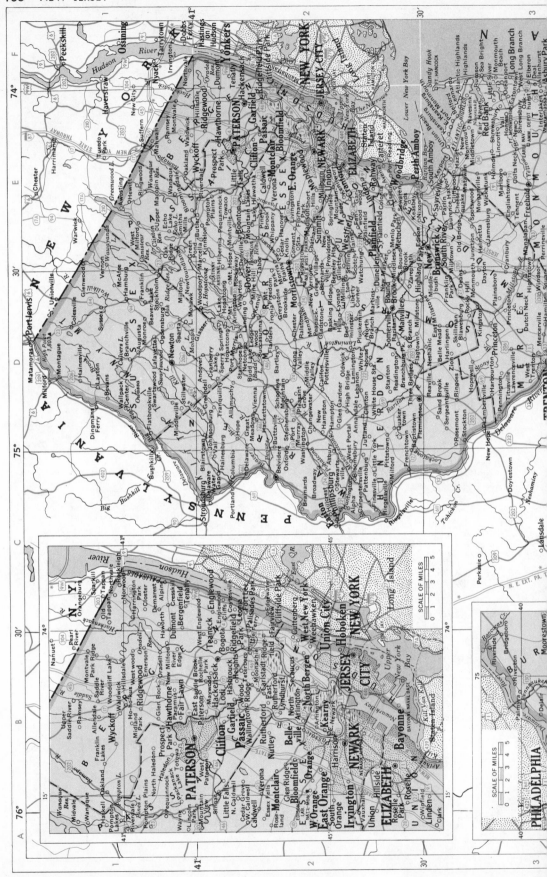

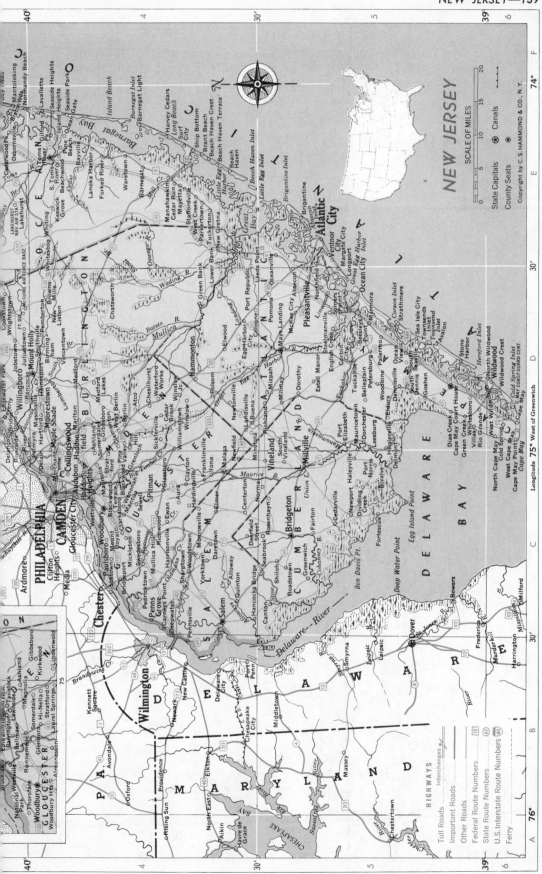

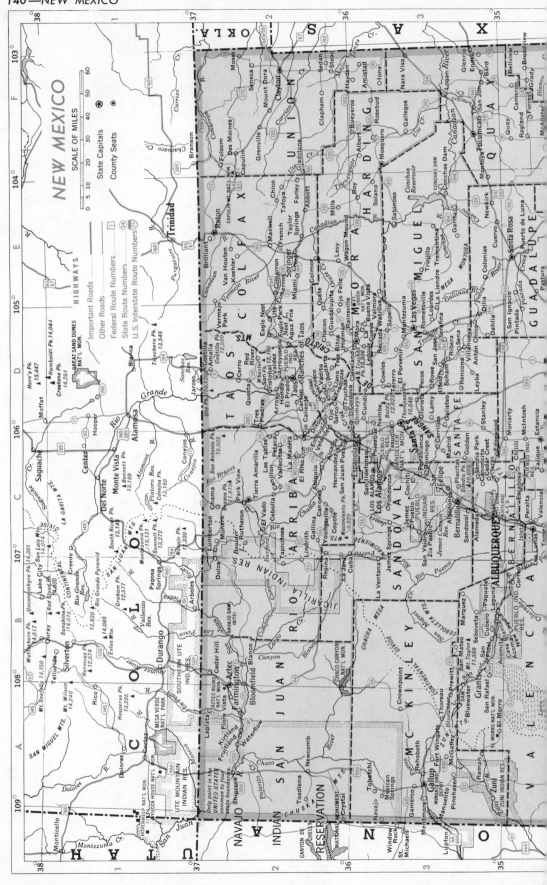

NEW MEXICO

SCALE OF MILES

0 5 10 20 30 40 50 60

⊛ State Capitals

◉ County Seats

HIGHWAYS

Important Roads

Other Roads

Federal Route Numbers ⑪

State Route Numbers ㉔

U.S. Interstate Route Numbers ㉕

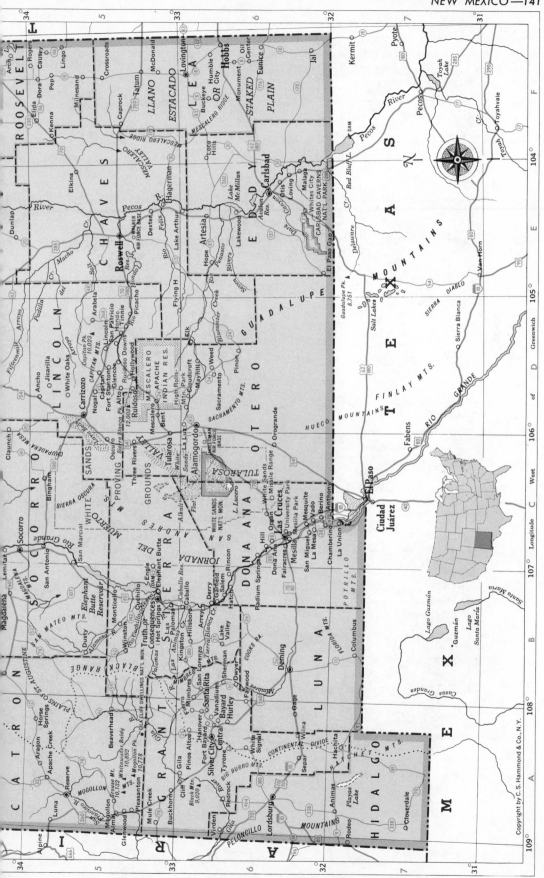

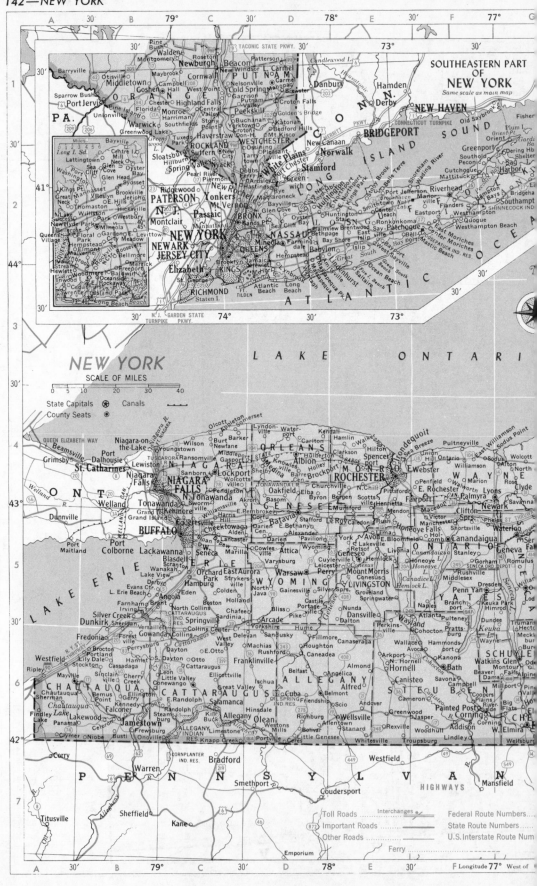

NEW YORK

SCALE OF MILES

State Capitals ⊛ Canals
County Seats ◉

SOUTHEASTERN PART OF NEW YORK
Same scale as main map

LAKE ONTARIO

LAKE ERIE

PENNSYLVANIA

HIGHWAYS

Toll Roads	Interchanges	Federal Route Numbers
Important Roads		State Route Numbers
Other Roads		U.S. Interstate Route Num
Ferry		

WESTERN PART OF
NORTH CAROLINA
Same scale as main map.

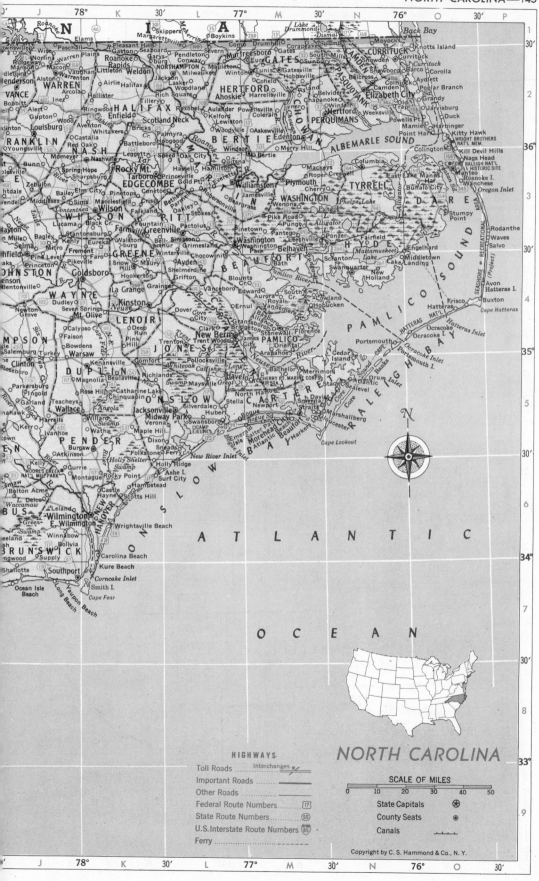

NORTH CAROLINA

SCALE OF MILES

HIGHWAYS

Toll Roads .... Interchanges
Important Roads ....
Other Roads ....
Federal Route Numbers 17
State Route Numbers 55
U.S.Interstate Route Numbers 85
Ferry ....

State Capitals .... ⊛
County Seats .... ◉
Canals .... ┼┼┼┼┼

Copyright by C. S. Hammond & Co., N. Y.

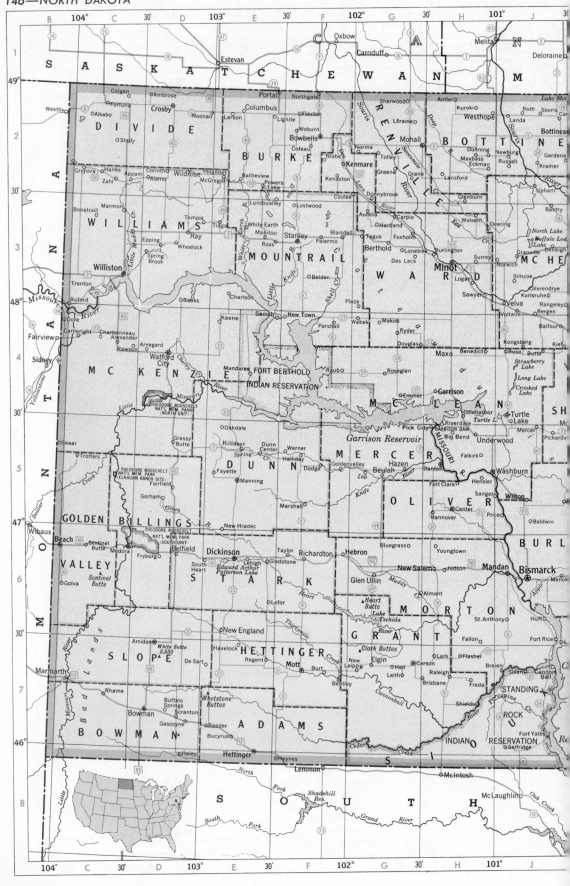

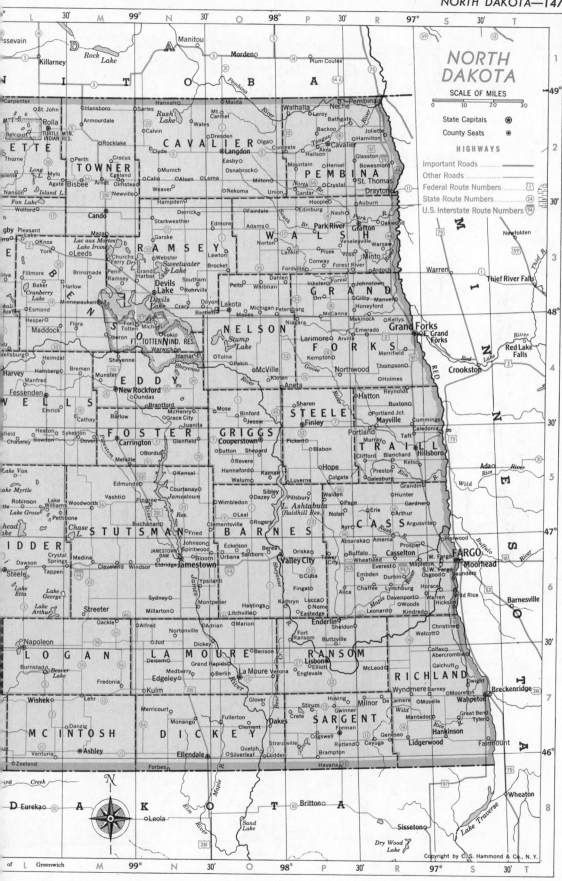

NORTH DAKOTA

SCALE OF MILES

0   10   20   30

⊛ State Capitals
◉ County Seats

HIGHWAYS

Important Roads ....
Other Roads ....
Federal Route Numbers 81
State Route Numbers 24
U.S. Interstate Route Numbers 94

Copyright by C. S. Hammond & Co., N. Y.

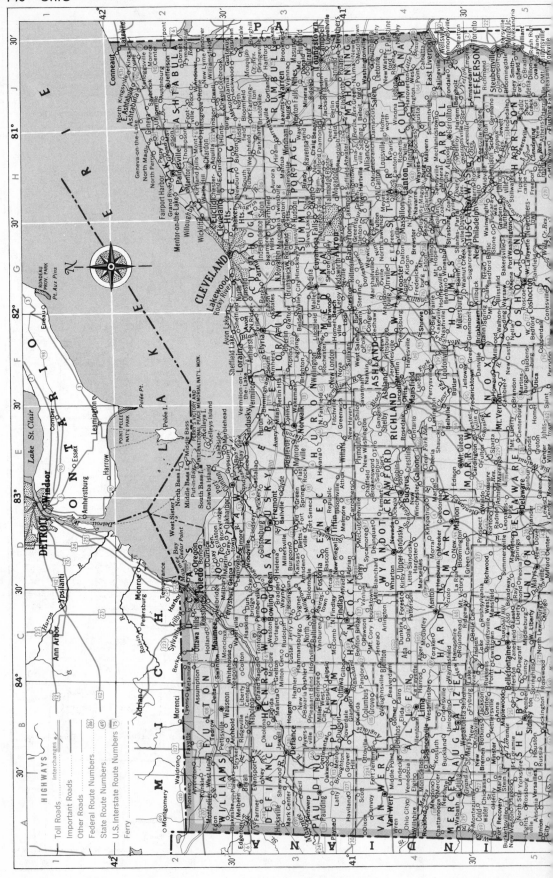

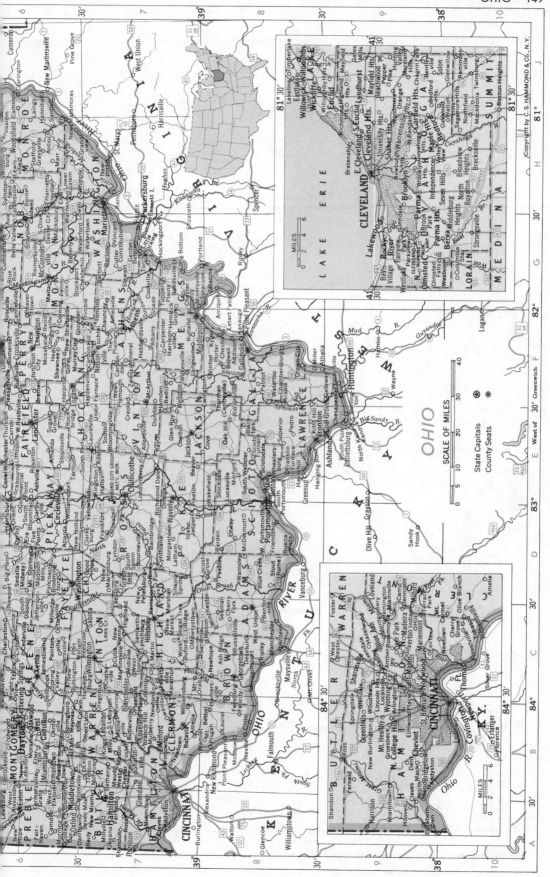

Copyright by C. S. HAMMOND & CO., N.Y.

OHIO

SCALE OF MILES

⊕ State Capitals
⊙ County Seats

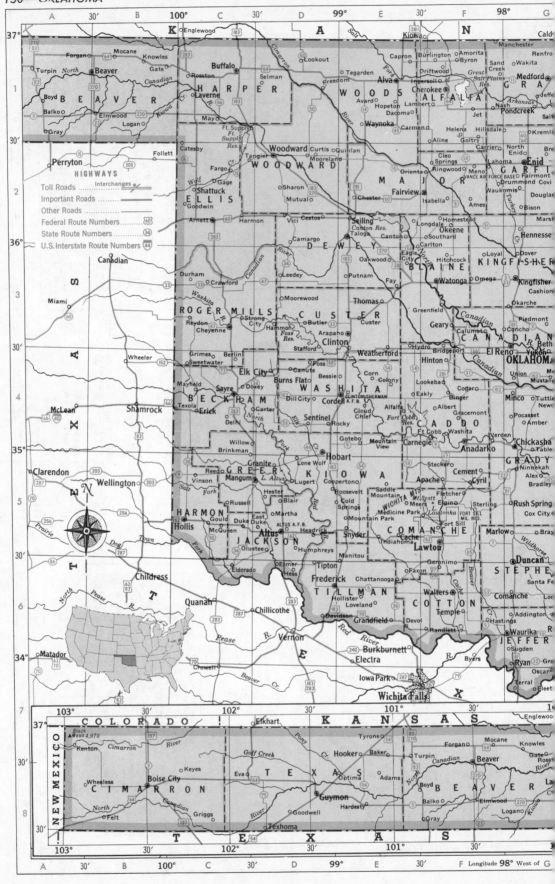

HIGHWAYS

Toll Roads .... Interchanges #
Important Roads ....
Other Roads ....
Federal Route Numbers........ 60
State Route Numbers 34
U.S. Interstate Route Numbers 44

OKLAHOMA
SCALE OF MILES
0 5 10   20   30   40

State Capitals ⊛
County Seats ◉

Copyright by C. S. Hammond & Co., N. Y.

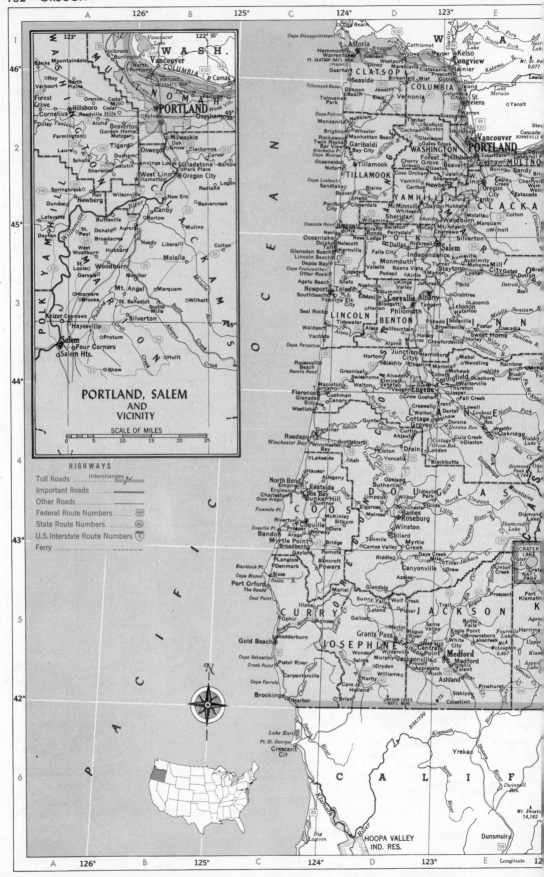

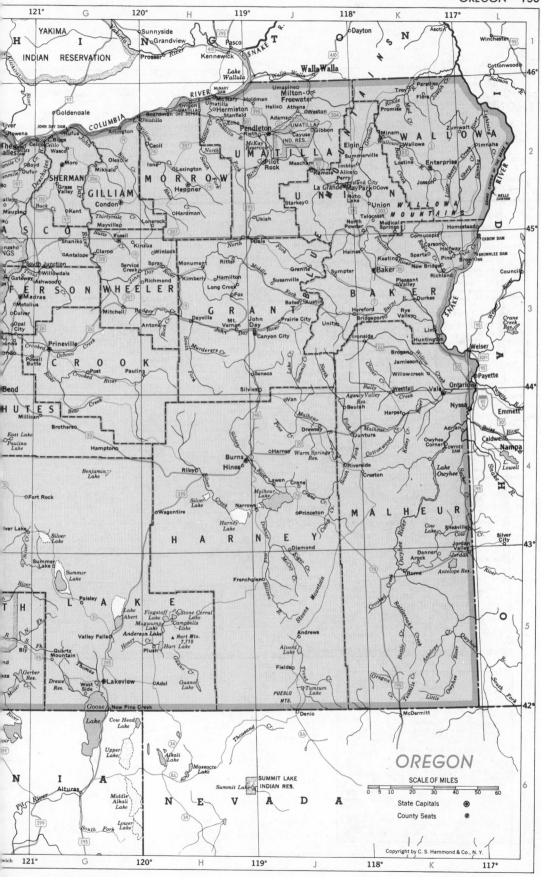

OREGON

SCALE OF MILES

0 5 10   20   30   40   50   60

State Capitals ⊛
County Seats ⊚

LAKE ERIE

NEW YORK

Counties and places (partial):

ERIE — Erie, North East, Harborcreek, Lawrence Park, Wesleyville, Kearsarge, Wattsburg, Fairview, Lake City, McKean, Girard, Platea, McLane, Waterford, Union City, North Springfield, East Springfield, West Springfield, Albion, Cranesville, Edinboro, Mill Village

CRAWFORD — Meadville, Conneautville, Saegertown, Cambridge Springs, Venango, Springboro, Blooming Valley, Harmonsburg, Fredericksburg, Linesville, Conneaut Lake Park, Geneva, Cochranton, Townville, Guys Mills, Hartstown, Adamsville, Atlantic, Centerville, Riceville, Spartansburg

WARREN — Warren, North Warren, Youngsville, Irvine, Sugar Grove, Clarendon, Tiona, Sheffield, Torpedo, Grand Valley, Garland, Pittsfield, Columbus, Lottsville, Bear Lake, Clymer, Russell, Corydon, Kinzua

MERCER — Sharon, Farrell, Greenville, Grove City, Mercer, Sandy Lake, Stoneboro, Fredonia, Transfer, Sharpsville, Clark, Wheatland, West Middlesex, Leesburg, Clarks Mills, Hadley, New Lebanon, Jackson Center, Sheakleyville, Pardoe

VENANGO — Franklin, Oil City, Seneca, Polk, Cranberry, Venus, Fertigs, Utica, Rouseville, President, Van, Emlenton, Clintonville, Kennerdell

FOREST — Tionesta, Marienville, Endeavor, East Hickory, West Hickory, Kellettville, Mayburg

ELK — Ridgway, Saint Marys, Johnsonburg, Kersey, Dagus Mines, Benezett, Byrnedale, Daguscahonda, Dents Run

McKEAN — Smethport, Bradford, Kane, Mount Jewett, Eldred, Port Allegany, Coudersport, Turtlepoint, Duke Center, Rixford, Larabee, Cyclone, Mount Alton, Ludlow, Kushequa, Marvindale, Hazel Hurst, Clermont, Crosby, Wrights, Colegrove, Betula

POTTER — Coudersport, Austin, Shinglehouse, Oswayo, Roulette, Keating Summit, Costello, Wharton

CAMERON — Emporium, Cameron, Sterling Run, Sinnamahoning, Driftwood, Sabula, Medix Run

CLARION — Clarion, New Bethlehem, Strattanville, Shippenville, Knox, Emlenton, St. Petersburg, Sligo, Rimersburg, Callensburg, Fryburg, Tylersburg, Leeper, Cooksburg, Lucinda, Corsica, Summerville, Reynoldsville

JEFFERSON — Brookville, Punxsutawney, Du Bois, Reynoldsville, Sykesville, Big Run, Falls Creek, Sandy, Anita, Walston, Hamilton, Baxter, Oak Ridge, Timblin, De Lancey, Worthville, Troutville, Helvetia

CLEARFIELD — Clearfield, Curwensville, Du Bois, Grampian, Mahaffey, Woodland, Lanse, Houtzdale, Madera, Osceola Mills, Ramey, Winburne, Munson, Morrisdale, Hawk Run, Smithmill, Glen Hope, Coalport, Irvona, Bigler, Wallaceton, Philipsburg, Chester Hill, S. Philipsburg, Brisbin, Woodland

CENTRE — State College, Philipsburg, Port Matilda, Warriors Mark, Pine Grove Mills

BUTLER — Butler, Ellwood City, Zelienople, Harmony, Evans City, Prospect, Chicora, Karns City, Petrolia, Bruin, Fairview, West Sunbury, Mars, Saxonburg, Renfrew, Lyndora, Cowansville, Herman, Connoquenessing, Valencia, Cabot, Callery, Marwood, Winfield, Cadogan, Templeton

ARMSTRONG — Kittanning, Ford City, Apollo, Leechburg, Freeport, Dayton, Adrian, Worthington, Rural Valley, Elderton, Manorville, Manor, Rayburn, N. Apollo, Ford Cliff, Sagamore, Dixonville, Smicksburg, Rosston, Atwood

INDIANA — Indiana, Homer City, Blairsville, Clymer, Marion Center, Saltsburg, Creekside, Shelocta, Clarksburg, Penn Run, Commodore, Cherry Tree, Glen Campbell, Heilwood, Lucernemines, Black Lick, Coral, Diltown, Ernest, Iselin, Aultman, Armagh

CAMBRIA — Johnstown, Ebensburg, Cresson, Portage, Nanty Glo, Patton, Carrolltown, Lilly, Gallitzin, Loretto, Spangler, St. Benedict, Wilmore, Summerhill, Ashville, Dysart, Hastings, Barnesboro, Vintondale

BLAIR — Altoona, Hollidaysburg, Tyrone, Roaring Spring, Bellwood, Williamsburg, Martinsburg, Duncansville, Claysburg, Newry, East Freedom, Tipton, Birmingham, Spruce Creek, Alexandria, Petersburg

BEAVER — Beaver Falls, Aliquippa, Ambridge, Beaver, Rochester, Monaca, Midland, New Brighton, Freedom, Conway, Baden, Industry, Koppel, Homewood, Frisco, Darlington, Hookstown, Georgetown, Ohioville, Hanover

LAWRENCE — New Castle, Ellwood City, Bessemer, New Wilmington, Volant, Pulaski, Edinburg, Wampum, Enon Valley, New Galilee, Hillsville, Slippery Rock

ALLEGHENY — **PITTSBURGH**, McKeesport, Sewickley, Coraopolis, Carnegie, McDonald, Oakdale, Bridgeville, Clairton, Elizabeth, Tarentum, Arnold, New Kensington, Springdale, Glenfield, Wilmerding, Wall, Trafford

WASHINGTON — Washington, Canonsburg, Donora, Monongahela, Monessen, Charleroi, California, Burgettstown, McMurray, Houston, Claysville, Finleyville, Bentleyville, Ellsworth, Marianna, West Alexander, Amity, West Middletown, Avella

WESTMORELAND — Greensburg, Jeannette, Latrobe, Monessen, New Kensington, Irwin, Murrysville, Derry, Ligonier, Mount Pleasant, Youngwood, Scottdale, Manor, Export, Delmont, Vandergrift, Hyde Park, Arona, New Stanton, Norvelt, Donegal, Bolivar, New Florence, Avonmore

FAYETTE — Uniontown, Connellsville, Brownsville, Masontown, Vanderbilt, Fairchance, Point Marion, Smithfield, Everson, Dunbar, Ohiopyle, Markleysburg, Perryopolis, Fayette City, Belle Vernon, Grindstone, Republic

GREENE — Waynesburg, Carmichaels, Nemacolin, Jefferson, Rices Landing, Clarksville, Sycamore, Nineveh, Greensboro, Mount Morris, Brave, Garards Fort

SOMERSET — Somerset, Meyersdale, Berlin, Windber, Boswell, Rockwood, Confluence, Central City, Jennerstown, Stoystown, Salisbury, Garrett, Ursina, Addison, New Centerville, Shanksville, Macdonaldton, Hooversville, Hollsopple

BEDFORD — Bedford, Everett, Hyndman, Schellsburg, Saxton, Woodbury, Hopewell, New Paris, Rainsburg, Buffalo Mills, Manns Choice, Breezewood, Wolfsburg, Clearville, St. Clairsville, Loysburg

FULTON — McConnellsburg, Needmore, Hustontown, Warfordsburg, Webster Mills, Big Cove Tannery, Harrisonville, Waterfall, Fort Littleton

HUNTINGDON — Huntingdon, Mount Union, Mapleton Depot, Orbisonia, Broad Top City, Saxton, Three Springs, Cassville, Entriken

Inset map:

PITTSBURGH — McKees Rocks, Wilkinsburg, Homestead, Munhall, Duquesne, McKeesport, Carnegie, Mt. Lebanon, Dormont, Swissvale, Edgewood, Turtle Creek, Forest Hills, Monroeville, Churchill, Penn Hills, Ingram, Crafton, Greentree, Rosslyn Farms, Heidelberg, Castle Shannon, Bethel, Baldwin, Whitehall, Brentwood, Pleasant Hills, West Mifflin, Dravosburg, Glassport, Clairton, Liberty, Jefferson, Lincoln, Versailles, White Oak, Port Vue, N. Braddock, Braddock, Rankin, Etna, Sharpsburg, Aspinwall, Blawnox, Verona, Oakmont, Fox Chapel, Glenshaw, West View, Bellevue, Avalon, Emsworth, Ben Avon, Millvale, Universal, Harmarville, Cheswick, Laurel Gardens, Ambridge, Leetsdale

SOUTH PK. MIL. RES.

MILES

W. VA. / **WEST VIRGINIA** — Frostburg, Cumberland, Keyser, Romney, Winchester, Martinsburg, Berkeley Spgs, Paw Paw, Westernport, Oakland, Deep Creek Lake, Youghiogheny River Res., Capon Bridge

MARYLAND — Cumberland, Hancock

VIRGINIA — Winchester, Berryville

Youghiogheny River

Potomac River

HIGHWAYS

Toll Roads (Interchanges)	
Important Roads	
Other Roads	
Federal Route Numbers	
State Route Numbers	24
U.S. Interstate Route Numbers	80
Ferry	

Longitude 78° West

PENNSYLVANIA

SCALE OF MILES

State Capitals ⊛
County Seats ⊙
Canals

Copyright by C. S. Hammond & Co., N.Y.

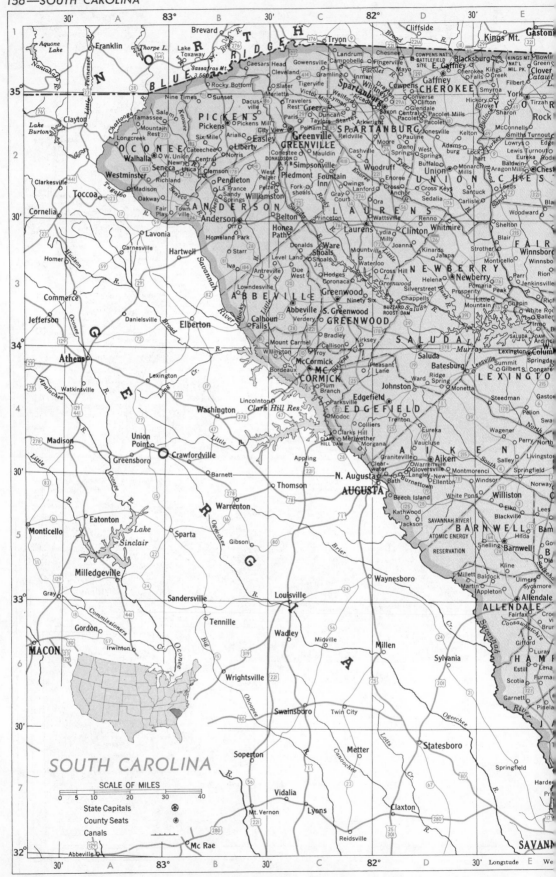

SOUTH CAROLINA

SCALE OF MILES

0   5   10   20   30   40

State Capitals ⊛

County Seats ◉

Canals

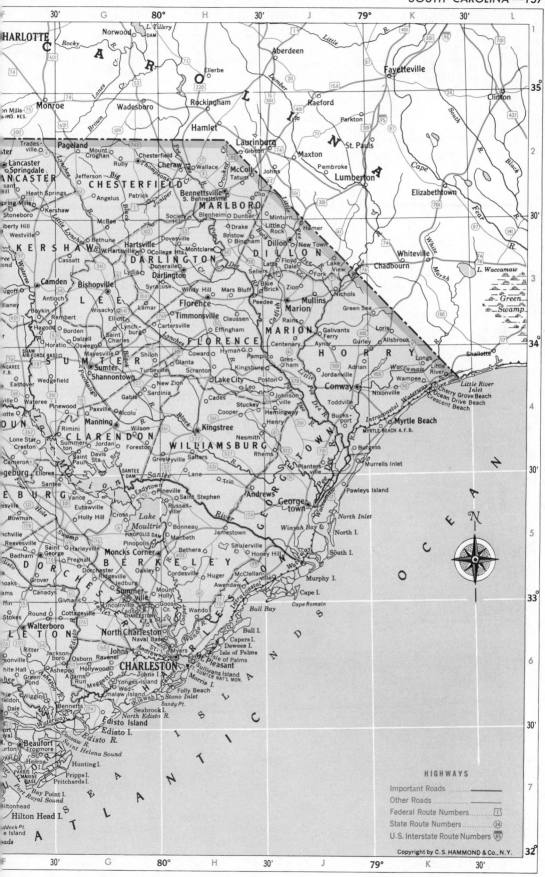

HIGHWAYS

Important Roads ....
Other Roads ....
Federal Route Numbers 73
State Route Numbers 24
U.S. Interstate Route Numbers 85

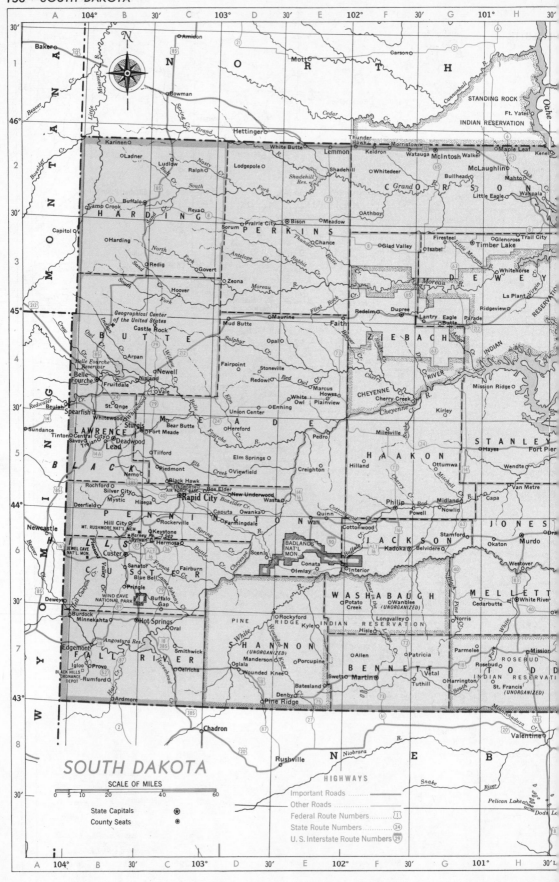

SOUTH DAKOTA

SCALE OF MILES

0 5 10   20   40   60

State Capitals ⊛
County Seats ◎

HIGHWAYS

Important Roads ....
Other Roads ....
Federal Route Numbers .... 🛡
State Route Numbers 24
U.S. Interstate Route Numbers 29

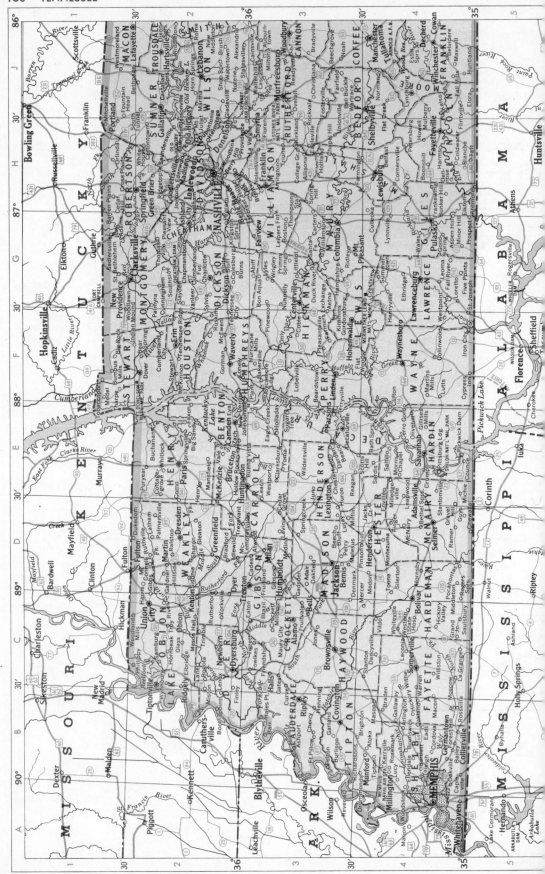

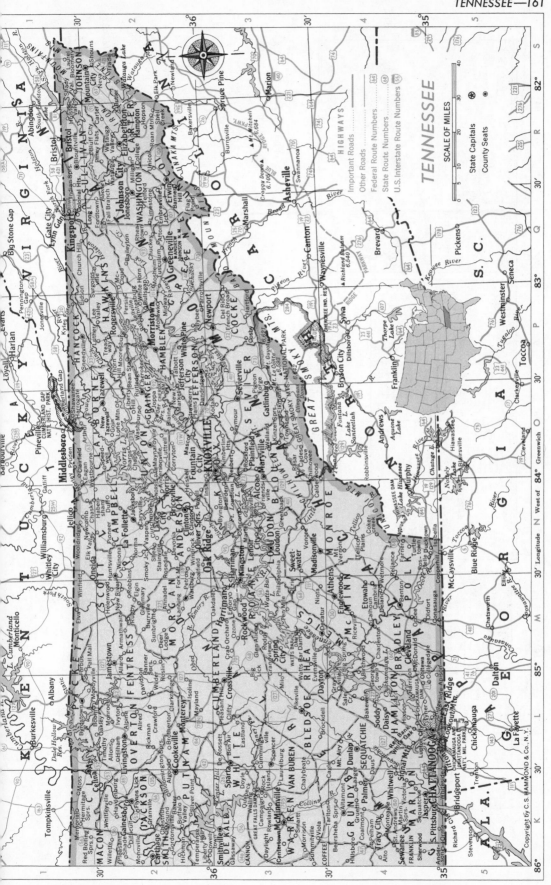

TENNESSEE

SCALE OF MILES

HIGHWAYS

Important Roads
Other Roads
Federal Route Numbers
State Route Numbers
U.S. Interstate Route Numbers

State Capitals
County Seats

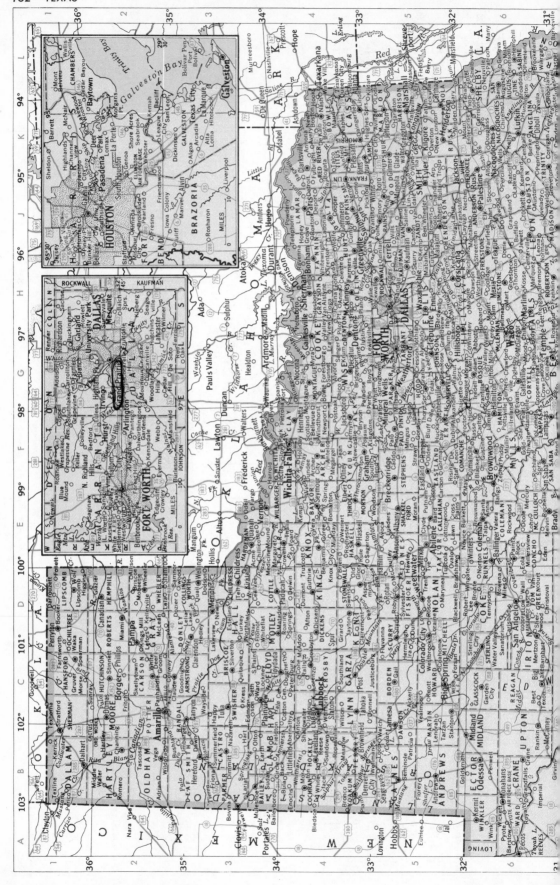

TEXAS

SCALE OF MILES

HIGHWAYS

Toll Roads .... Interchanges
Important Roads ....
Other Roads ....
Federal Route Numbers 77
State Route Numbers 27
U.S. Interstate Route Numbers ... 35
Ferry ....

State Capitals
County Seats

Copyright by C. S. HAMMOND & Co., N.Y.

WESTERN PART
OF
TEXAS
Same scale as main map

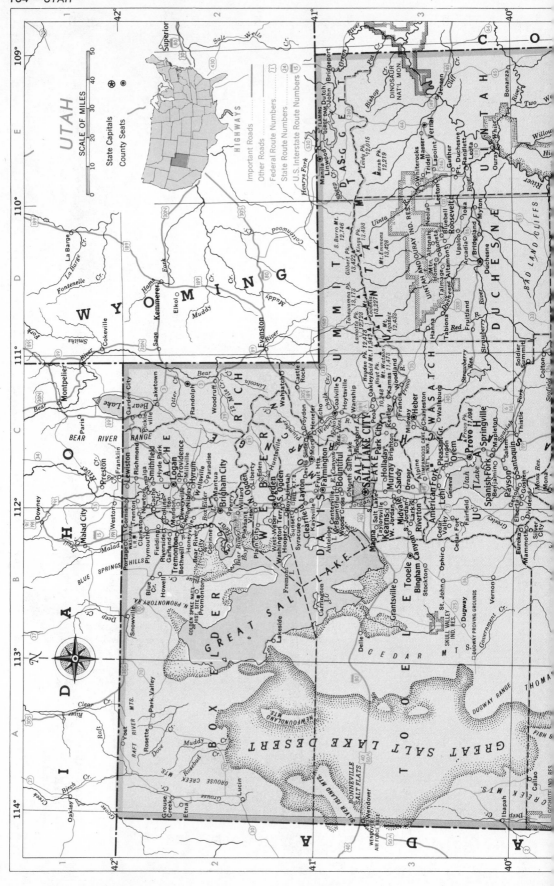

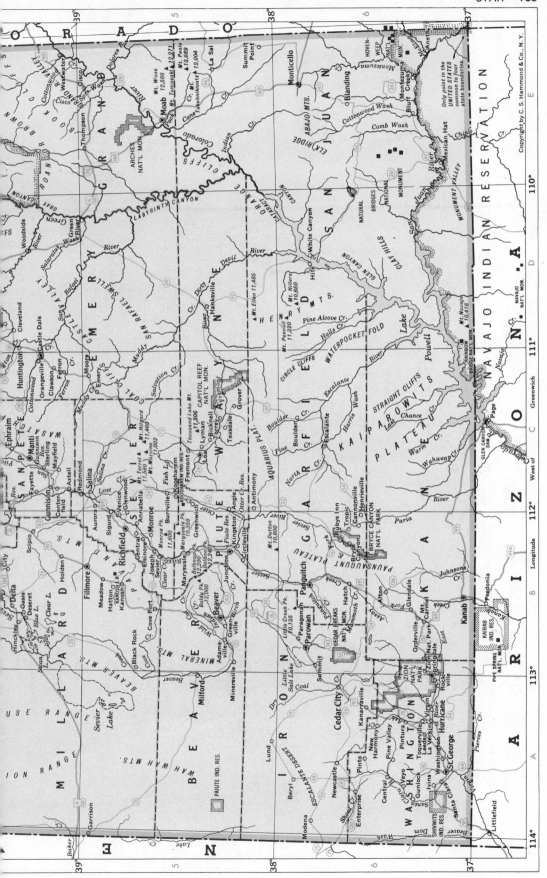

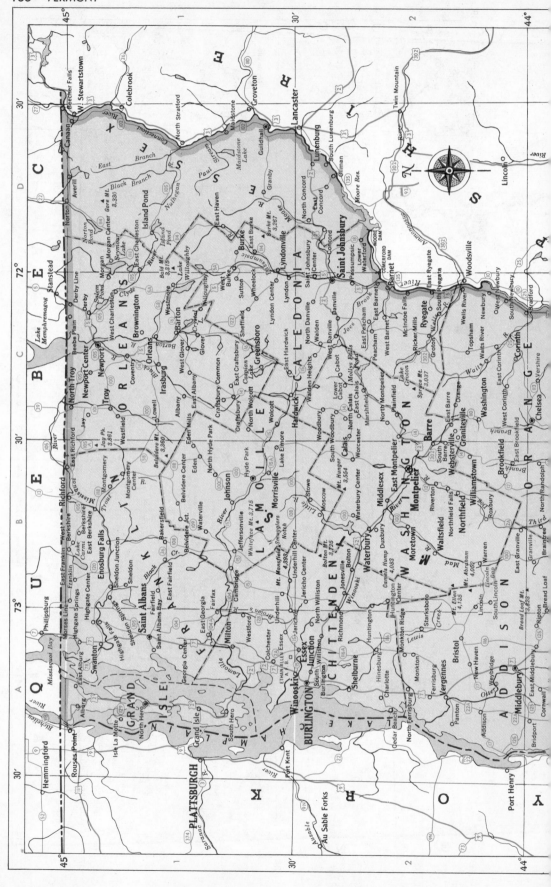

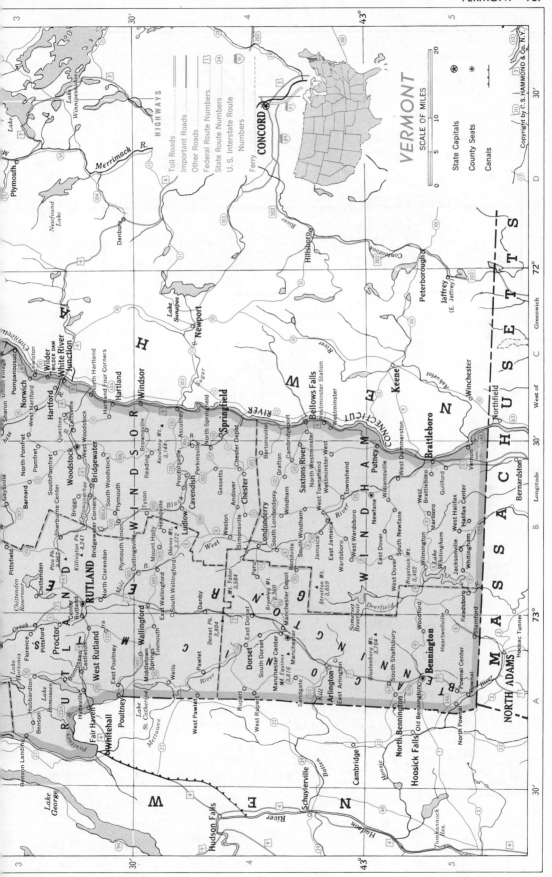

VERMONT
SCALE OF MILES

State Capitals
County Seats
Canals

Copyright by C. S. HAMMOND & Co., N.Y.

HIGHWAYS

Toll Roads
Important Roads
Other Roads
Federal Route Numbers
State Route Numbers
U. S. Interstate Route
    Numbers
Ferry

CONCORD

WESTERN PART
OF
VIRGINIA
Same scale as main map.

HIGHWAYS

Toll Roads .... Interchanges
Important Roads ....
Other Roads ....
Federal Route Numbers.... 15
State Route Numbers....... 47
U.S.Interstate Route Numbers 85
Ferry ....

Copyright by C. S. Hammond & Co., N.Y.

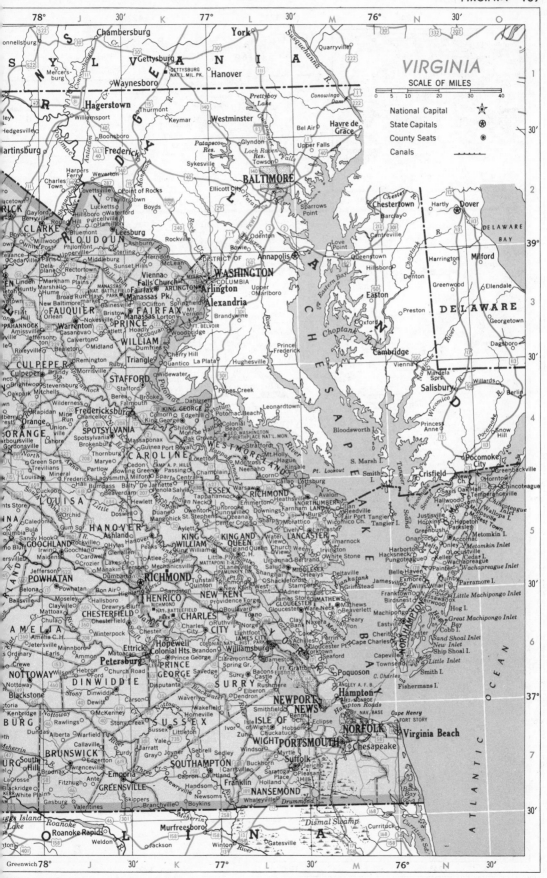

VIRGINIA
SCALE OF MILES

0 5 10 20 30 40

National Capital
State Capitals
County Seats
Canals

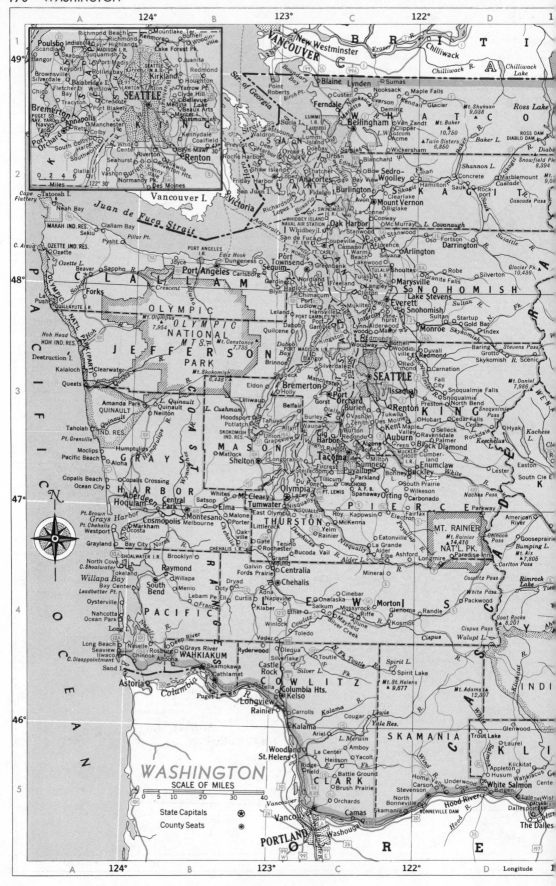

WASHINGTON
SCALE OF MILES

State Capitals
County Seats

COLUMBIA

Oliver
Christina L.
Grand Forks
D
Rossland
Fruitvale
Trail
49°

N

Night-hawk
Osoyoos L.
Molson
Chesaw
Ferry
Danville Laurier
Rossland
Mt. Abercrombie 7,308

Remmel Mtn. 8,690
Oroville
Curlew
Orient
Northport
Leadpoint
Metaline
Metaline Falls

Palmer L.
Loomis
Mt. Bonaparte 7,267
Wauconda
Malo
Boyds
Bossburg
Evans
Box Canyon Dam
Ione
Sullivan L.
Priest L.

OKANOGAN
Mazama
Conconully
Tonasket
Republic
Snow Pk. 7,109
Kettle Falls
Marcus
Coulee Dam Nat'l Recreation Area
Tiger
PEND OREILLE

Tiffany Mtn. 8,275
Riverside
Aeneas
Kettle Falls
Colville
Lost Creek
Ruby
2

Winthrop
Omak
Synarep
FERRY
Rice
Orin
Park Rapids
Cusick
KALISPEL IND. RES.

Twisp
Okanogan
COLVILLE
Arden
Addy
Usk
ALBENI FALLS DAM
Priest River

Carlton
Malott
INDIAN RESERVATION
Incheilum
Daisy
Bluecreek
Chewelah
Dalkena
Newport

Methow
Monse
Nespelem
Twin Lakes
Covada
Gifford
Coulee Dam Nat'l Recreation Area
Valley
Sacheen
Diamond
Priest River
48°

Brewster
Pateros
Rufus Woods Lake
Kewa
Keller
Hunters
Cedonia
Springdale
Deer L.
Clayton
Loon Lake
Deer Park
Milan
Mt. Spokane 5,878

Chelan
Azwell
Bridgeport
Chief Joseph Dam
Electric City
Coulee Dam
Elmer City
Fruitland
SPOKANE IND. RES.
Ford
Denison
Chattaroy
Colbert
JOA 95

Manson
Pearl
Grand Coulee Dam
Grand Coulee
Miles
Lincoln
Wellpinit
Turnbull
Newman L.
Coeur d'Alene

Chelan Falls
Leahy
Wilbur
Creston
Davenport
Reardan
Nine Mile Falls
WRIGHT A.F.B.
Spokane
Millwood
Greenacres

Entiat
Waterville
Withrow
Banks
Hartline
Almira
Mondovi
Rocklyn
Deepcreek
Espanola
FAIRCHILD A.F.B.
Medical Lake
Opportunity
Dishman
Veradale
Liberty Lake
3

Orondo
Douglas
Farmer
DOUGLAS
Coulee City
Long Lake
LINCOLN
Waukon
Four Lakes
Cheney
Yardley
Mica

East Wenatchee
Rock Island
Mansfield
Blue L.
Lenore L.
Stratford
Wilson Creek
Harrington
Edwall
Tyler
Marshall
Spangle
Fairfield

Malaga
Soap L.
Ephrata
Marlin (Krupp)
Coal
Lamona
Sylvan L.
Amber
Plaza
Waverly

Quincy
Trinidad
GRANT
Wheeler
Odessa
Marcellus
Sprague
Sprague L.
Lamont
Rock L.
Rosalia
Malden
47°

Vantage
Burke
George
Moses L.
Mae
Westlake
Moses Lake
LARSON AIR FORCE BASE
Ruff
Ritzville
Paha
Lind
Ralston
Benge
Marengo
Lancaster
Ewan
Sunset
Saint John
Thornton
Belmont
Farmington

SADDLE
Royal
O'Sullivan Dam
Warden
ADAMS
Cow Cr.
Steptoe
Garfield
Elberton

Beverly
Lower Smyrna
Royal Camp
Othello
Cunningham
Hatton
Washtucna
Hooper
WHITMAN
Dusty
Albion
Moscow

Mattawa
PRIEST RAPIDS DAM
Connell
Kahlotus
Snake
Riparia
Lacrosse
Pullman

YAKIMA
Cold Creek
HANFORD ATOMIC ENERGY RESERVATION
Mesa
LOWER MONUMENTAL DAM (SITE)
Ayer
Starbuck
Hay
Almota
Mayview
Johnson
Colton
Uniontown
4

Union Gap
Zillah
Granger
FRANKLIN
Eltopia
Ice Harbor
Clyde
Tucannon
GARFIELD
Pataha
Pomeroy
Clarkston
Lewiston

Sunnyside
Grandview
W. Richland
Richland
Pasco
Burbank
ICE HARBOR DAM
Eureka
Prescott
Huntsville
Dayton
COLUMBIA
ASOTIN
Asotin
Cloverland

Prosser
Benton City
Kennewick
Finley
WALLA WALLA
Dixie
Waitsburg
Walla Walla
Anatone
46°

Mabton
BENTON
Lake Wallula
Wallula
Lowden
Touchet
College Place
WHITMAN NAT'L MON.
BLUE MTS.

Bickleton
Paterson
Plymouth
McNARY DAM
Milton-Freewater

Alderdale
Umatilla
Boardman

Roosevelt
Willows
Arlington
Pilot Rock
5

HIGHWAYS
Toll Roads .... Interchanges
Important Roads ....
Other Roads ....
Federal Route Numbers 99
State Route Numbers 22
U.S. Interstate Route Numbers 5
Ferry ....

Greenwich 120° F 119° G 118° H 117°

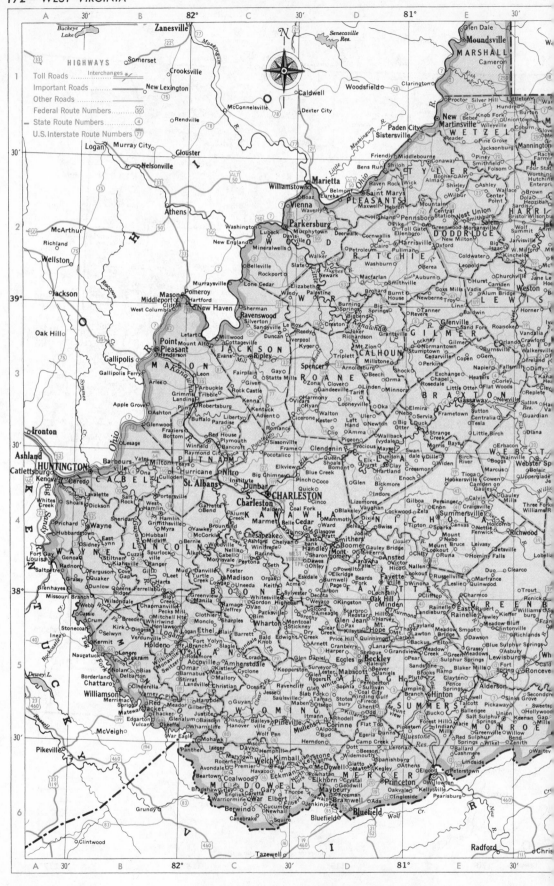

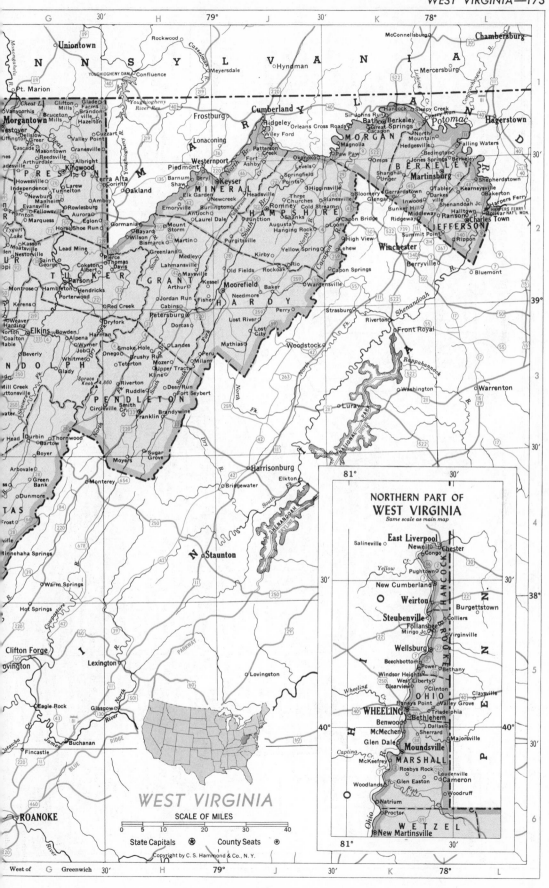

WEST VIRGINIA

SCALE OF MILES

0 5 10 20 30 40

State Capitals ⊛   County Seats ⊙

Copyright by C. S. Hammond & Co., N.Y.

NORTHERN PART OF
WEST VIRGINIA
Same scale as main map

West of   G   Greenwich   30'   79°   30'   K   78°   L

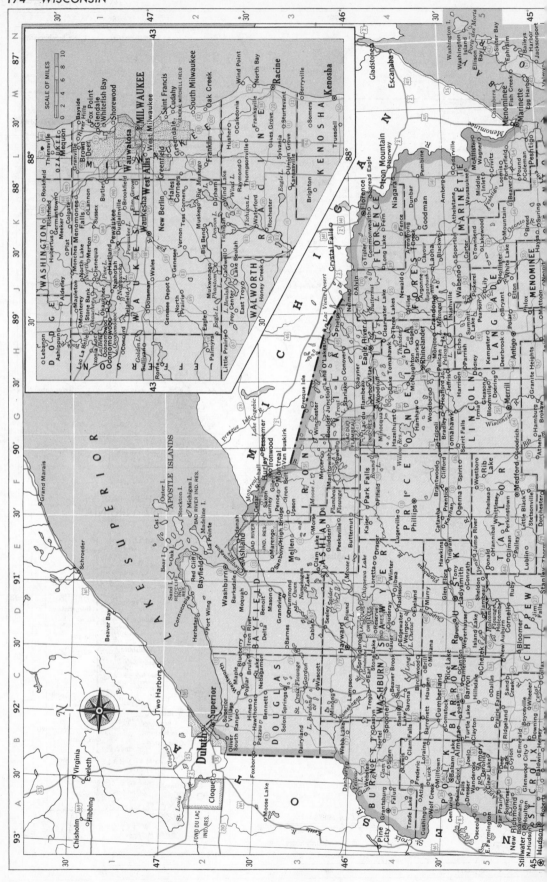

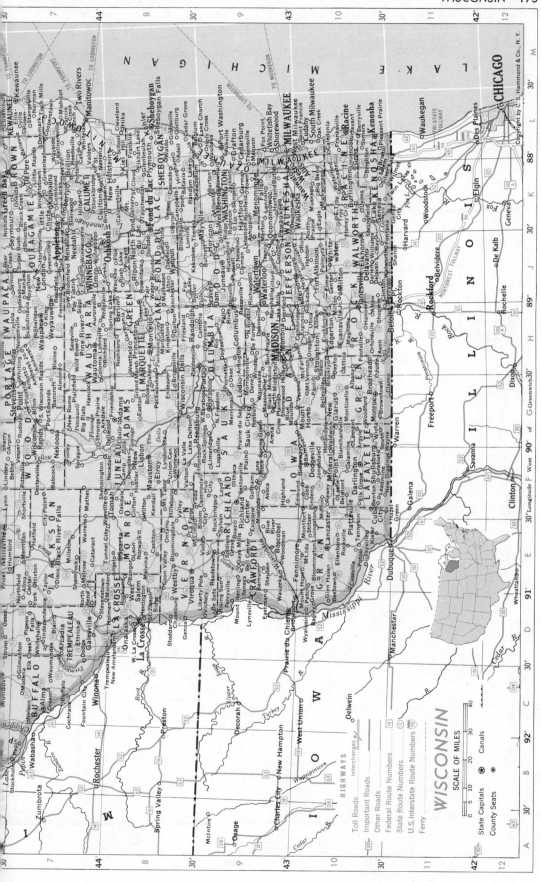

WISCONSIN

SCALE OF MILES

HIGHWAYS

Toll Roads
Interchanges
Important Roads
Other Roads
Federal Route Numbers
State Route Numbers
U.S. Interstate Route Numbers
Ferry
State Capitals
County Seats
Canals

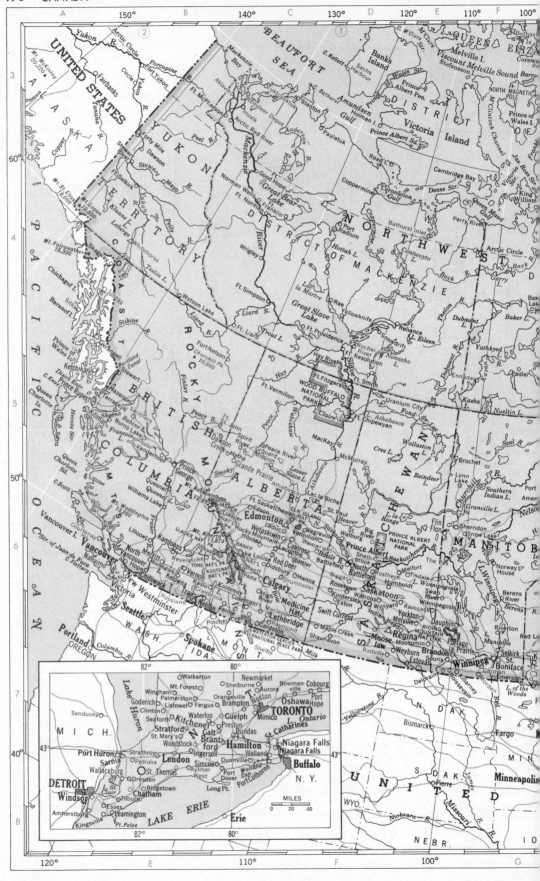

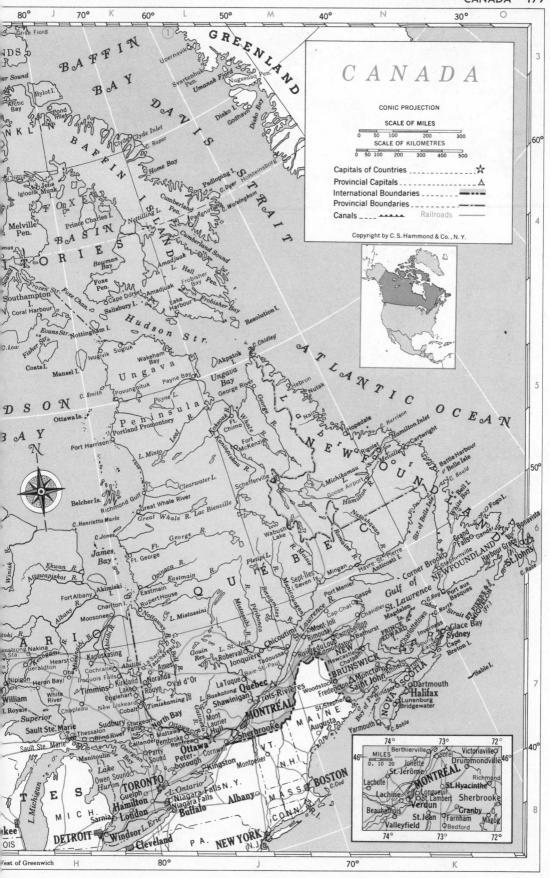

CANADA

CONIC PROJECTION

SCALE OF MILES

| 0 | 50 | 100 | 200 | 300 |

SCALE OF KILOMETRES

| 0 | 50 100 | 200 | 300 | 400 | 500 |

Capitals of Countries .... ☆
Provincial Capitals .... △
International Boundaries ------
Provincial Boundaries ------
Canals ....----- Railroads

Copyright by C.S. Hammond & Co., N.Y.

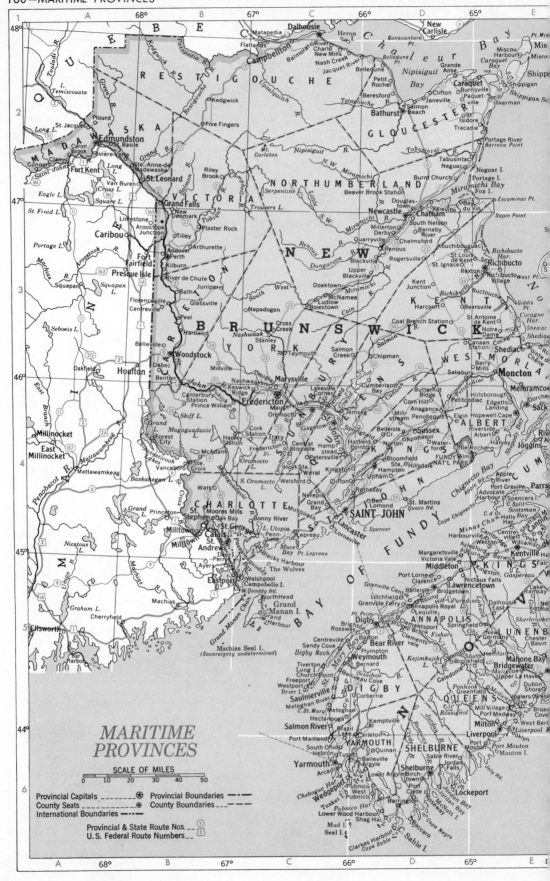

MARITIME
PROVINCES

SCALE OF MILES

0   10   20   30   40   50

Provincial Capitals .... ⊛ Provincial Boundaries — — —
County Seats .... ◉ County Boundaries — — —
International Boundaries — — —

Provincial & State Route Nos. ①
U.S. Federal Route Numbers ⊕

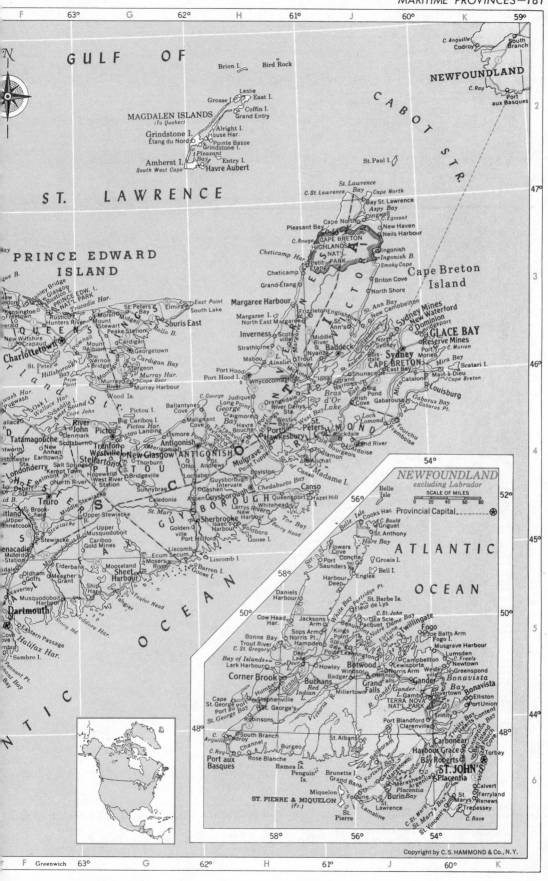

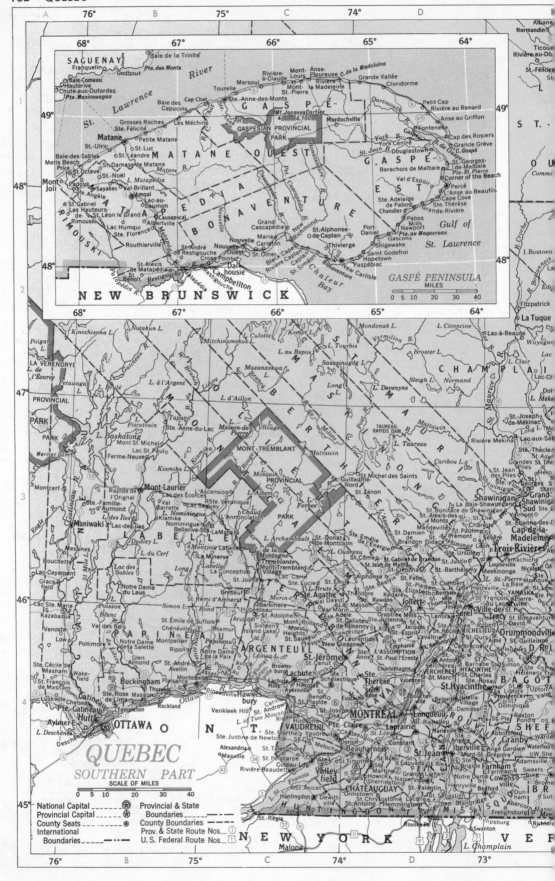

GASPÉ PENINSULA

MILES

0 5 10   20   30   40

QUEBEC
SOUTHERN PART

SCALE OF MILES

0 5 10   20   30   40

National Capital
Provincial Capital
County Seats
International
Boundaries

Provincial & State
Boundaries
County Boundaries
Prov. & State Route Nos.
U.S. Federal Route Nos.

COUNTIES
indicated by numbers:

1 Iberville — D4
2 Napierville — D4
3 Laprairie — D4
4 Chambly — D4
5 Jacques-Cartier — D4
6 Deux-Montagnes — C4
7 Soulanges — C4
8 Beauharnois — C4
9 Hull — B4
10 Hochelaga — D4

Internal divisions represent Municipal Counties

Copyright by C.S. HAMMOND & Co., N.Y.

West of Greenwich

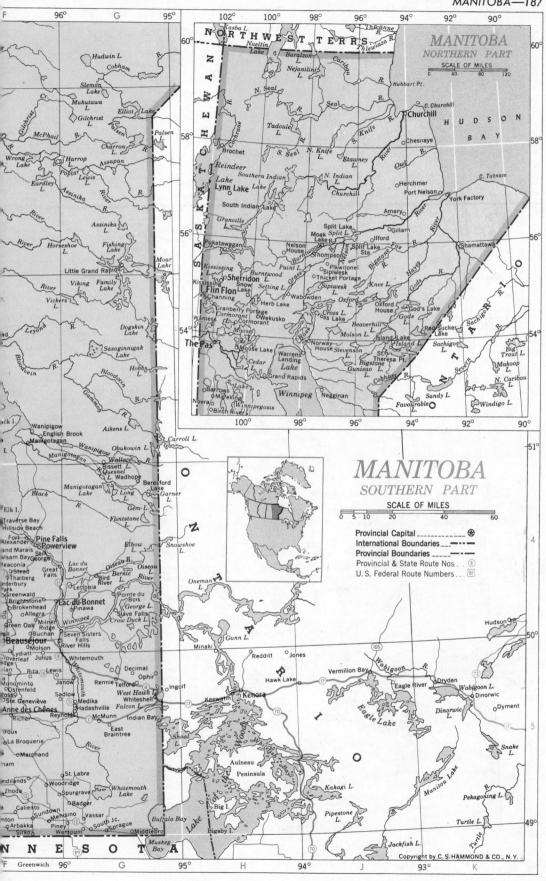

MANITOBA
SOUTHERN PART
SCALE OF MILES
0 5 10   20   40   60

Provincial Capital	⊕
International Boundaries	—··—··—
Provincial Boundaries	—·—·—·
Provincial & State Route Nos.	⑧
U.S. Federal Route Numbers	[81]

Copyright by C. S. HAMMOND & CO., N.Y.

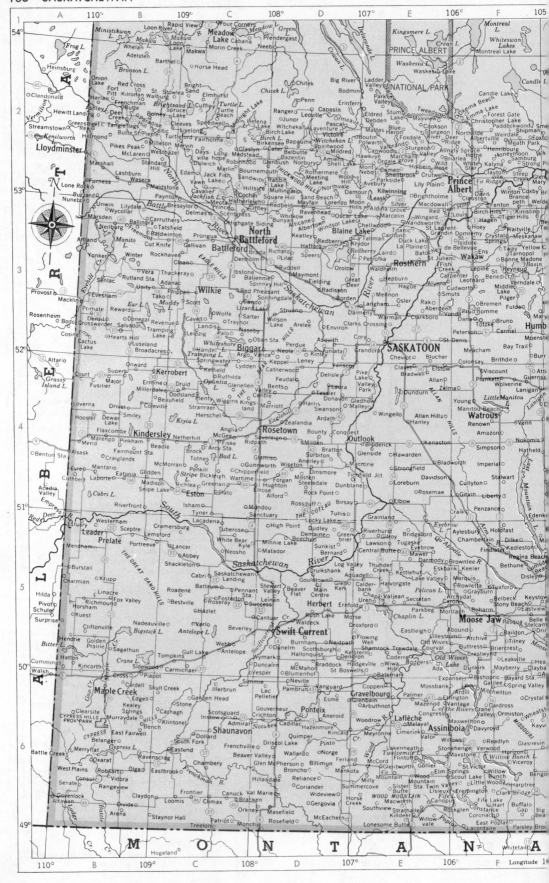

SASKATCHEWAN
NORTHERN PART

N. W. TERR'S.

0 20 40 60 80 100
MILES

SASKATCHEWAN
SOUTHERN PART

SCALE OF MILES

0 5 10 20 40 60

Provincial Capital .... ⊛
International Boundaries .—·—·—·—
Provincial Boundaries .—.—.—.
Provincial & State
Route Numbers .... ①
U.S. Federal Route Numbers ... 🔟

Copyright by C. S. HAMMOND & CO., N.Y.

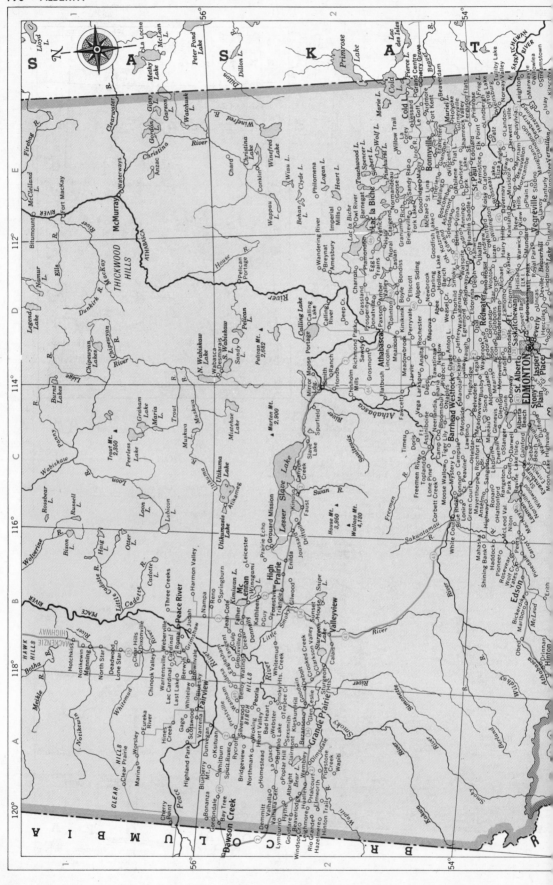

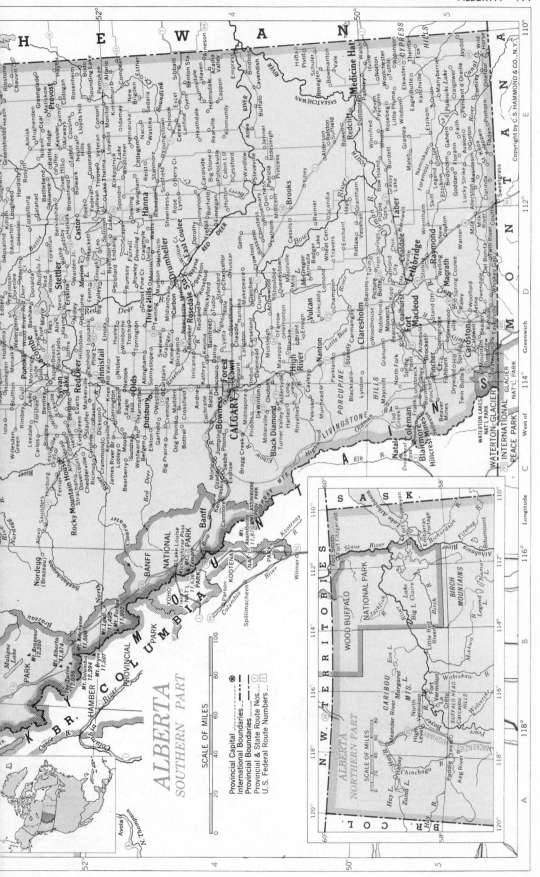

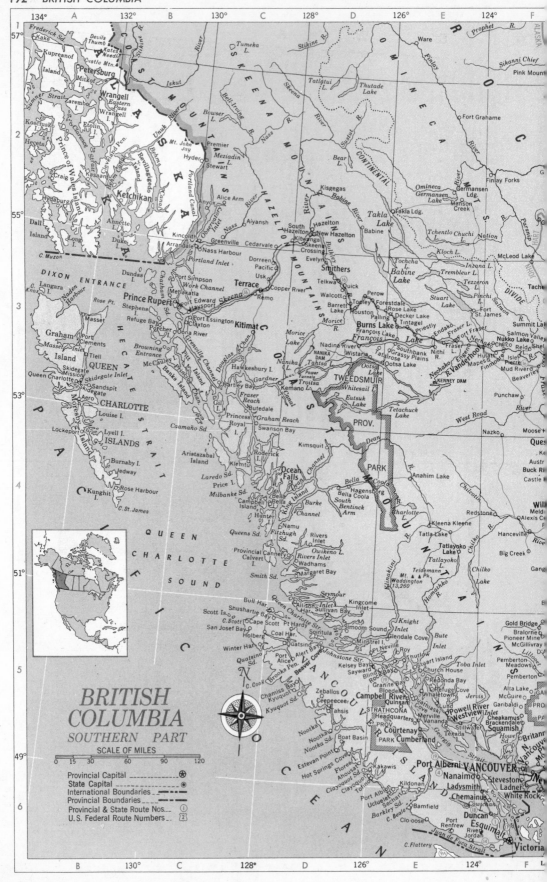

BRITISH
COLUMBIA
SOUTHERN PART

SCALE OF MILES

0   15   30   60   90   120

Provincial Capital .... ⊛
State Capital .... ⊚
International Boundaries ...... — —
Provincial Boundaries .... — · —
Provincial & State Route Nos... ①
U.S. Federal Route Numbers ... ②

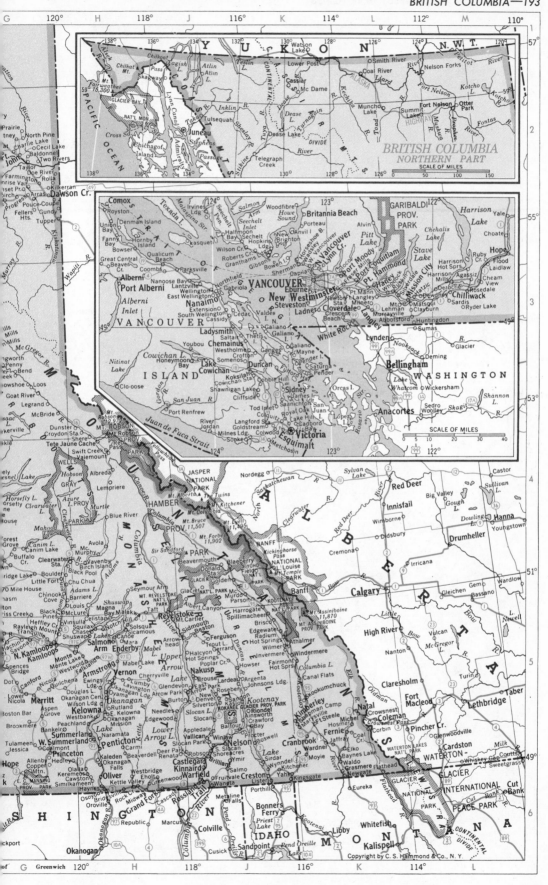

BRITISH COLUMBIA
NORTHERN PART
SCALE OF MILES
0   50   100   150

SCALE OF MILES
0 5 10   20   30   40

Copyright by C. S. Hammond & Co., N.Y.

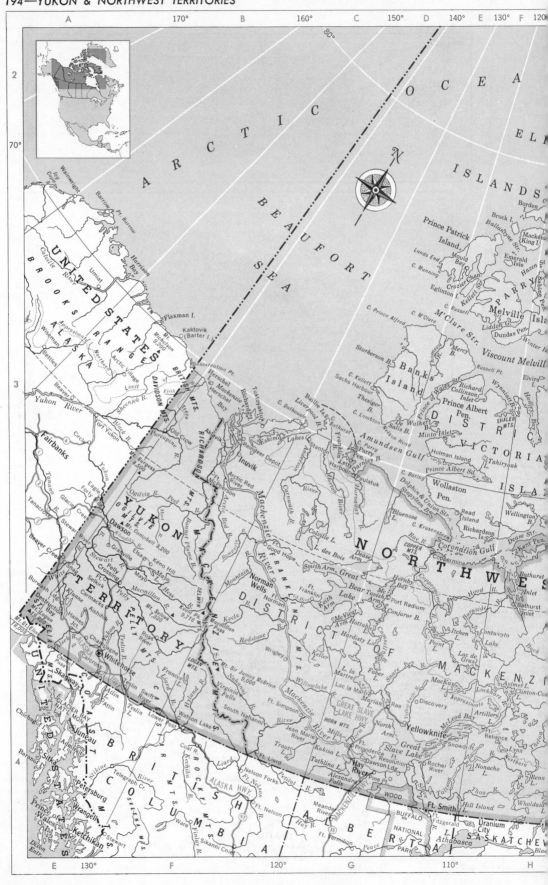

YUKON AND NORTHWEST TERRITORIES

SCALE OF MILES

0   50   100   200   300

Territorial Capitals .... ⊛
Administrative Center (N. W. Terr.) .⦿
International Boundaries ....
Provincial & Territorial Boundaries ...
District Boundaries ....
Provincial & State Route Nos. ....①

All islands in Hudson and James Bays
lie within the District of Keewatin.

© Copyright by C. S. HAMMOND & Co.

Longitude West of Greenwich

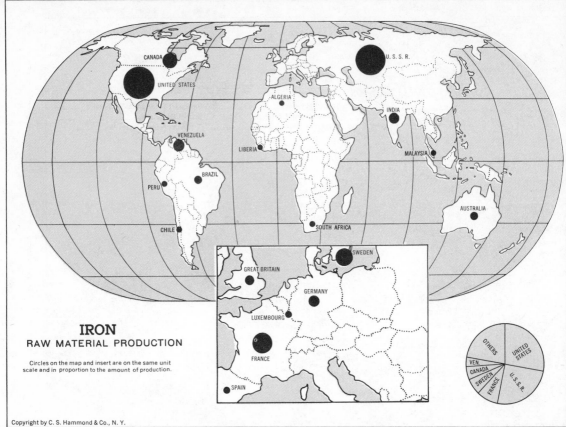

IRON
RAW MATERIAL PRODUCTION

Circles on the map and insert are on the same unit
scale and in proportion to the amount of production.

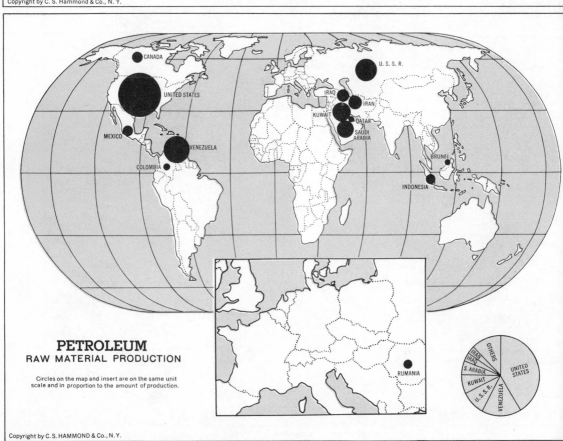

PETROLEUM
RAW MATERIAL PRODUCTION

Circles on the map and insert are on the same unit
scale and in proportion to the amount of production.

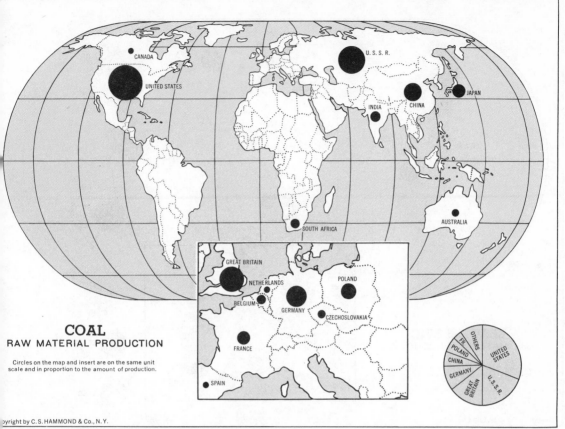

COAL
RAW MATERIAL PRODUCTION

Circles on the map and insert are on the same unit scale and in proportion to the amount of production.

Copyright by C.S. HAMMOND & Co., N.Y.

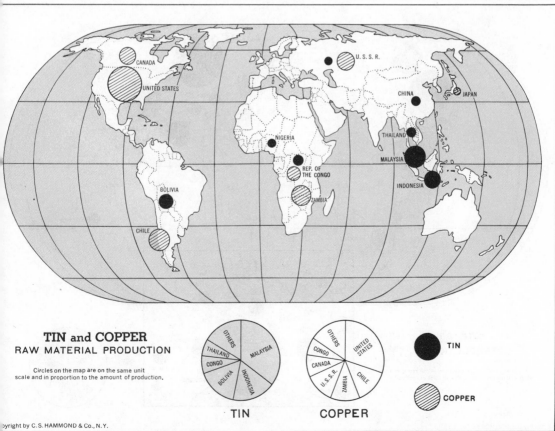

TIN and COPPER
RAW MATERIAL PRODUCTION

Circles on the map are on the same unit scale and in proportion to the amount of production.

Copyright by C.S. HAMMOND & Co., N.Y.

Production data based on Monthly Bulletin of Statistics
Statistical Office of the United Nations

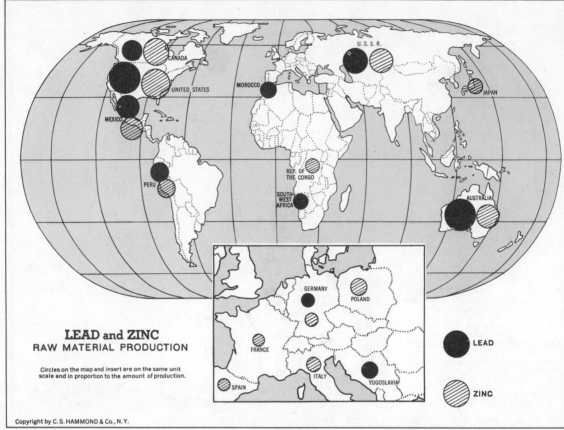

LEAD and ZINC
RAW MATERIAL PRODUCTION

Circles on the map and insert are on the same unit
scale and in proportion to the amount of production.

LEAD

ZINC

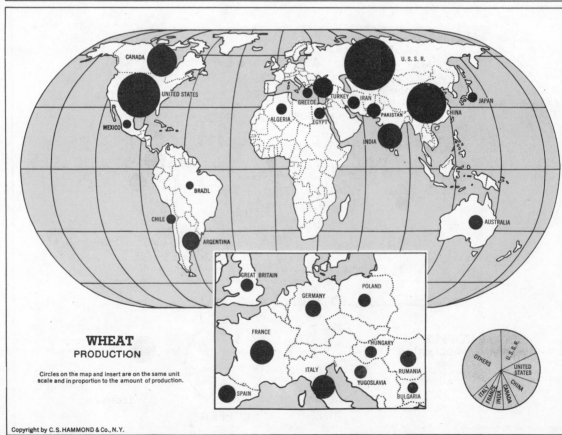

WHEAT
PRODUCTION

Circles on the map and insert are on the same unit
scale and in proportion to the amount of production.

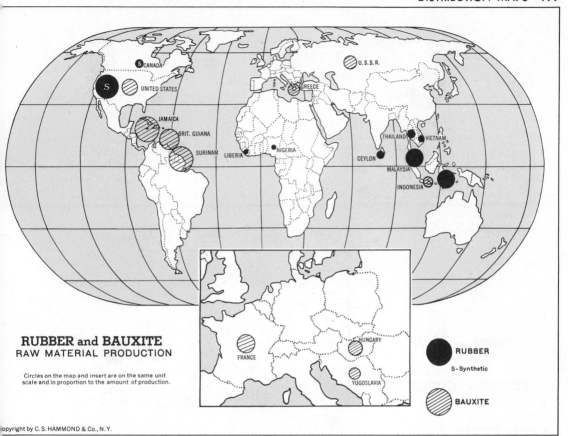

RUBBER and BAUXITE
RAW MATERIAL PRODUCTION

Circles on the map and insert are on the same unit
scale and in proportion to the amount of production.

RUBBER
S- Synthetic

BAUXITE

MEAT and FISH
PRODUCTION

Circles on the map and insert are on the same unit
scale and in proportion to the amount of production.

MEAT

FISH

Production data based on Monthly Bulletin of Statistics,
Statistical Office of the United Nations.

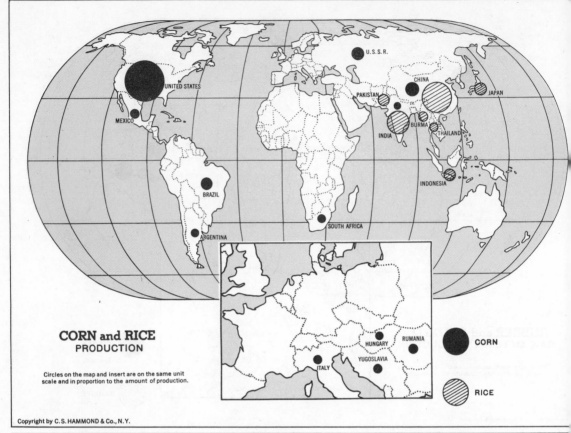

CORN and RICE
PRODUCTION

Circles on the map and insert are on the same unit scale and in proportion to the amount of production.

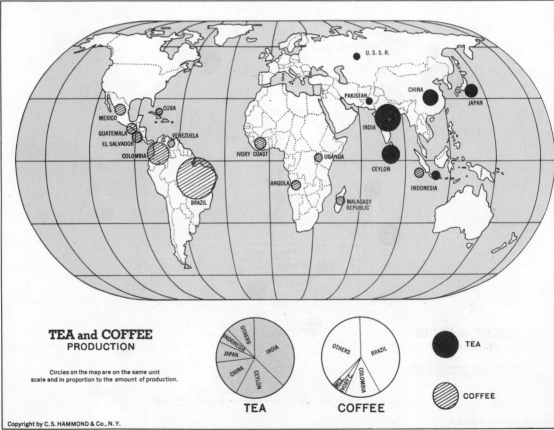

TEA and COFFEE
PRODUCTION

Circles on the map are on the same unit scale and in proportion to the amount of production.

TEA

COFFEE

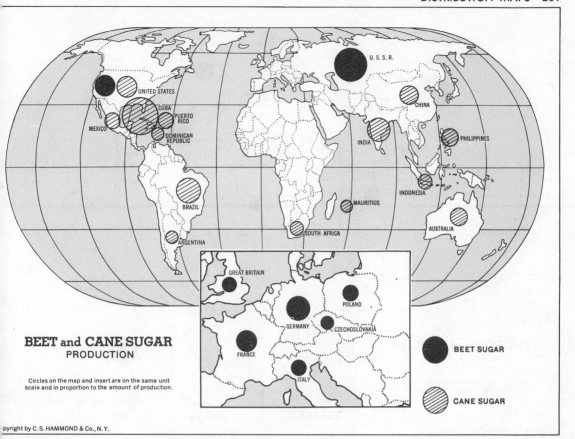

BEET and CANE SUGAR
PRODUCTION

Circles on the map and insert are on the same unit scale and in proportion to the amount of production.

● BEET SUGAR

▨ CANE SUGAR

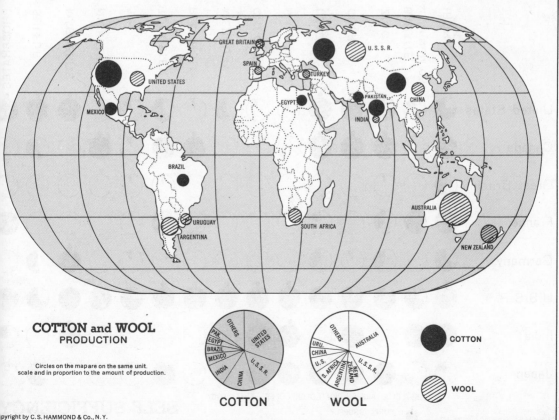

COTTON and WOOL
PRODUCTION

Circles on the map are on the same unit scale and in proportion to the amount of production.

● COTTON

▨ WOOL

COTTON

WOOL

Production data based on Monthly Bulletin of Statistics, Statistical Office of the United Nations.

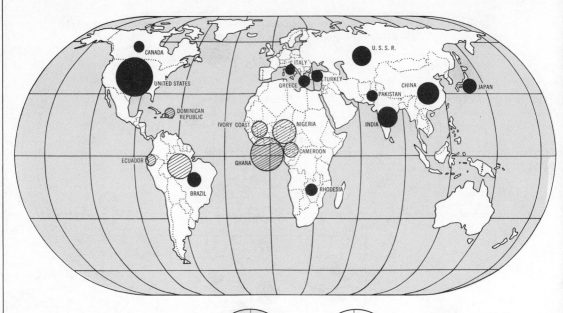

TOBACCO and COCOA
PRODUCTION

Circles on the map are on the same unit scale and
in proportion to the amount of production.

TOBACCO

COCOA

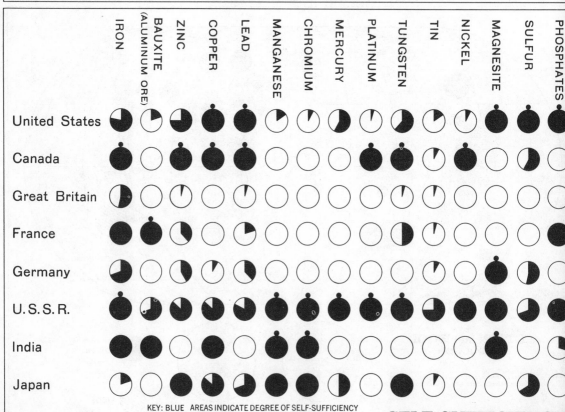

KEY: BLUE AREAS INDICATE DEGREE OF SELF-SUFFICIENCY

= SURPLUS SUPPLY

SELF-SUFFICIENCY

Prepared by C.S. HAMMOND & Co. Inc., N.Y.

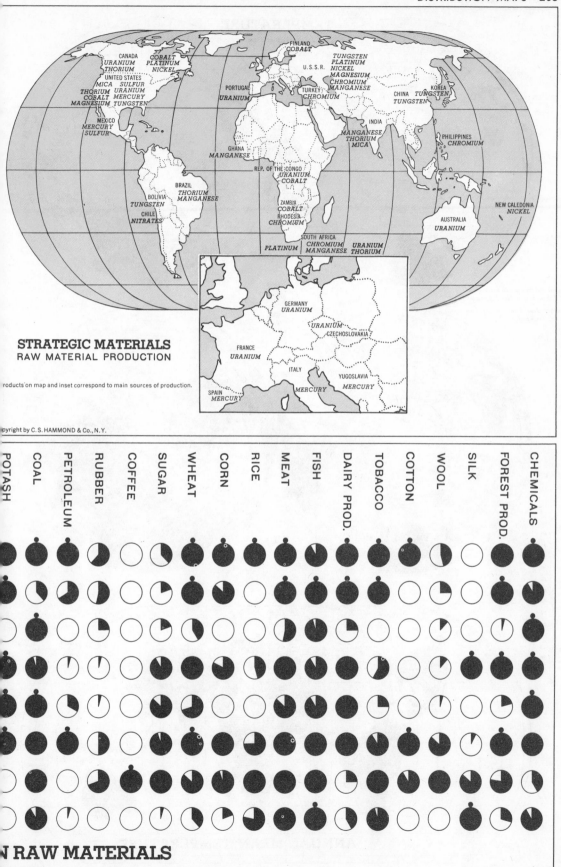

STRATEGIC MATERIALS
RAW MATERIAL PRODUCTION

...roducts on map and inset correspond to main sources of production.

CANADA
URANIUM
THORIUM

**COBALT
PLATINUM
NICKEL**

UNITED STATES
MICA SULFUR
THORIUM URANIUM
COBALT MERCURY
MAGNESIUM TUNGSTEN

MEXICO
MERCURY
SULFUR

BRAZIL
THORIUM
MANGANESE

BOLIVIA
TUNGSTEN

CHILE
NITRATES

FINLAND
COBALT

PORTUGAL
URANIUM

TURKEY
CHROMIUM

GHANA
MANGANESE

REP. OF THE CONGO
URANIUM
COBALT

ZAMBIA
COBALT

RHODESIA
CHROMIUM

SOUTH AFRICA
CHROMIUM URANIUM
MANGANESE THORIUM

PLATINUM

U.S.S.R.

**TUNGSTEN
PLATINUM
NICKEL
MAGNESIUM
CHROMIUM
MANGANESE**

CHINA
TUNGSTEN

KOREA
TUNGSTEN

INDIA
MANGANESE
THORIUM
MICA

PHILIPPINES
CHROMIUM

NEW CALEDONIA
NICKEL

AUSTRALIA
URANIUM

GERMANY
URANIUM

URANIUM
CZECHOSLOVAKIA

FRANCE
URANIUM

ITALY

YUGOSLAVIA
MERCURY

SPAIN
MERCURY

MERCURY

POTASH
COAL
PETROLEUM
RUBBER
COFFEE
SUGAR
WHEAT
CORN
RICE
MEAT
FISH
DAIRY PROD.
TOBACCO
COTTON
WOOL
SILK
FOREST PROD.
CHEMICALS

...N RAW MATERIALS

TEMPERATURE
after Napier Shaw

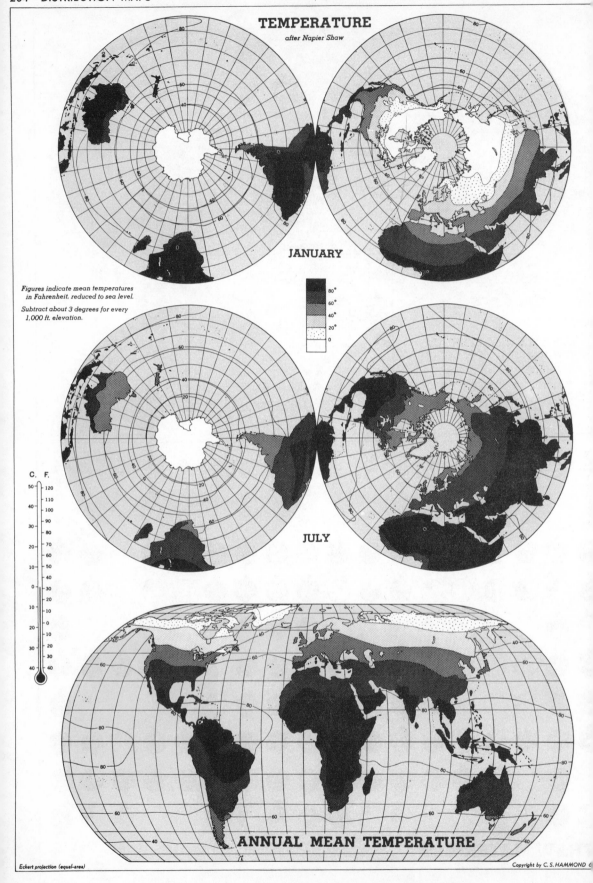

JANUARY

Figures indicate mean temperatures
in Fahrenheit, reduced to sea level.

Subtract about 3 degrees for every
1,000 ft. elevation.

JULY

ANNUAL MEAN TEMPERATURE

Eckert projection (equal-area)

Copyright by C.S. HAMMOND

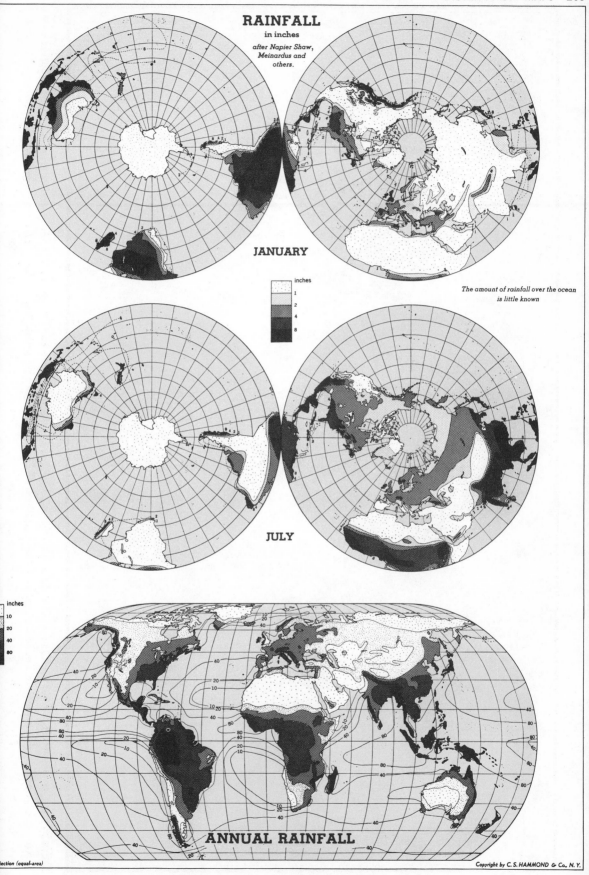

RAINFALL
in inches
*after Napier Shaw,
Meinardus and
others.*

JANUARY

inches
1
2
4
8

*The amount of rainfall over the ocean
is little known*

JULY

inches
10
20
40
80

ANNUAL RAINFALL

ojection (equal-area)

Copyright by C. S. HAMMOND & Co., N. Y.

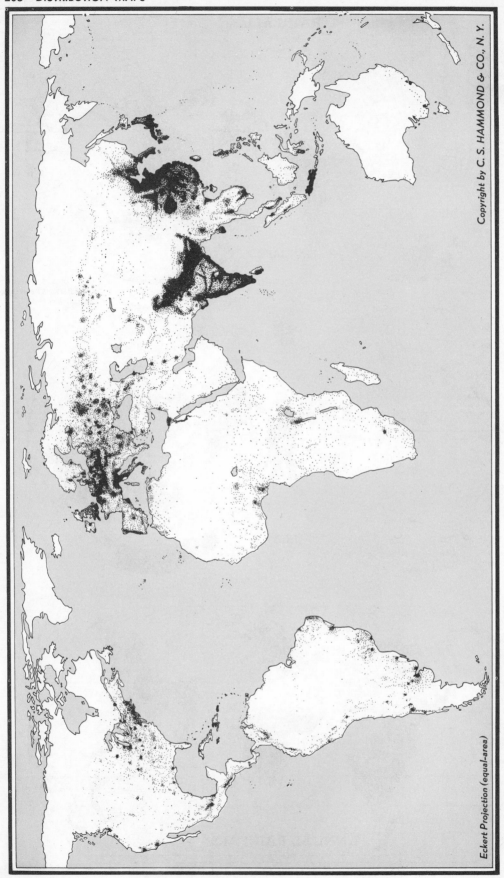

Eckert Projection (equal-area)

Copyright by C. S. HAMMOND & CO., N. Y.

DENSITY OF POPULATION. One of the most outstanding facts of human geography is the extremely uneven distribution of people over the Earth. One-half of the Earth's surface has less than 3 people per square mile, while in the heart of India, China, Java and Japan and despite reaches the incredible congestion of 2000-3000 per square mile. Three-fourths of the Earth's population live in four relatively small areas; Northeastern United States, North-Central Europe, India and the Far East.

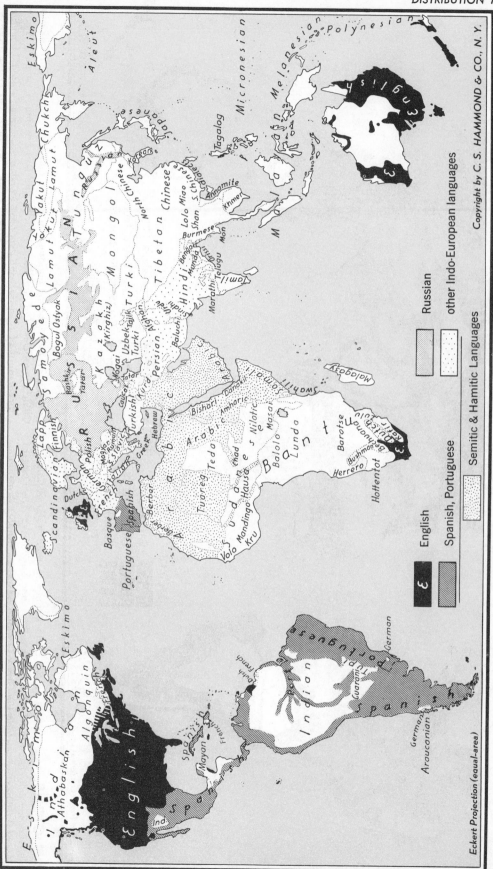

Eckert Projection (equal-area)

LANGUAGES. *Several hundred different languages are spoken in the World, and in many places two or more languages are spoken, sometimes by the same people. The map above shows the dominant languages in each* locality. English, French, Spanish, Russian, Arabic and Swahili are spoken by many people as a second language for commerce or travel.

Copyright by C. S. HAMMOND & CO., N.Y.

English

Spanish, Portuguese

Russian

other Indo-European languages

Semitic & Hamitic Languages

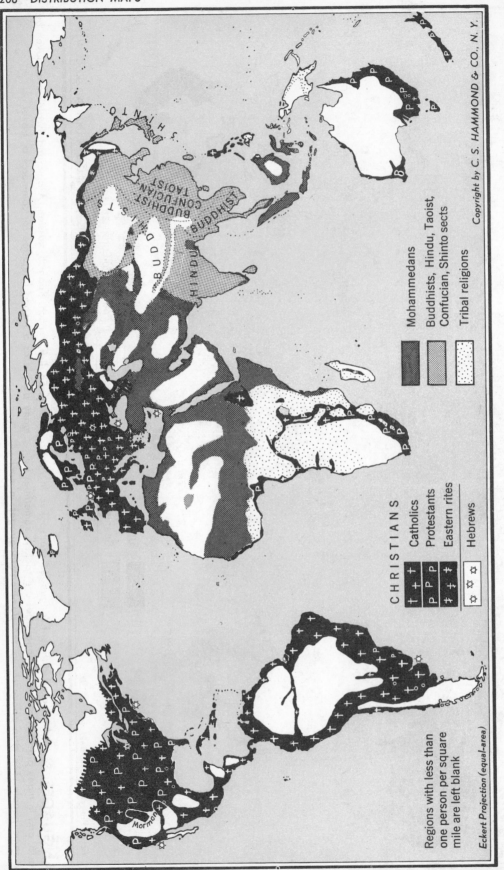

CHRISTIANS

Catholics	✝✝
Protestants	P P
Eastern rites	✝✝

Hebrews ✡ ✡

Regions with less than
one person per square
mile are left blank

Mohammedans

Buddhists, Hindu, Taoist,
Confucian, Shinto sects

Tribal religions

Eckert Projection (equal-area)   Copyright by C. S. HAMMOND & CO., N. Y.

RELIGIONS. Most people of the Earth belong to four major religions: Christians, Mohammedans, Brahmans, Buddhists and derivatives. The Eastern rites of the Christians include the Greek Orthodox, Greek Catholic, Armenian, Syrian, Coptic and more minor churches. The lamaism of Tibet and Mongolia differs a great deal from Buddhism in Burma and Thailand. In the religion of China the teachings of Buddha, Confucius and Tao are mixed, while in Shinto a great deal of ancestor and emperor worship is added. About 11 million Hebrews live scattered over the globe, chiefly in cities and in the state of

ILLUSTRATED GEOGRAPHY OF THE WORLD

Introduction

The headline events of the last half-century have made the average American acutely curious of the vast world beyond the national borders of the American homeland. Constant repetition has tended to make this thought a cliche, yet it is one of the most significant truths of our time. This new national concern for the external world and its problems is one of the hopeful signs pointing to a better future for mankind.

One of the main roads to a better knowledge of this fascinating planet is a thorough indoctrination in the golden lore of geography. This science is not a narrow and limited scholarly discipline but a universal department of knowledge drawing on the sum total of man's explorations in the field of thought. The very pervasiveness of earth science makes it intriguing reading for the average non-specialist. At the same time that it entertains, it also builds a permanent edifice of information for the general reader. As more individuals discover this golden key to understanding the tumultuous happenings of the day, our collective actions in the field of enlightened citizenship will gain immeasurably in effectiveness.

CONTENTS

Canadian National Railroads
Ragged peaks and stoney crags form the watercourse for Emperor Falls in British Columbia.

NORTH AMERICA

NORTH AMERICA — Lying across the wide expanse of the Atlantic Ocean, was a new World waiting discovery and recognition. Europe was completely unaware of its existence for many centuries. Its discovery was destined to change the whole course of history and affect the fortunes of men and nations the world over. More than that, its discovery ushered in a whole new era of civilization, and marked the first faltering step towards the exploration and charting of all lands and waters of the world.

No discovery, before or since, has added more to man's opportunities and the wealth of the world; or played a more important part in shaping a world's destiny. Yet, its discoverer died in ignorance of his epoch-making contribution to the world. It remained for those who followed to prove the existence of a New World.

Landing on one of the Bahamas, how was Columbus to know that his quest for a new route to the East Indies had led him to an island outpost of two fabulous empires ? . . . now but a bare few hours by air travel from the sister continents of North and South America. In his wildest dreams Columbus could not have conceived of a land extending virtually from the North Pole to the South Pole, for a distance of some nine thousand miles.

We can imagine Balboa's thrill twenty-one years later, when he fought his way across the rocky Isthmus of Panama to gaze upon the Pacific. But, how was he to know that this narrow ribbon of tapering land joined two vast domains ? That, from where he stood, an unbroken expanse of land reached northward for forty-five hundred miles, and actually spread out into a gigantic fan three thousand miles wide ? Also, that, to the south a similar, though lesser triangle of land, reached thousands of miles below the equator to the icy waters of the Antarctic ?

Today these are historical incidents of common knowledge, thanks to the intrepid discoverers, explorers and map-makers. We take their hard won glories for granted, and even forget the adventure and romance that has gone into the making of our geographical maps.

We must be constantly reminded that, of all the continents of the world, North America is the most favored for natural wealth, climate and position on the earth. Being situated between the two largest oceans has protected the people of North America from enemy invasion, and also enabled them to develop an extensive commerce. The millions of square miles of fertile soil and untold mineral wealth has provided a standard of living unknown elsewhere in the world. Hence, composed of peoples from all over the world, its inhabitants have enjoyed peace and plenty, without fear of their independent ways of life being encroached upon, or destroyed by jealous and covetous neighbors. We can be assured that such a fortunate people will not easily relinquish what they have come to hold so dear.

The principal geographical features of North America are its two mountain ranges and the intervening central plains. The high and rugged mountains to the westward extend from the tip of Alaska to the base of the Isthmus of Panama, or from the northern to the southern extremity of the continent. These mountain ranges include the Coastal system that hugs the Pacific Coast, and the Rocky Mountains that branch out eastward and southward across the United States to become, in Mexico and Central America, the Sierra Madres. The Cascade Mountains, which farther south become the Sierra Nevada, are separate ranges that work inland from the coastal mountains. These diverging mountain chains in the east and west, form the bulwark for a number of high plateaus that lie between. The land adjoining the Cascade Mountains is the Columbia Plateau, while farther south lies the Colorado Plateau. In between is the arid region of the Great Basin. The Great Salt Lake is all that remains to reveal that this vast area was once a geologic lake.

In the east, extending from the Gulf of Saint Lawrence to the Gulf of Mexico is the Appalachian Range. These mountains are older and less rugged than the Rockies. Time has worn them down and rounded their peaks. On the side toward the Atlantic Ocean, they merge with the Piedmont Plateau, which slopes off into a coastal plain.

The great central plains that slope towards the center, and lie between the Rocky Mountain and Appalachian Highlands describe a giant "V" which extends from the Arctic Ocean to the Gulf of Mexico.

More varieties of climate prevail in North America than in any other land in the world. The greater part of the continent, however, enjoys a temperate and invigorating climate. The inhabitants of the far north must adjust themselves to the rigors of Arctic weather, Mexico endures sub-tropical temperatures, and Central America a tropical heat. Even from the east to west there is a wide variety of climate due to difference in altitude, and other conditions not affected by latitude.

To an airman soaring above the shifting panorama of North America, the realization must come that this is indeed a rich land of fertile soils, spreading forests, rolling plains, inland lakes, and mighty rivers. There is hardly an area of any size on the entire continent but contains, on the surface or beneath it, a species of natural wealth. On the western coast, the great Pacific Ocean, generally a protective barrier, separating

North Carolina News Bureau

The American South contains unusually picturesque mountain scenery.

most of North America from the shores of Asia, offers little promise of isolation at its far northwest corner. While eight thousand miles separate the peoples of China from the United States, Russia and Alaska almost meet at the Bering Strait, which is only fifty-seven miles wide.

ALASKA—Purchased from Russia in 1867 for a pittance proved to be the most valued of U.S. possessions and it is now the 49th state. The Senate voted June 30, 1958 for Alaskan statehood. Although partially in the Arctic Circle, it is by no means the frozen and inhospitable land its latitude would suggest. Alaska has a wide area of equable climate. Along its mountainous and island-fringed coast, the warm Japanese Current keeps the temperature at all times above zero. This rises in the summer to a seasonal heat of 80°. These sections endure drenching rain, caused by the condensation of warm winds striking the snow-capped peaks of the mountains. In the center of Alaska is a broad upland where grasses, flowers and mosses grow.

The Yukon River, rising in Canada, swings across Alaska for fifteen hundred miles, twelve hundred of which are navigable. Although frozen for two-thirds of the year, this river is a main artery of travel. Dog sled teams replace the large steamers during the months when it is ice-bound. A half million acres of land is cultivated in the Yukon Valley, and even though the growing season is short, the Arctic days provide long hours of sunshine.

First known as "Seward's Folly," Alaska justified its purchase within a few short years and has proved a veritable storehouse of treasure. Each year it produces more than twice its purchase price, in minerals alone.

The popular conception of the Arctic does, however, exist in the northern regions. Here the ground thaws only a few inches at the surface during the summer. Except for a few Eskimo and reindeer, there is comparatively no life or vegetation able to survive the rigors of the frigid climate.

While at one time Alaska was a remote and unexplored country, today with ever increasing population and extensive building and improvement of roads, development is steadily expanding.

The Aleutian islands are strung out in a broad arc off the tip of Alaska for a thousand miles and separate the Bering Sea from the North Pacific. Numbering about one hundred and fifty islands, they are the tops of submerged mountains. Included in the purchase of Alaska, they have great strategic value as air bases and weather observing stations for the United States.

CANADA—The over 5000 mile boundary between the United States and Canada is convincing proof that two great nations may live side by side in peace and harmony. For over a hundred years this boundary line —the longest in the world—has been free from fortification of any kind by either nation. In a world that has been repeatedly torn by war during the past century here is lasting evidence that national progress, pride and ambition can exist without adjoining countries being tempted to encroach on the other's domain.

Canada is the largest domain of the British Commonwealth. It extends from the icy waters of the Arctic to the borders of the United States, and from east to west its greatest distance is 3,700 miles. Its area is greater than that of the United States and nearly as large as the continent of Europe.

Canada is a vast diversified land of fertile plains, of mountains and rivers, and countless lakes. Over 6 per cent of the total is water area, affording ready power for her ever increasing industrial development. Like the United States it can be roughly divided into three sections; the eastern highlands, a great level central plain, and mountain ranges extending from the Rockies to the Pacific.

In the east the Appalachian region is a beautiful land of hilly or mountainous terrain with very heavily forested sections and fertile farm lands. Just west of the highlands lies the St. Lawrence Valley including the Ontario peninsula, the hub of Canada's industry. In this area, rich in minerals, forests, water power and fertile land, is the highest concentration of population. Moderate climate combined with valuable accessible resources have made this section of the greatest economic importance. Northwest of the Valley is the Canadian Shield, an area characterized by low hills, countless lakes connected by streams and rapids. Here is Canada's greatest store of resources, minerals, forests, furs and water power. In the interior Plains is the great wheat belt. In the west, parallel to the Pacific, is the magnificent mountain country formed by the Cordilleran Mountain System. In addition to minerals and valuable forests, this area, in the fertile valleys, produces much of Canada's fruit and vegetable crops.

Although primarily an agricultural country, Canada has developed rapidly in recent years as an industrial country. Lumbering is of great importance, which is to be expected, for the forests of Canada are among the largest in the world. Furs have been an important source of wealth since the early days of the Hudson's Bay Company, and the fishing grounds of Canada are the largest and most productive on earth. Wheat is the principal crop of the prairie provinces, and Canada is one of the biggest producers and exporters of this grain.

The provinces in the southern sections of Canada enjoy much the same climate as exists in the Great Lakes regions of the United States. The southern parts of Ontario and Quebec have less severe winters, but the northern sections of these provinces have very severe winters, with short, hot summers. The prairies experience great extremes in temperature, while moderate rainfall in this region favors wheat production.

About half of the population is of British origin and one quarter is French. The remaining fourth is principally Russian, German, Austrian and Scandinavian. Some hundred thousand Indians live mostly on reservations.

UNITED STATES —Within the span of the last two hundred years, the United States of America has written an amazing chapter in history. In that brief period a wilderness has been tamed, and a powerful nation has arisen to take its place among the foremost countries of the world. A land populated by every race, creed and color, and a haven of refuge for the oppressed, its phenomenal growth has never been equalled. Far removed from the traditions and hampering fetters of the Old World, it has charted a new course in government. Its freedom loving people have devoted their energies to developing the riches that Nature has so lavishly supplied.

The United States has reached its present position of greatness because of a number of reasons. It is blessed with a climate that cannot be surpassed elsewhere in the world, and is rich in mineral wealth beyond that of any other country. With a coastline on three sides well supplied with harbors, it is ideally situated for trade with the rest of the world. Its rivers and lakes are navigable and give easy access into the interior of the country. The variety of climate and the fertility of the soil make a great diversity of crops possible.

Climate has made the people of the United States energetic, and Nature has endowed the land with more than enough to meet their needs. This country's way of life has provided the incentive for continually bettering the standards of living of its people. All this has brought continued economic, cultural and scientific progress.

The United States, the world's greatest manufacturing nation, with over half the

The Pyramid of the Sun, San Juan Teotihuacan, Mexico.

population depending upon industry for a living. It has the finest systems of transportation and communication, including the great majority of the automobiles in the world. A large part of the world's coal and iron reserves as well as substantial deposits of almost all important minerals are found here.

The three principal geographical features are a continuation of those in Canada. They are the eastern highlands, comprising the Appalachian Range, the broad central plains, and the Rockies and Coastal ranges in the Far West.

A closer study of the geography of the United States does much to explain the growth of the nation. For example, the stony soil of New England discouraged farming and caused the early settlers to turn to manufacturing and commerce. The swift streams furnished water power and the jagged coastline provided bays for harboring the ships from Europe. Farther south, the coastal plains widen out into broad stretches of fertile land, and the rivers are short and deep. This led to the development of the large plantations in the deep South, where the climate is favorable to crops that require long hot summers. Here the coastal plain includes half of Georgia, all of Florida, and extends along the Gulf of Mexico. It reaches into the interior as far north as southern Illinois.

The lake and prairie region of the upper Mississippi Valley is one of the most fertile in the world, and is linked by waterways with the East and South through the Great Lakes and the Mississippi River system. The Great Plains region, depending upon the nature of the topsoil and the amount of rainfall, is either grain or grazing country, with valuable deposits of oil in Texas and Oklahoma. With Alaska becoming a state (in 1958), the United States now embraces land reaching into the Arctic, while the statehood of Hawaii, voted for by Congress in March, 1959, adds a region of tropical island climate and vegetation. Because they seemed inexhaustible, the resources of the United States were exposed to great waste. Today, conservation measures are increasingly applied.

MEXICO—Beyond the southern border of the United States and across the Rio Grande, where North America begins to taper sharply to a point, lies Latin America. It is difficult to conceive of the contrast to be found beyond this man-made boundary with the rest of the continent. It is another world, with a totally different culture, another language, and traditions and customs which set it apart from its northern neighbors.

Over one-fifth the area of the United States, Mexico swings south for about eleven hundred miles, ending in the narrow hook of the peninsula of Yucatan.

While half of Mexico lies in the torrid zone, its climate is determined more by elevation than latitude. Along the coast the weather is hot and humid, with luxuriant tropical vegetation. As the land rises the climate changes to temperate and the mountain peaks are snow-clad. Two mountain chains, that are a continuation of those in the United States, converge and meet at the southern tip, leaving a flat tableland between. The average altitude of this plateau is about 6,500 feet. Mexico's highest concentration of population is here where the fertile land, ideal climate and favorable rainfall afford excellent conditions for agricultural crops. Although industrial development has increased rapidly in recent years

and most of Mexico's wealth is derived from her mines and petroleum, the great majority of the people are still employed in agricultural pursuits. Except for the coastal plain bordering the Gulf of Mexico, mountains and plateaus occupy the greater part of Mexico. Lying in both the temperate and torrid zones allows the country to produce a greater variety of crops than is possible in most other countries.

Mexico is a beautiful and picturesque country with ancient ruins of pyramids and temples still standing as mute evidence of a flourishing civilization that existed before the coming of the Spanish invaders in the early fifteenth century.

CENTRAL AMERICA—As North America decreases in size from a land of magnificent distance to a slender neck of land where the Isthmus of Panama joins South America, the sizes of its nations shrink to even greater extent. In Central America a string of six small countries, Guatemala, Honduras, El Salvador, Nicaragua, Costa Rica and Panama, is confined to an area less than that of the State of Texas. Their total population is somewhat more than 12,000,000.

The Cordilleras, a continuation of the mountain chains starting far north in Alaska, extend the entire length of the land. Many of the peaks are volcanic and frequent eruptions occur. These mountains have formed many high and fertile plateaus which provide fine pasturage for livestock and rich soil for a diversity of crops. As in Mexico, the tropical climate of the lower regions is tempered by the elevation of the high plateaus. There are a number of harbors on both coasts, with the principal seaports on the Caribbean Sea. Most of the rivers that flow into the Caribbean are navigable.

These agricultural nations have become increasingly important in the past few years. With the organizing of the Pan-American Union, the growth of air travel, and the fostering of a new spirit of co-operation between the republics of North and South America, Central America's future became one of promise. When global war shut off supplies of many important crops to the Western world from the East, it was found that here in the Americas could be grown many necessities that formerly had been imported from afar. Great variation in soils, rainfall, and terrain afford an enormous variety of tropical, semi-tropical and temperate crops. Experiments have successfully produced important quantities of spices, fibres, and essential oils for medicinal and industrial purposes that were introduced from the East. Among the important crops exported almost exclusively to the United States are bananas, natural rubber, coffee, rope fibres, cacao and sugar.

Although there is potential mineral wealth in most of the countries of Central America this resource, for the most part, has been unexploited. Much of the land is heavily forested and some of the world's most valuable woods such as mahogany, rosewood, teak and ebony are found here. However, only a very small part of the forests have been as yet cut for commercial purposes.

ISLANDS OF THE CARIBBEAN—The

Caribbean Sea is a vital water link between the Americas and the West Indies. With the opening of the Panama Canal it took on added importance as a trade route for the ships of the world.

The island republics and colonies lying in the Caribbean have likewise become increasingly important with the passing years, both for their economic and strategic value.

The West Indies, numbering hundreds of islands, extend in a sweeping arc beginning near southern Florida and ending off the coast of Venezuela. Columbus named the islands, in the belief that he had reached India. Most of the islands, forming two main groups, the Greater and the Lesser Antilles, are mountainous. However, there is sufficient fertile land to afford a variety of tropical products. In general the climate is hot but is tempered by the sea breezes. All the islands are subject to tropical hurricanes and in many regions there are occasional volcanic eruptions.

As with the Central American republics the West Indies have enjoyed increased production and trade with the importation of new crops from the East that are now grown

Pan-American-Grace Airways

Peru's cultural past is evident to all who visit her attractive cities.

throughout Middle America. Nearness to markets and the great manufacturing centers and cheap ocean transportation are added advantages.

A number of these islands not independent are dependencies of the United States or Great Britain, while some belong to France and the Netherlands.

SOUTH AMERICA—It is a common error

to think of South America as being directly south of the United States. A glance at the globe will show that this is far from the truth. Except for the bulge to the west and the southern tip, all of South America is east of the Atlantic coast boundary of the United States. This places South America much closer to Africa than North America is to Europe. A theory has been advanced, though never proved, that at one time Africa and South America were joined.

Smaller than North America by over two million square miles, and representing one-eighth of the world's total land area,

South America is the fourth largest continent.

With the equator crossing South America on a line with the Amazon River, two-thirds of this southern neighbor is in the tropics and the balance in the temperate zone. In common with other lands situated in the Southern Hemisphere, it has the further disadvantage of being far removed from the principal world markets. These factors, together with the history of the continent, explain why it has not developed as rapidly as the United States, although discovered at the same time. But in spite of the handicaps of climate, position and history, South America has an extensive trade with the United States and Europe. And, although for centuries the Spaniards robbed it of its buried treasures, South America still possesses great mineral wealth.

South of the Isthmus of Panama, the great line of mountains which extends the entire length of North America becomes the mighty Andes. Second only to the Himalayas, they follow the western coast to Cape Horn, rising steeply from the Pacific in long ranges of snow-capped peaks and wide plateaus. Mount Aconcagua is the highest peak in the Americas and rises to a height of twenty-three thousand feet. Several lesser peaks are active volcanos. To the south the range begins to narrow and the coast is bordered by a tattered fringe of islands clothed with pines and swept by fierce northwesterly winds.

On the east are two broad plateaus, the Guiana and Brazilian highlands, which might be compared with the Laurentian highlands and the Appalachian chain of North America. Between the eastern slope of the Andes and these plateaus lie broad lowlands. The grassy, tree dotted plains, or *llanos,* of the Orinoco Basin in Venezuela and Colombia, provide fine pasturage between the dry and rainy seasons. In the dry season they practically revert to desert. To the south are the dry plains, or *pampas,* of Northern Argentina, which is the great cattle country of the continent.

The Amazon—largest river system in the world—drains over one-third of the continent. This area is equal to two-thirds that of the United States. This mighty river is thirty-five hundred miles long and in places is over fifty miles wide. It flows through the densest tropical forest in the world and much of it is unexplored.

The La Plata River is actually the estuary for three rivers, the Parana, with a drainage area almost as large as that of the Mississippi, the Uruguay and the Paraguay. Buenos Aires, metropolis of the Southern Hemisphere is situated on the south bank of the La Plata 175 miles from the Atlantic. Buenos Aires is one of the world's most beautiful cities and important seaports. The above mentioned rivers drain Northern Argentina, Uruguay and Paraguay.

Other rivers of less importance are the São Francisco of Brazil, the Magdalena of Colombia, the Orinoco of Venezuela, and the Río Colorado of Argentina.

Lying in the Andes at an altitude of over twelve thousand feet is Lake Titicaca. With an area over half that of Lake Erie, it is the highest navigable lake in the world.

Much of Argentina and Chile are in southern latitudes that compare with the northern latitudes of the United States, but there are only sections where the climate is similar. Parts of Chile have a climate that compares with the Pacific coast states, and sections of Argentina and Uruguay are comparable to the east coast of the United States.

The heat is insufferable and the rainfall extremely heavy in the low Orinoco and Amazon Valleys. In the northern countries, while hot, the climate is tempered by the highlands. At the extreme southern tip the seasons are exactly the opposite of those in North America, but there is not the variation in temperature. This is due to the influence of oceans and mountains.

The only important indentations on the Pacific are found along the rugged coast of southern Chile and the Gulf of Guayaquil in Ecuador.

The high temperature and humidity of the tropical regions, together with many insects and diseases, discourage the activity of white people and even sap the strength of the natives. Large areas of swamp and rugged mountains have made the development of transportation difficult and expensive. Only with the growth of air travel has it been possible for the Andean countries to contact one another with relative ease.

In the main, South America is sparsely settled, with the greatest density of population along the coasts. The original inhabitants were Indians, but, due to the early colonization by the Spanish and Portuguese, many of the present inhabitants are *mestizos,* a mixture of Indian and Spanish or Portuguese blood. The remainder is largely composed of Italian and German immigrants. Except in Brazil, where the official language is Portuguese, Spanish is spoken in all the other independent countries.

The three countries of Chile, Argentina and Uruguay, where there has been the largest European immigration, are making rapid industrial progress. The rest of South America is still largely agricultural. Most of the countries produce only one or two major products and there is little diversity of crops. Practically all exports are raw materials, while imports are manufactured goods.

With the exception of the three colonies of British, French and Dutch Guiana, all of South America is composed of independent republics. In spite of a common language and form of government there is little interchange between countries. In general they are more concerned with world trade than dealing with each other.

Since the early coming of the Spaniards, South America has continued to yield great stores of precious metals. The Andes are rich in minerals, and the eastern highlands contain iron, gold, and diamonds. Some coal is found in Brazil, Chile and Colombia, but not in great quantity. Water-power and oil are being utilized to make up for this lack.

Ecuador, Peru and Chile are all west coast countries, which, until the opening of the Panama Canal, were practically isolated from the rest of the world. Bolivia, having no outlet to the sea, moves nearly all of her exports through the seaports of Chile and Peru.

CHILE—Sometimes called the "Shoestring Republic," Chile stretches along the west coast for twenty-six hundred miles, from the

Brazilian Government Trade Bureau

Although in the torrid zone, Brazil's climate is tempered by rainfall, favorable winds and altitude.

borders of Peru to Cape Horn. It has a variety of climate ranging from frigid to torrid. This long, narrow and mountainous country is one of the most progressvie in South America. It is one of the three republics where there are more white people than natives. The other two are Argentina and Uruguay.

From north to south Chile is divided into three regions: the desert, a dry sub-tropical region which includes the coast, and a section that is forested. The greatest mineral region lies between Santiago and the Peruvian border. In the northern half of this area are the nitrate fields which have produced almost the entire world's supply of this important fertilizer. The nitrate beds located in the Pacific coastal desert (Atacama) were wrested from Peru during the War of the Pacific (1879-83) from which Chile emerged victorious. Chile's fame as a nitrate region has waned with the introduction of synthetic nitrate into world industry. The country is now seeking to stimulate the

The Taj Mahal, Agra, India.

Italian State Tourist Office

Night view of the Colosseum, Rome, Italy.

Egyptian State Tourist Administration

The Sphinx at Giza, Egypt.

TWA-Airline Photo

The Abbey of Mont-Saint-Michel, France.

export of wine, honey and livestock. In the southern half there are deposits of copper, iron, gold and silver. Chile ranks high among the world's producers of copper; this metal is the country's most important export.

PERU—This country is an extension of the narrow and arid coastal plain in northern Chile, with the Andes occupying fully half of the land. A densely wooded tropical region drops down in the east to meet the low plains of Brazil.

About a fourth of the population is white, most of whom are Spanish. The balance are *mestizos* (mixed) or Indians. Descendants of the ancient Incas, the Indians of Peru, are found principally living on the high mountain slopes of the Andes, and sailing their strange fiber craft on Lake Titicaca. These Indians have domesticated the llama and the alpaca, two animals which are native to this region, and which have never been raised successfully elsewhere. The llama is a sure-footed animal upon which the Indians depend for food, clothing and transportation. Used as a beast of burden in this lofty arid country, the llama, like the camel, can go several days without water. The alpaca is too small to carry loads and is raised for its very long wool.

ECUADOR—Peru and Ecuador have a similar climate and topography except for the northern part of the coastal plain of Ecuador. This plain is as fertile as any area in South America and is the principal agricultural section of Ecuador. Among this country's chief export crops are bananas, cacao and coffee. Ecuador's coffee has been increasing in importance since its cacao, blighted by witches'-broom, has suffered an appreciable decrease in export. Tagua, a substitute for ivory, is produced in limited quantities. Ecuador is world-famous for its amazing variety of wild birds. The country contains one-fourth of all recorded species in South America.

BOLIVIA—Shut off from the sea by Chile and Peru, Bolivia is one of the most sparsely populated countries in the world. It consists of a high plateau in the southwest that is cold and dry, and wet tropical lowlands in the north and east. Though Bolivia's surface is three-fifths lowlands, the country includes one of the highest inhabitable regions in the world. The Andes spread out into two great chains of mountains which enclose a plateau nearly as high as the peaks themselves. Lake Titicaca, one of the highest of the larger lakes in the world, is situated on this plateau.

Bolivia, ranking after Malaya, Indonesia, and Mainland China in its tin deposits, is well supplied with nearly all known metals. Strangely enough, although having local supplies of coal, necessary in smelting, it is usually cheaper to import coal.

Lack of capital, the high cost of transportation, and the scarcity of labor, have retarded mining in all the countries of the Andes. Only the natives can do manual labor in the high altitudes and the people are not inclined toward mining. However, mining is the chief industry. Aside from tin, there is abundant amounts of gold, copper, bismuth, antimony, lead, zinc, wolfram and oil. Tobacco, wine and vanilla, together with quinine and rubber, are exported.

BRAZIL—Covering nearly half the continent and with half the population, Brazil lies almost entirely in the tropics. This republic is only 10 per cent smaller than the United States and has three times the area of Argentina.

The Amazon and its tributaries have a total length of over nineteen thousand miles, of which thirteen thousand are navigable. This huge system extends through more than half the country's area.

The great plateau country, known as the Brazilian Highlands, lies in the south and east. It is composed of numerous mountain ranges and river valleys. Rio de Janeiro, South America's third largest city, is adjacent to this region. Hemmed in by mountains and a wide bay, it has one of the finest and most beautiful harbors in the world.

Brazil at one time was the greatest rubber-producing country. Brazil has embarked on a program of intensified manufacturing. Silk, cotton and woolen mills have sprung up all over the eastern seaboard. Shoes and hats are becoming major products. Many paper mills are being built to utilize some of the billion acres of forests that cover half the land area. Its greatest mineral wealth has yet to be exploited, though one of the largest estimated deposits of iron ore in the world is now being developed. The country produces about fifty percent of the world's coffee. Efforts to do away with the one-crop system are gaining success and coffee is no longer the economic tyrant that it was. A growing cacao industry now ranks second in the world, while tobacco, rice, cotton and sugar are attaining commercial significance.

URUGUAY—This is the smallest republic in South America. It has a fine climate with the winds of the ocean modifying the temperature.

Since the Spanish brought sheep and cattle to the grassy plains of Uruguay in the 17th century, it has been a stock raising country. Today it is one of the leading meat producers of the world. Only a small percentage of the arable land is devoted to the raising of crops and it is limited in both minerals and manufacturing.

PARAGUAY—One of the two republics of South Amercia that is completely surrounded by other nations. Little has been done to develop its natural resources.

Most of the surface of western Paraguay is a low, swampy and unhealthy plain. The climate in the north is hot and unsuited to the white man. Most of the people live in the southern area east of the Paraguay River. It is a country of small villages, grazing, and farm lands, which depends upon the rivers for means of transportation.

Extending from Bolivia, across the western third of Paraguay, and south into Argentina, is the Gran Chaco, a great plain.

THE ARGENTINE REPUBLIC — T h e early colonists' anticipation of finding silver and gold in Argentina prompted them to name the country for the Latin word meaning silver. Although the colonists' search for great mineral wealth was in vain, the fertile soil and temperate climate have fostered the country's great economic progress. The Re-

Pan-American-Grace Airways

The most cosmopolitan city of South America, Buenos Aires has been strongly influenced by Europe.

public is the second largest of the South American countries.

The Gran Chaco, in the northern part, is a land of forests, lakes and swamps, which is largely unexplored. The grassy plains of the *Pampas* occupy a large area of Argentina. This cattle country and farm land extends from the Atlantic coast to the Andes in the west, and northwest to the highlands which reach into Brazil. The rich grazing lands, which have led to Argentina becoming a large exporter of meat and wool are in the center of the *Pampas;* the largest meat refrigerating plant in the world is at Buenos Aires.

Only a small part of the land is under cultivation, although it has been said that 80 per cent is capable of producing crops, grass or forests. An idea may be gained from this of the great possibilities for future development that lie ahead.

Argentina is an agricultural and commercial, rather than an industrial country. It has been hindered in the development of manufacture by a shortage of coal, the lack of water power, and an inadequate supply of minerals.

Descendants of the Spanish settlers are

the leaders of the country, with most of the farm population consisting of Italians. Immigrants from the British Isles have taken to sheep raising, and many Germans have migrated to Argentina. Today half of the population is foreign-born or are descendants of immigrants.

NORTH COAST COUNTRIES—Colombia, Venezuela, and the British, French and Dutch Guianas, are all on the north coast.

COLOMBIA—The only South American country having a coastline along both the Atlantic and Pacific oceans. Half the country is high in the rugged Andes; the other half lies in unhealthy tropical plains. Three cordilleras of the Andes traverse in a parallel line from north and south which forms a barrier between the seacoast and the rich inland valleys. The chief source of wealth is coffee. Colombian coffee is the finest in the world and the bean is jealously guarded. Almost all of the exported coffee is shipped to the United States. A type from the area around Medellin commands the highest price per pound in the world. Surpassed by Brazil in quantity, Colombia's coffee yields to none in quality. Next to coffee in export value is oil. The fields are to a large extent a continuation of those in Venezuela. Production in recent years has been more than 40 million barrels annually. Other resources include platinum, emeralds and coal.

VENEZUELA—One of the most productive oil regions in the world, is on the coast of the Caribbean. Easy access to this coast from the interior affords great possibilities for commercial and industrial development. Venezuela's land area is distinguished by its llanos or wide lowlands along the Orinoco River. The river is navigable for a course of 700 miles and is connected to the Amazon system by a canal. Coffee, chiefly from the basin of the Maracaibo, is second only to that of Colombia. A ranking producer of petroleum, Venezuela's exploitation of oil is fraught with difficulties which have never been successfully surmounted. Virgin forests cover the country and include about 600 species of wood. At Margarita is located a profitable pearl industry. Iron, asphalt, coal and gold figure as the main mineral resources.

THE GUIANAS—On the north coast of South America are the only European possessions on the continent. Their combined area is 178,000 square miles. The surface is composed of an alluvial plain at sea-level and another plain farther south which is distinguished by hills and forested mountains. The climate is tolerable except in the south where the northeast trade winds do not prevail. Though their topography is similar their economic importance varies greatly from east to west. British Guiana, about the size of Great Britain, is the most highly developed. Dutch Guiana (Surinam) has no important industries except the mining of bauxite. French Guiana, the easternmost colony, is of little importance economically. Its sparse population and the excessive emphasis placed on the mining of gold has led to the neglect of its fertile soil. Mineral resources in the form of gold and diamonds are equally divided among the Guianas.

EUROPE—Eurasia is the world's largest land mass and includes both Europe and Asia. Europe occupies about a third of the western end of Eurasia, and, with the exception of Australia, is the smallest continent. It is the most densely populated for its size and no other continent has so many separate nations. Nearly all of these countries have distinctive customs and speak different languages. This does much to explain Europe's turbulent history.

Actually Europe is a huge peninsula, subdivided into a number of lesser peninsulas, caused by the oceans and inland seas which encroach upon it. Its irregular form, together with the mountain barriers, and the presence of important islands near the continent, have contributed to the growth of individual nations. Differences in language and customs have a natural tendency to arouse a strong nationalistic spirit. This keeps people apart and makes them suspicious of those with different customs, and who speak alien tongues. Among mountain people an independent spirit and love of freedom is even more pronounced.

In the northwest, two peninsulas are

formed by the Baltic Sea. The countries of Norway and Sweden occupy the Scandinavian Peninsula. Denmark is on the Jutland Peninsula between the Baltic and North Seas. To the south, Portugal and Spain comprise the Iberian Peninsula. The peninsular boot of Italy thrusts out into the Mediterranean, and the Balkan Peninsula is surrounded by the Black Sea and the Adriatic, Ionian and Aegean Seas of the Mediterranean.

Great Britain is prevented from being a peninsula only by the narrow English Channel, and was once a part of the mainland. The entire course of history has been changed by this strip of water which made England an island. The same may be said for the Straits of Gibraltar separating Europe from Africa. But for this nine-mile passage, the Mediterranean would have had no outlet to the Atlantic.

Europe may be divided into five natural regions: (1) the Northwest Highlands, (2) the Central Plains, (3) the Central Highlands, (4) the Southern Mountains and Plateaus, and (5) the Southern Lowlands.

Most of the British Isles, a section of France, and a good part of the Scandinavian Peninsula are included in the Northwest Highlands. This is the coastal region with excellent harbors where men have made their living by the sea, and commerce has become most important. In those places where coal and iron are found it has led to an industrial life. This highland region enjoys a cool, temperate climate and people are energetic.

The great Central Plains extend from the British Isles to the Ural Mountains that separate Europe from Asia. These plains range from the tundra regions of the Far North to the Caspian Sea, the Caucasus Mountains, and the Black Sea of the Southeast. In the Southwest they reach into southern France. Within such an extensive area there are naturally great differences in climate. There is also great diversity of vegetation and the occupations of the people.

South of the Arctic tundra belt are extensive evergreen forests that reach westward to the Scandinavian Peninsula. In the grasslands to the south of the forests are large areas used for the growing of grain,

British Travel Association

England's rolling countryside is specked with tiny cottages which augment the natural beauty of the landscape.

and stock grazing is the chief occupation in the drier southeastern sections. This is the region of the dry and treeless steppes.

The Central Highlands include the plateau in central France and take in parts of Belgium, southern Germany, Austria, and the most of Czechoslovakia. It is the region of forest, water-power, and varied mineral resources. The industrial districts of Central Europe are the outgrowth of the great deposits of coal and iron found here.

The impressive peaks of the Alps rise south of the Central Highlands, forming one of the many ranges of Southern Europe. The Apennines extend the length of Italy, and other ranges follow the eastern coast of the Adriatic through Yugoslavia and Albania to the southern tip of Greece. Spreading out to the east they include most of the Balkan Peninsula. To the north the Carpathian Mountains swing east and north around the valley of the Danube and then run northeast to almost circle the Plain of Hungary. Farther to the east, the Caucasus Mountains reach from the Black to the Caspian Sea. Separating France and Spain are the Pyrenees, and the Sierra Nevadas are in southern Spain bordering the Mediterranean.

The Alps are particularly famous for their scenic grandeur. The Sierra Nevadas and Carpathian Mountains are rich in mineral resources, and some of the world's greatest oil fields are in the Caucasus. The mountains of Italy lack valuable ores and have been largely stripped of their forests.

The Southern Lowlands of the Danube Valley and the Plain of Hungary represent some of the finest farming and grazing land in the world.

The extreme irregularity of the European coastline has been of great importance to the life of the people. With the North and Baltic Seas, the Mediterranean and Black Seas, penetrating far into the interior, only Central Europe and Eastern Russia are very far from the coast. Although the combined areas of South America and Africa are nearly five times that of Europe, the coastline of Europe is longer.

A majority of the great seaports of the world are in Western Europe. Its people have led the world in sea-faring.

Europe has a generally mild, temperate climate, particularly in the western areas, which are warmed by ocean currents and the winds blowing over these waters. Even the British Isles have a mild climate in spite of being in the same latitude as Labrador. Greater extremes of temperature exist in eastern Europe where these winds lose their moderating effect.

Due to the Alps blocking the cold north winds, and the influence of the warm waters of the Mediterranean, the southern shores of Europe enjoy a mild year-round climate. Excepting in eastern Europe, where the rainfall is light, there is generally sufficient moisture for agriculture.

An abundance of mineral resources, fine forests, rich farmlands, water-power, and the seas plentifully supplied with fish, have encouraged Europe's growth. An invigorating climate, waterways, harbors and access to the oceans of the world, have contributed to its commercial importance.

The climate and natural resources of each country have largely determined their individual occupations and prosperity.

GREAT BRITAIN AND NORTHERN IRELAND—The British Isles and the British Commonwealth of Nations owe much of their commercial and industrial growth to the daring and initiative of their early mariners. Although we usually think of the British Isles as comprising Great Britain and Ireland, it actually consists of nearly five thousand islands. Within the small compass of the islands there is a considerable variety of topography.

In Northern Ireland there are many lakes, including the largest one of the island, Lough Neagh, as well as a range known as the Mourne Mountains. A large portion of the country consists of the basalt plateau of Antrim.

Northern Ireland, or Ulster, as the six counties are sometimes called, is the seat of a very extensive lace and linen industry. In County Down and County Antrim there are highgrade deposits of granite and bauxite which are being exploited. Shipbuilding is a major industry centered in the capital, Belfast.

In Scotland the three well-marked divisions stand out, the highlands, the southern uplands, and between these two, the central lowlands, into which four-fifths of the population is crowded. The lowlands contain the richest agricultural land, as well as the coal fields. They are penetrated by three great estuaries, the Firths of Tay and Forth on the east, and of Clyde on the west, so that communication coastwise or overseas is everywhere easy.

Scotland has some of the largest shipbuilding yards in the world on the Firth of Clyde. Sheep and cattle are raised in large numbers since the land is not well suited to agriculture.

The Welsh cliffy upland is flanked to the north and east by small coal fields, but the greatest field lies to the south. A belt of limestone running from Bill of Portland to Tees Bay, and bearing at many points valuable iron ores, serves as a rough boundary of industrial England, for to the south and east of it, apart from the metropolis, agricultural interests predominate. Lying to the west of the limestone band is the Devon-

Cornwall peninsula, where great bosses of granite and slate form the famous moors.

Wales, after 700 years as a part of the English kingdom, retains its individuality and is nationalistic in speech, dress and customs. The Welsh language is Celtic, akin to the Gaelic of Ireland. It is the only speech of nearly one-tenth of the people.

Channel Islands, lying across the English Channel off the coast of Normandy, and Scilly Islands, lying southwest of Land's End, enjoy an almost complete freedom from frost and severe weather.

Because of the density of population Great Britain is far from self-sustaining and must depend upon the raw materials and products of other countries. This has led to the development of her world-wide commerce, a large part of which is carried on with her far-flung and numerous colonies. Agriculture is intensive with much importance placed on livestock. Many of the world's most valuable breeds of farm animals have been developed on English farms. This is exemplified by such names as Guernsey, Shropshire, Jersey, Hereford, Hampshire and Plymouth.

IRELAND

IRELAND—Except for coastal hills and mountains, the country is largely an ill-drained plain dotted with lakes and peat-bogs, and crossed by the sluggish Shannon. In the southwest is the beautiful Killarney Lakes region which attracts many tourists each year. Although little of the land is suitable for large scale agriculture, grass and fodder crops are abundant and provide stockraising needs which is the major industry of the country. The Shannon River, Royal Canal, and the Grand Canal provide an excellent inland waterway system of transportation. Shannon airport, near Limerick, is a major international airway terminal. Horse-breeding is the most famous of Irish farm industries. A prosperous tourist trade is developing.

NORWAY AND SWEDEN

NORWAY AND SWEDEN—With its saw-toothed coast, great fiords, and neighboring islands, it is natural that Norway, occupying the western part of the Scandinavian peninsula, would be a maritime country. Norway's long coast line, facing the

Belgian Government Information Center

The European peasant has long been a factor in the economic development of the Old World.

Atlantic, is edged with lofty cliffs and seamed with deep fiords. Islands, countless in number, fringe the coast. Most of the country is a rocky, rugged and barren land, about one-fifth of which is forested. The rivers are short and torrential, but provide the finest salmon fishing in Europe. The Kjolen Mountains which form the backbone of the peninsula separate Norway from Sweden. These mountains rise in many parts to over 6,000 feet, the highest peaks being over 8,000 feet.

Norway is the land of the "midnight sun". From Trondheim northward at least a part of the disk of the sun is visible from May through July. But the winter nights are 17 hours long and midday seems like twilight during the winter months. Another striking feature is that much of the area above the Arctic Circle is warmer than some regions further south. Northeast Norway is the warmest part of the country in the summer.

Sweden consists primarily of a tableland sloping from the Kjolen Range to the Baltic. No less than 8 per cent of the surface of Sweden is water, the immense number of lakes covering almost 15,000 square miles. The two largest, Vanern and Vattern, in the southern portion of the country, are connected by a system of canals. Besides the large number of small islands which fringe

Suomen-Matkat

The snow-encrusted northlands of Scandinavia force its northernmost inhabitants to lead nomadic existences.

the coast, Sweden includes the two large Baltic islands of Gotland and Oland. Most of the people live in the southern part of their country while the Norwegians have settled chiefly near the fiords. Hydro-electric development is in an advanced stage in both countries.

In Sweden, iron deposits are among the richest in the world. Swedish steel is universally famous for its fine qualities. The making of machinery for export is a major industry. Swedish agriculture is in a very high state of development, and exports wheat, bacon and butter in large quantities. In forestry and sawmilling the nation has evolved such advanced methods that foreign technicians in the industry often go to Sweden to study logging and forestry. Nearly half of her exports are in pulp and paper products.

DENMARK—Denmark occupies a peninsula and numerous islands lying at the entrance to the Baltic. It is a lowland country characterized by many lakes, ponds and short rivers. Its sandy shores are shallow, with lagoons shut in by shifting sand bars. Most of Denmark is farm land, about half of which is used for grazing. The Faeroe Islands produce fish, mutton and wool for the homeland.

Dairy farming is the country's chief industry, the products of which comprise nearly all her exports. Greenland, the largest island in the world, is a part of the Danish realm.

ICELAND—The republic is an island in the north Atlantic consisting of a great tableland averaging 2,000 feet above sea level. Of its whole area barely a quarter is habitable. The surface is dotted by over 100 volcanic peaks. There are many boiling springs and the geysers are world-famous. It is too cold for agriculture but has rich grazing land for sheep and cattle.

FINLAND—Finland consists of a great plateau, ranging from 400 to 600 feet in elevation. The southern half of the plateau has about 25 per cent of its area occupied by thousands of shallow lakes, many of them linked by short natural or artificial channels, providing many miles of navigable waterways. Forests cover the greater part of the country which has led to lumbering, paper-making and the manufacture of woodenware. Over half the population is engaged in agricultural pursuits which are carried on under great difficulties.

THE NETHERLANDS—The tiny kingdom of the Netherlands, lacking natural resources has been largely a nation of seafarers for centuries. Along the canals, the meadows are often ten or twelve feet below the water line, and between the land and the sea at high tide there may be a difference of twenty-five feet or more. The land is protected by embankments and dikes, and it may be pictured as a great trough, the floor of which slopes down from east and southeast toward the North Sea. The rivers which flow across the country from the higher continent beyond, are at their mouths, frequently below the level of the sea, into which they have to be lifted by canals and locks across the dams or dikes. A large part of the land has been reclaimed from the sea and little by little it has become a fertile country.

BELGIUM—Smaller than Holland, Belgium is the most densely populated country in Europe. Situated between England, Holland, France and Germany, it is in the very center of industrial Europe. The country is well watered, and has two principal rivers, the Scheldt and the Maas. The country does not raise sufficient food to feed her people. Belgium's intensive industrialization has been at the expense of its agriculture, for the valley of the Sambre-Meuse, the chief industrial center, is also the richest farming land. Besides coal mining, steel manufacturing, and iron milling, Belgium's industrial output is increased by the age-old textile industry (once noted for tapestries and lace) which produces synthetic fabrics, wool and linen. The nation furnishes a great variety of farm products and a world-famous breed of horses. Little wildlife remains except in the forested area of the Ardennes where deer still roam.

LUXEMBOURG—The Grand Duchy of Luxembourg, smaller than the state of Rhode Island, is one of Europe's oldest states. An abundant store of iron ore has encouraged mining, smelting and some manufacturing. International trade of the duchy has been carried on through a customs union with Belgium.

LIECHTENSTEIN—Only 27 square miles larger than San Marino, Liechtenstein is separated from Switzerland by the Rhine river and is bounded by Austria in the east. The population is largely German but Switzerland administers its postal and telegraph facilities, and its currency is Swiss. It also belongs to the Swiss customs union. The tillable soil, a long strip along the Rhine river, yields grapes, grains and pasturage for a small cattle industry.

FRANCE—France is largely an agricultural country where the farmers, instead of living on their farms, usually live in nearby villages. Although rich in minerals, it has lagged behind both England and Germany as an industrial country. The surface is diversified, but much of it is lowland, with a few level plains. In the center is a triangular plateau called the Auvergne Mountains, with a height of something over 3,000 feet. The Cévennes form the eastern edge of this plateau, and from them to the Vosges, the tableland continues. There is a mountainous area in Britany, but the greatest heights are on the

Austria State Tourist Dept.

Austria's small villages are nestled among the deep valleys of its mountainous countryside.

frontiers, the Jura, the Pyrenees, and the Alps separating it respectively from Switzerland, Spain and Italy. The Ardennes in the northeast are less lofty. The Seine drains the north, the Loire and the Garonne the west, and the Rhone the east and south. France enjoys a delightful climate. Only in the region of the Alps is real winter encountered. Protected by the mountains to the north, the balmy area along the Mediterranean is a magnet that has drawn countless vacationers. Many semi-tropical plants and fruits are grown in this section. Indeed, France's greatest resource is her soil. Grape culture is by far the leading agricultural pursuit, for France produces a billion gallons of wine in a vintage year. Yet, the country imports millions of gallons. Textile production, particularly the silk industry centered around Lyons, is a valuable undertaking in the country; cotton mills are the leading producers of goods.

MONACO—The Principality of Monaco is one of the smallest states in the world. It possesses the administrative organs and institutions of larger nations in miniature. It has no taxes for it is supported by the gambling casino of Monte Carlo from which its own citizens are barred. The most striking feature of this 370 acre state is the Monagasque Acropolis on a headland 200 feet above the water. The Prince's Palace, a magnificent structure, is located on it. On the Mediterranean coast, surrounded by the Riviera of France, Monaco offers to the tourist auto-racing, skiing, bathing, sailing, and of course, gambling. There is also an oceanographic museum.

SWITZERLAND—This rugged little country is a completely land-locked republic nestling among the beautiful Alps. It has succeeded in maintaining its neutrality and independence while the rest of Europe engaged in costly and devastating wars. Between Lake Constance on the Rhine and Lake Geneva on the Rhone are Lakes Neuchatel, Zurich, Lucerne, Brienz, Thun, all of which drain to the Aar. Lake Geneva and Lake Constance each exceed 200 square miles in area. Many of Switzerland's mountains are permanently covered with snow. Capitalizing upon its wonderful mountain and lake scenery, and making the most of its limited resources, Switzerland has become one of the most prosperous of the smaller nations. With its snow-capped peaks rising from ten to fifteen thousand feet, it has been the playground of Europe for many years.

GERMANY—There are two natural regions in Germany, the northern plain and southern highlands. The former is the most extensive agricultural region. The land which borders Denmark is favorable to the grazing of cattle, and, in the northeast, large numbers of sheep and goats are raised. The minerals found in the central highlands have had the greatest influence upon the development of Germany in the last fifty years.

Except for ample supplies of coal and potash, Germany is deficient in natural resources. During the glacial period, sand was deposited over the plains region and as a result the soil is not naturally fertile. Only by intensive cultivation and the heavy use of fertilizers, made from potash, is much of the soil made productive. Germany's great scientific development has been largely the result of solving agricultural problems, and

of searching for new uses to utilize the coal reserves.

Germany's only access to the ocean, and world trade, is through the Baltic and North Seas. To make the most of this she has developed a remarkable system of waterways. The Rhine rises in the Alps and flows through the fertile lowlands of western Germany to the border of Holland, and thence to the sea. The Elbe, Weser, and the Oder flow north across the low plain of Germany. The Oder empties into the Baltic. The Elbe and Weser flow into the North Sea. All three are navigable far inland for ocean-going vessels. The rivers, together with fifteen hundred miles of canals, form a network of waterways which provide cheap transportation.

AUSTRIA AND HUNGARY—Austria is characterized by its beautiful mountain scenery, over 90 percent of the land is classified as mountainous, which has contributed to development of one of its largest industries— tourist and resort trade. However, over 80 per cent of the land is productive and half of this is under cultivation. In contrast Hungary is largely comprised of a low fertile plain. The country is primarily agricultural and is a great grain and wine producer.

CZECHOSLOVAKIA—This land - locked country contains strategic routes between north and south Europe of economic and political value. The country has two large mountain ranges, the Carpathian in the east and the Sudeten in the west. Czechoslovakia is famous for its subterranean caverns and its spas and mineral springs. The people are energetic and progressive and there are valuable forest resources, fertile soil and varied mineral deposits.

THE BALKANS—They include Rumania, Yugoslavia, Bulgaria, Albania, Greece and European Turkey. Located at the gateway to Asia, and on a natural route connecting the two continents, this region has been a battleground for centuries. Repeated invasions from various directions have resulted in a number of racial groups and religious beliefs. The rugged nature of the country has isolated the people into many rival factions with intense racial and national spirit.

YUGOSLAVIA consists essentially of a mountainous core, which stretches from the Dinaric Alps in the northwest to the Balkan Mountains on the Bulgarian frontier. The only valley which cuts the mountains and forms a passageway is that of the Morava River, which with that of the Vardar, leads from Belgrade to Salonika. Beyond the Sava-Danube, as far as the northern boundary, the land is low and swampy near the rivers, with a few minor elevations. The chief concentrations of people are around Zagreb and Belgrade. Yugoslavia has recently experienced a crisis resulting from a boycott by the Cominform countries and the Soviet Union. Forced to turn to the West, the nation has signed trade agreements with several Western European states. Its greatest problem is the lack of communications between its regions. The more highly developed coastal areas have access to outside markets, but the distribution of economic aid further inland is hampered by the mountains which impose a rugged barrier between the provinces.

RUMANIA—In western Rumania the Carpathian Mountains from the northwest and the Transylvanian Alps from the southwest meet in the center to form a crescent. To the north and west of this crescent is the Transylvanian plateau; to the south and east are the plains of Moldavia and Walachia. The principal rivers are the Danube in the south which enters the Black Sea at Sulina, and the Prut in the northeast and the Siret in the southeast—both of which connect with the Danube.

BULGARIA—The country is hilly and well watered by numerous streams, of which the Iskur, Struma and Maritsa are the most important. Although nearly one-third of the country's area is in forests, only a small part of the wood is used commercially since about one-fourth of the forest area is completely unproductive. Many of the forests consist of scrub timber and a sizeable portion of the good forests are inaccessible. Eighty percent of Bulgaria's population is employed in agriculture, the chief crops being tobacco and cereals. Attar of rose and silk are important products.

TWA Transworld Airline

The coastal cities of Portugal draw heavily on the sea for their principal commodity.

ALBANIA—Albania is a mountainous country on the western side of the Peninsula. In the center, part of the plateau is cultivable, and in the south there is fertile alluvial soil with grazing land on the slopes.

GREECE—With a very long coast line on the Aegean and Ionian Seas, and a large number of islands, including Crete, Mytilene, Dodecanese and Chios, the area is generally mountainous. The mountains, though not very high, divide the country into a number of small districts, between which communication is difficult. It is the sea which links the different regions of Greece.

ITALY—Once the hub of the known world, Italy's importance declined as the age of exploration and discovery opened up the ocean routes of the world. Taking no part in this period of conquest and empire building, she did not acquire colonies. Lacking unity she was in no position to demand her share of the rich prizes of newly discovered land being acquired by other European nations.

With the opening of the Suez Canal and tunnels through the Alps, her trade somewhat improved, but the absence of the necessary minerals prevented her from keeping pace with industrial development elsewhere in Europe.

The south slope of the Alps belongs to Italy. At the point where the Alps reach the Mediterranean, the Apennines begin. These mountains follow the length of Italy and form a rugged backbone which extends through the island of Sicily. The southern and western parts of the peninsula have been subjected to volcanic eruptions, and Vesuvius, Etna, and Stromboli are still active volcanoes. The chief lowlands are in the Po Valley with narrow coastal plains east and west of the Apennines. The majority of the people, and most of the agriculture and manufacturing, are located in the Po Valley. Consequently Northern Italy does not experience the poverty to be found in Southern Italy. It is from the south that most of the immigrants to the United States have come.

Italy's colorful history, scenery and balmy climate have attracted many tourists which has in some measure offset an unfavorable balance of trade.

SAN MARINO—San Marino is one of the oldest republics in the world and is the smallest. It has always been on good terms with its big neighbor, Italy, by whom it is surrounded. The state was founded in the fourth century by Marinius of Dalmatia, a stonecutter. Except for a few invasions, its liberty has been respected, even by Napoleon. During World War II it declared war against Germany and was occupied by the Germans and subsequently liberated by the British. Much of its revenue is obtained through the sale of its postage stamps issued for the benefit of collectors.

SPAIN AND PORTUGAL—About three-fourths of the Iberian Peninsula is a granite plateau with a range of mountains dividing it in the center. The rivers that flow through this region through deep gorges block transportation and are unsuited for navigation, waterpower or irrigation. The dry climate, lack of water, a rugged land formation, poor soil and an absence of transportation have been great obstacles standing in the way of the economic development of both Spain and Portugal. A portion of the land in the valleys

and plains has been made fertile through irrigation and farming is the main industry. Fishing is important along the Portugal coast, although a great part of the coast is too rugged for harbors. There are forests in most of the higher areas where half the world's supply of cork is produced.

ANDORRA—Tiny Andorra is in the Pyrenees Mountains between France and Spain. It is not a republic, as is often supposed, but a joint dependency of France and the Bishops of Urgel in Spain. Its mountains are high and arid, and its valleys contain poor soil so that the people are nearly all engaged in pastoral pursuits. The one product of the soil is tobacco. Sheep-herding is the main industry, and the need of hay for winter forage further limits the use of soil for any other crop.

POLAND—Poland was for many years a chiefly agricultural country but good supplies of coal, lead, iron and zinc have helped her industrial progress to such an extent that industry is now more important than agriculture. Most of the land is comprised of a plain, although there are low hills in the northwest in Pomerania. The lower regions of the Vistula have marshes, sand dunes and lakes. The central plain of Poland with an elevation of about 500 feet is traversed by great rivers, the most important being the Oder and the Vistula. Her strategic position near the Baltic Sea, and the lack of natural boundaries and barriers, have long made the people of this country, as well as those of the former Baltic States, the victims of stronger nations seeking an outlet to the sea.

U. S. S. R.— Almost 2½ times the size of the United States and comprising more than one-seventh of the world's land surface, the Union of Soviet Socialist Republics sprawls across two continents. Most of Russia is a great plain reaching from the Pacific to its western boundaries. Its position in northern latitudes and the absence of protecting barriers result in an extreme climate with long, cold winters. Vladivostok, on the Pacific coast, and the ports on the Arctic Ocean and Baltic Sea are closed by ice during the long winter months. Vladivostok, however, is kept open the year round by ice-breakers. In no part of the land is the rainfall heavy, and there are frequent and widespread droughts, which bring hunger and starvation to its people.

From the Black Sea in the south to the Arctic Ocean, and from the Baltic Sea to the Ural Mountains, which divide Asiatic Russia from European Russia, is a vast lowland. To the east of the Urals is Siberia, two-thirds of which is a flat, unbroken plain. In the far north the ground has been found to be frozen to a depth of over six hundred feet. This presents peculiar problems, if the government is to succeed with plans to mine the ores found there and industrialize this Arctic region. Here in the tundra country the moss, upon which the reindeer of the nomadic tribes feed, is often five feet thick.

South of the tundra belt is a great evergreen forest covering billions of acres, where lumbering and fur-trapping are the chief occupations.

Russia's supply of minerals is so great and widely scattered that the extent of many of the deposits is still unknown. There are immense reserves of coal in both European and Asiatic Russia. Copper, platinum, iron, gold, manganese and other minerals are found in the Urals. Some of the richest petroleum deposits in the world are located in the Baku region of the Caspian Sea and in the Urals.

Great strides have been made in industrial development, with the manufacture of iron and steel, machinery, textiles and leather goods in the lead.

In spite of climate, high cost of manufacture and difficulties of transportation, the U. S. S. R. is a country that is largely self-sustaining, and has become increasingly important industrially.

AFRICA—This continent, once called a sleeping giant, is awakening, as more and more of its peoples enter the world stage as independent nations. Africa, the second largest continent, is rich in natural resources. But many regions are desert or tropical forest and are thinly settled. Although Egypt and Carthage flourished along its northern shores in antiquity, the rest of the continent long

TWA—Trans World Airline .

Many natural phenomena, like these hot springs, are present in Africa's terrain.

remained shrouded in mystery.

Joined to Asia by a land bridge at the Isthmus of Suez, and only separated from Europe by the narrow Strait of Gibraltar, it was not until the nineteenth century that Europe finally set about the conquest of the "Dark Continent." For centuries an unfavorable climate and natural barriers combined to guard its secrets and hold back development.

Almost midway of its length Africa is crossed by the equator. Being triangular in shape, this places most of the continent in unhealthy torrid regions. Added to this its coastline is steep and regular, and offers few places for ships to anchor. The rivers as regards navigability cannot be considered in the same light as the great rivers of Europe, Asia and the Americas. None, except the Nile and the Congo, has unimpeded entrance to the sea.

The deltas of the Niger and the Zambezi are choked by silt and, on nearly all, navigation is impeded by shoal or cataract. Nevertheless the Congo and the Nile with their tributaries have many thousands of miles of navigable waterways, as have the Niger, the Benue and the Zambezi.

To the north, the Sahara Desert proved an effective barrier of sand and intense heat, which for hundreds of years prevented any important exchange of ideas or trade between the white man of the north and the black man in the south. Extending from the Atlantic to the River Nile, and reaching from the Mediterranean to the Sudan, the dry Sahara is a region of desolation. What trade existed between Asia, Europe and Africa followed caravan routes which led from oasis to oasis. The only life to be found there is at these scattered oases.

Africa is a great plateau, over four thousand miles long from north to south. The average height of the entire continent is over two thousand feet above sea level. Its loftiest peak is nearly twenty thousand feet high, while the Qattara Depression in the Libyan Desert sinks to four hundred feet below sea level.

The Atlas Mountains parallel the north coast of Africa, with their southern slopes dropping down to the Sahara. The Sudan belt, which extends south from the Sahara to the Gold Coast and the Gulf of Guinea, is a lower region of hills, valleys and plains. To the southwest are the low Cameroon Mountains; and another chain in the eastern part follows the Red Sea.

In Eastern Africa, a ridge of highlands reaches below the equator to form a series of mountain ranges. It is here that the great lakes region is found. Only in North America are there lakes which compare to these in size. Unlike the mountain ranges of other continents, those of Africa do not follow a regular pattern. This, together with their location, provides an unusual drainage system. A mountain ridge separates the lakes that drain into the three great rivers, the Nile, the Congo and the Zambezi. This ridge dictates the direction of their courses, with the Nile flowing north toward the Mediterranean, the Congo twisting and turning to finally reach the Atlantic to the west, and the Zambezi flowing east to empty into the Indian Ocean. Each river follows a devious course through the mountains before finding a way over the edge of the plateau to reach the sea. This results in many falls and rapids which interrupt transportation. The Victoria Falls on the Zambezi, the rapids of the Congo, and the cataracts of the Nile are typical.

The Congo, winding through the gloomy depths of the fever-infested forests, is three thousand miles long. It is second only to the Amazon of South America in the volume of water it empties into the sea. The Nile travels four thousand miles before reaching the Mediterranean, and today, as in ancient times, makes Egypt a habitable country. As the Nile winds slowly through the Sahara, the evaporation is so great that the river would dry up before reaching the sea were it not fed by rivers from the high Ethiopian Highlands. It is these waters of the Blue Nile which bring the great Nile floods and supply the water for irrigation to make of Egypt a fertile strip of land hemmed in by cliffs and burning sands. Africa's fourth large river, the Niger, while rising only one hundred and fifty miles from the ocean, flows twenty-five hundred miles before reaching the Atlantic.

Africa is a land of climatic contradictions. At the equator the temperature ranges from typical jungle weather at the lower levels, to a climate similar to that found well over a thousand miles to the north. This occurs in the high altitudes of the mountains. Along the Mediterranean, the weather compares with that of southern Europe. The weather in the Congo Basin is always hot and humid, although to the east, in the mountain and lake region, it is tempered by the higher altitudes. In the far south, around Cape Town, the weather is mild and sunny like the climate of southern California. The same extremes exist in rainfall. At the equator it is excessive, with periods of torrential rains. Traveling north or south from this wet center there is less and less rain, with parts of the Sahara never getting a drop.

Plant life varies with the rainfall. The dense, matted tropical jungles, which are exceeded only in size by the forests of the Amazon, give way to grassy plains and open forests. The only vegetation in the Sahara is around the springs that nourish the oases. Because the hot winds of the south are blocked by the Atlas Mountains, the entire coastal area of North Africa from the Atlantic to the Nile River is agriculturally productive.

Africa still has many wild animals, especially in its deep jungles. These teem with monkeys, among them gorillas and chimpanzees, and there are snakes and many birds. In the open woods and semi-arid grasslands of the savanna (called veldt in South Africa) live elephants, lions, giraffes, rhinoceroses, zebras and antelopes. Crocodiles and hippopotamuses are found in the rivers. The savanna is also the region for the raising of cattle. The desert has a very sparse animal population of a special kind, such as camels and jackals.

Africa is a strange mixture of white and black races. The four original races of Hamites and Semites, Negroes and Hottentots have become so intermingled that it is no longer possible to draw clear lines between racial groups. The Hamites and Semites of North Africa are white and Mohammedans. The Negroes and Hottentots are the black people of Central and South Africa. While probably members of the Negro race, the Hottentots have distinctive characteristics which put them in a class by themselves. These native tribes have a barbaric form of worship. The Sudanese, blackest of the Negroes, were sought by the early slave traders. For over three hundred years millions of these poor blacks were seized and transported to strange lands.

The slave trade was started by the son of a man who accompanied Columbus to America. Needing labor in her New World colonies to replace the Indian slaves, who preferred death to captivity, Spain granted each Spanish colonist the right to import twelve African Negroes. A year later the king of Spain bestowed a grant upon the Dutch allowing them to take four thousand slaves a year. Soon the "black ivory trade" had grown to huge proportions, and it has been estimated that as many as two million slaves were removed from Africa within one hundred years.

It was only following the explorations of Livingstone, Stanley and others in the last century, that Europe became aware of the possibilities existing in Africa. Then, sud-

TWA—Trans World Airline

Africa's varied topography lends itself to all sorts of livelihoods ranging from the industrial to the pastoral.

denly awakened to the great wealth that had been overlooked, European powers rushed in to carve out vast empires. When they had finished only two sections remained which were not possessions or dependencies of the white man, the Republic of Liberia (established in 1822 by the American Colonization Society for freed American Negroes, becoming a republic in 1847), and the Kingdom of Ethiopia. Later Egypt became independent and South Africa (which administers South-West Africa) entered the British Commonwealth as a dominion.

Following World War II Africa entered a period of political unheaval which is still going on. The colonial empires are breaking up and new nations are emerging. At the present time Africa includes about sixty political units.

Tunisia and Libya early became independent. The huge areas comprising the French colonial empire have been split into many countries — Algeria, Mauritania, Mali, Niger, Chad, Senegal, Guinea, Ivory Coast, Upper Volta, Dahomey, Morocco, Cameroon (which includes former British Cameroons), Central

The Rhumel Gorge from above, Constantine, Algeria.

African Republic, Republic of Congo (Brazzaville), the Gabon and Malagasy Republic.

The former British areas have one by one been achieving statehood — Sudan, Uganda, Kenya, Tanzania (Tanganyika and Zanzibar), Sierra Leone, Ghana, Nigeria, the Gambia, Togo (comprising former British and French administered territories), Zambia (Northern Rhodesia), Rhodesia (Southern Rhodesia), and Malawi (Nyasaland). Basutoland, Bechuanaland and Swaziland are still British dependencies.

The Somali Republic was formed from British and Italian Somaliland. Ruanda-Urundi, formerly under Belgian administration, split to become Rwanda and Burundi.

Since Algeria attained independence, the only remaining areas in Africa still belonging to France are the island of Réunion, an overseas department, and the overseas territories of the Comoro Islands and French Somaliland. In the French referendum of 1958, these areas voted to remain in the French Community.

The largest of Portugal's African possessions is Angola, a huge, treeless, mostly arid plain. Diamonds and coffee are exported. Mozambique with a coast line of 1500 miles has an unhealthful climate. Many of its people work in South African mines. Portuguese Guinea is a small territory on the west African coast. In the Atlantic Ocean lie the Portuguese islands of São Tomé and Príncipe and the Cape Verde Islands. Small Spanish provinces in Africa are Ifni, the Spanish Sahara, Fernando Po and Río Muni.

Along with political change has come technical change. Improved transportation in the form of railroads, motor roads, and airline service continue to reach out and draw distant points closer together. While railways have been extended, Africa still has relatively fewer miles of railroad than have the other continents. The greatest growth in transportation has been in motor and air transportation. Today areas which only a few years ago were inaccessible can be reached within hours. Modern engineering genius is overcoming the obstacles imposed by climate and land formation, and Africa is rapidly developing its huge, untapped natural resources. As the difficulties of climate, communications and diseases are overcome and education increases, Africa with its rich natural resources and its remarkably vital peoples is rapidly joining the modern world.

Sorghum and other grains are staple foods in Africa. Other important products, especially for export, are coffee, cocoa, tea and tobacco. Cotton is grown in many places, and from various regions. Hides, ivory and timber are exported. The rain forests furnish rubber, mahogany and teakwood.

Some of Africa's mineral resources are of the richest in the world. Almost all gem diamonds for the world market are found here; gold is mined on a large scale, and one of the world's richest uranium mines, the Shinkolobwe of the Republic of the Congo, lies in this continent. Zinc, silver, tin, copper, chromium, vanadium and manganese are also found. There is very little oil, which poses a serious problem for modern transportation needs. However, Africa has a great potential source of industrial power in its mighty rivers.

AUSTRALIA—This island continent of the South Seas is the smallest, and last to be discovered of all the continents.

The United States and Australia are nations of about the same age and size, and in other respects have much in common. The loss of America as a British Colony directly led to the settling of Australia. It was first claimed for the British Crown in 1788 as a settlement for British convicts who had previously been sent to America. Landing in a virgin country, the early pioneers of the two countries had to conquer the wilderness before creating a nation. In the process of so doing the people of both lands developed similar characteristics. In later years Australia even patterned its constitution after that of the United States.

But, whereas the United States became a melting pot for all the races and creeds in the world, Australia has been peopled almost entirely by British stock. Today 97 per cent of the population are descendants of British colonists, and 86 per cent are Australian born. Strict laws have confined immigration to the white race. Few of the natives who originally inhabited Australia remain. These aborigines are similar to the African Negro but not so intelligent, and are believed to be a separate race.

Almost half of Australia lies within the tropics, but being surrounded by great oceans, the continent has a mild climate throughout the year. Snow normally falls only in the high mountains in the winter. Since the seasons are the reverse of those in the United States, this occurs in their winter months of June, July, and August.

Australia is said to be most level in surface and regular in outline of all the continents. There is an entire absence of towering mountains. The highest peak is only about seventy-three hundred feet above sea level. The mountains parallel the east coast, with, by far, the greater part of the continent a vast, irregular, and undulating plateau.

Australia can be regarded as falling into four well-defined regions: (1) The Great Plateau in the west extends over about half of the continent; (2) The Eastern Highlands follow along the whole of the eastern coastline, rarely exceeding a distance of a hun-

New Zealand Consulate

Modified by ocean currents, New Zealand's climate remains moderate.

dred miles inland; (3) The Central Basin is a lowland area much of which was once a sea-bed; and (4) the Coastal Plains, which form a rim surrounding most of the continent.

Despite rich coastal lands and an immense grazing area in the interior, much of this interior is unsuited for agriculture. It is a great arid region of desert and semi-desert which is sparsely settled and will never support a dense population. The heaviest rainfall is in the tropical regions of the north, and there is adequate moisture along the south coast and southern part of the highlands. Elsewhere there is insufficient rain. But for the presence of innumerable artesian wells scattered over wide areas, much more of the country would be without water. It is these wells that make stock-raising possible, but because of its mineral content, the water is seldom used for agriculture or human use.

The major rivers of Australia are of two types—those which flow toward the coast and are similar to such rivers in other parts of the world; and the inland rivers which gradually lose their water as they flow away from the coastal regions. The headwaters of most of these inland rivers are in the Eastern Highlands.

The Murray River with its tributaries is the main river system and flows into the ocean on the south coast. The Gilbert, Norman and Flinders are the principal streams flowing into the Gulf of Carpentaria in the north. On the west the Murchison, Gascoyne, Ashburton and Fitzroy empty into the Indian Ocean.

The rivers which flow inland vary greatly in volume during the year. For long periods they are mere strings of waterholes, but during floods their waters spread out over the flat country for many miles. Most of their waters evaporate or soak into the ground before they flow very far. In the center of the continent the rivers flow into Lake Eyre when there is sufficient water in them, but generally they are merely beds of dry sand.

The lakes that appear to be scattered so liberally over the land are also a disappointment as they are little more than shallow basins that carry water only after rains.

Great Barrier Reef, the largest of all coral formations, follows the northeast coast for twelve hundred miles of Australia's twelve-thousand-mile coastline. Except in a few places this reef is impassable to ships, but it does provide an inner passage for coastal navigation. There are good harbors on the southeastern coast.

Wherever there is sufficient moisture for grass to grow, the land is especially adapted to grazing. This land has proved the most suitable in the world for raising sheep. Merino sheep, which produce a very fine quality of wool, comprise most of the flocks. The heavy fleece from these sheep exceeds that of breeds raised elsewhere, so, although Australia produces less than one-sixth of the world's sheep, the wool yield is more than a quarter of the world's requirement.

Lacking navigable rivers, most of the transportation is by railways. These have been of first importance in developing the country, but one great drawback of railroad transportation is that there are several gauges. During the last twenty-five years there has been a steady expansion of motor roads, and air routes are rapidly increasing.

In addition to the mainland and the island of Tasmania, Australia has extensive territorial interests. These comprise the Trust Territory of New Guinea, Papua, Nauru and Norfolk Island.

The Trust Territory of New Guinea includes the northeastern section of New Guinea, the Bismarck Archipelago, and the northern islands of the Solomon group. Scattered over a sea area of more than one million square miles, these islands are mountainous with limited coastal areas suitable for cultivation.

NEW ZEALAND—Two large islands and several small ones make up New Zealand. Situated about twelve hundred miles southeast of Australia, New Zealand is a lonely member of the British Commonwealth.

The two principal islands, North and South Island are separated by Cook Strait which is ninety miles wide. Close as they are to each other, these islands have little in common except that they are both mountainous. North Island is of volcanic origin and consists chiefly of forested hills and plateaus. South Island is more rugged with glaciers and snow-clad peaks that rival the Alps of Switzerland.

PACIFIC ISLANDS—The Pacific Islands fall into three major regions: Polynesia, Micronesia and Melanesia.

Polynesia, or "many islands," consists of widely scattered groups and a few isolated islands forming a rough triangle. The Hawaiian Islands are at the northern point, twenty degrees north of the Equator. The Fiji Islands, at the western point of the triangle, are the meeting place of Polynesian and Melanesian cultures, the people being of mixed stock. The easternmost point lies in the Gambier group of the Tuamotu Archipelago, although isolated Pitcairn Island, inhabited by Anglo-Tahitian descendants of the mutinous crew of the "Bounty," is generally included geographically. Within this area lies the most highly developed group of Pacific peoples, a mixture of white, black and yellow racial stocks, the Polynesians. Famous as navigators, they crossed the Pacific from Asia hundreds of years ago, and sailed their canoes eastward to their present homes. For the most part, the islands are mountainous, volcanic and covered with dense vegetation, often fringed by coral reefs. Along the equator and in the southeast, low coral atolls predominate, often only a few feet above sea level, and frequently torn by hurricanes.

The people, often easy-going to the point of idleness, are not always used in local production, some Chinese having been hired to do manual work. Famous for dancing and feasting, the generally happy Polynesians strive to maintain their early customs against the inroads of European traders, missionaries and government regulations.

In the western Pacific, for the most part north of the equator, lies Micronesia, or "little islands," confined to the Marianas, Carolines, Marshall Islands, and Gilbert and Ellice Islands. Except for the latter islands, they are mostly volcanic and coral-fringed, and are peopled by a light-skinned group—the latest arrivals in the Pacific. These inhabitants show more evidence of a recent black and yellow mixture.

The earliest inhabited area of the Pacific, New Guinea and the islands spreading to the southeast of it, is known as Melanesia, the "black islands." Of early Negroid stock, this area was generally by-passed by the later Polynesians and Micronesians, as settlement was already established. Melanesia is a rapidly developing area, rich in minerals as well as the usual coconuts. Today the people range from Europeanized workers in the plantations of New Caledonia and Fiji, and the missions of the New Guinea coast, to half-naked savages, often head-hunters and cannibals, in the higher regions of New Guinea.

ASIA—To say that this is the largest continent in the world gives no idea of its immensity. Covering one-third of the land area of the world, Asia is more than a million square miles larger than the combined areas of North and South America. It extends from the ice-bound regions of the Arctic Circle to the sun-burnt islands of the Tropics. It claims the highest and lowest elevations, as well as the wettest and driest areas in the world. Mount Everest is the highest and the Dead Sea the lowest. Assam is the wettest, and Northern Siberia the driest. Asia is the cradle

The Eastern Gate to the Old City of Damascus, Syria.

of the earliest civilization and is now the home of over half the population of the world.

Man has drawn a line separating Asia from Europe but the only natural division is the low Ural Mountains and a depression extending from the mountains to the Caspian Sea. Only a man-made canal at the Isthmus of Suez separates Asia from Africa.

Washed by three oceans and a number of seas, Asia has a coast line over thirty thousand miles in length. Deep indentations along the irregular coast form seas, such as the Bay of Bengal and the Arabian Sea. Twisting and pointed peninsulas reach far out into the oceans. The shores are dotted with archipelagos and island groups. Among the island groups are Japan, the Philippines, and Indonesia, all of which have become as important as mainland countries.

The mountain ranges that sweep across Europe from west to east continue in long parallel lines through Asia. These mountain chains rise in height, first curving away from one another, and then closing in abruptly in a knot of massed mountains which has been referred to as "the roof of the world." Eastward, the awe-inspiring Himalayas reach to the plateau of Tibet, turn suddenly south through Indochina in long lines of deep, forested ravines, and disappear in a string of islands, drowned by the waters of the Indian Ocean. The Himalayas, covered with eternal snows and scored by mighty glaciers, are the highest mountains in the world. From Mount Everest, their loftiest peak, they drop steeply down to the low river plains below.

To the north of the mountains lies the great plain of Northern Asia, a continuation of the North European plain. Broken only by the Urals it sinks slowly to the frozen Arctic shore. To the south, in India and Arabia, are two low plateaus with steep sides, and the river lowlands of Mesopotamia and the Ganges plain.

This enormous continent is drained by many large rivers. Flowing toward the Arctic Ocean are the Ob, Yenisei and Lena Rivers. They are often blocked with ice for months and flood the surrounding country in thaw. In the east the silt carried down by the rivers has built the wide alluvial plains of China. The Hwang Ho, or Yellow River, flows into the Yellow Sea. Yellow is a sacred color, for this is the color of the silt deposited by the great river on the fertile plain, where crowded millions of Chinese grow their crops and find their livelihood. The Yangtze Kiang, or Blue River, rises in Tibet and passes through deep walls before winding sluggishly across the lowlands of China. These rivers often overflow in disastrous floods and have changed their courses many times.

The Ganges, Indus and Brahmaputra have built up the fertile lowlands of North India and are slowly extending it in broad, swampy deltas, out to sea.

Covering so many degrees of latitude, the climate of Asia would naturally show great variation. There are great extremes of cold and heat in the Siberian lowlands and Northern China. Great areas in the center of the continent, far from the sea, are dry; with tropical conditions prevailing in the south. The heaviest rainfall anywhere in the world is in some localities of Southeastern Asia and everywhere in the eastern region there is sufficient moisture for agriculture. In Assam, India, the rainfall averages about thirty-five feet a year.

There is every type of vegetation, ranging from tundra mosses in the extreme north to tropical plant life in the south. There are great stores of mineral wealth, but much of this is still undeveloped. Asia has been slow to awaken to the possibilities of an industrialized civilization.

Southwestern Asia is that section of the continent lying between India and the Aegean Sea. It is a rugged, mountainous country which includes the two desert plateaus of Iran and Arabia, and the rich lowlands of the Tigris and Euphrates valley.

Great nations flourished in Southwestern Asia several thousand years before the birth of Christ. Composed almost entirely of the white race, their civilizations contributed much to the early nations along the Mediterranean. Mongolian hordes invaded these lands in the thirteenth century, almost destroying the civilizations which they found. Growing in power, a mighty nation which spread into Africa and Europe came into being. The Turks are descendants of these war-like people.

TURKEY—Surrounded by mountains on three sides is a high, dry plateau which slopes to the fertile shores of the Mediterranean. Among the chief mountains are the Taurus range, stretching from the southwestern shore of the Aegean to the north of Syria, their principal peaks rising from 7,000 to 10,000 feet; the Bulgar Mountains rising over 10,000 feet; and the Ala Mountains, north of Seyhan, rising 8,000 to 10,000 feet high. The highest peak in the country is Mt. Ararat, 16,945 feet. Flowing into the Black Sea are the Coruh, the Yesilirmak, the Kizilirmak and the Sakarya. Into the Mediterranean flow the Seyhan and Ceyhan. In the east of Asia Minor are the headwaters of both the Euphrates and the Tigris as well as of the Araxes.

ISRAEL—After 2,000 years the Jewish people realized their dream of an independent homeland with the establishment of the new state of Israel in 1948. Lying between Egypt and Jordan on the eastern shores of the Mediterranean, the country is a hot and arid land. The new nation's economy is based on the cultivation of citrus fruit for export made possible by extensive irrigation of the lands of Zionist sponsored settlements. Oil refining, chemical production and light industry are also important to the economy.

SYRIA AND LEBANON—The occupations of the people of these countries have not changed since Biblical times, and are similar to those of Turkey. Mostly agricultural, there is little mineral wealth, and manufacturing is largely for local markets. Lebanon is mainly mountainous with a fertile valley lying in the center between the Lebanon Mountains on the west coast and the Anti-Lebanon Mountains which form the eastern border between Lebanon and Syria. Syria consists largely of desert surrounded by mountains. In the northeast, the Euphrates flows across the desert and irrigates a valuable strip of agricultural land. Other fertile areas are found near Homs and Hama, both in the northwest, and Damascus and the Jebel Druze district in the southwest.

TWA—Trans World Airline

Flocks of sheep and goats are the economic mainstay of the Arab's life.

IRAQ—Once the site of the Babylonian Empire, the Tigris and Euphrates valley is part of the "Fertile Crescent" of ancient times. The country is a great alluvial plain, bounded on the north by Kurdistan, on the east by Iran, on the south by the Persian Gulf, and on the west by the Syrian and Arabian Deserts. Northern Iraq has a valuable supply of oil which is piped to Haifa and Tripoli.

IRAN (Persia)—Most of the country is plateau, surrounded by mountain chains, except in the east where huge salt deserts are found. An extension of the mountain ranges, locally known as the Khorasan Mountains of the Hindu Kush, enters on the northeast from Afghanistan and merges into the Elburz Range south of the Caspian, the highest peak being Mt. Demavend. Except for narrow fertile areas along the Caspian Sea and Persian Gulf the land is too dry to sustain many people.

ARABIA—The Arabian Peninsula is a land composed almost entirely of desert, mostly of a barren and stony type, with an abundance of sand in the southeast. Besides scattered oases there are only a few small areas in Arabia with enough rainfall to permit the growing of crops. Saudi Arabia, which occupies the central two-thirds of the peninsula, has experimented with modern, mechanized methods of irrigation to improve farming conditions, and a modern railroad now reaches the interior from the Persian Gulf. The finest Arabian horses and camels are raised in the central highlands. Discovery of valuable oil reserves in the desert near the Persian Gulf fostered new economic development, and many local sheikhs, or tribal rulers, have become suddenly rich. Pearling, once important in the Gulf, is now declining. In the mountain valleys of Yemen is the most fertile soil of the peninsula, and its Red Sea ports, such as Mocha and Hodeida handle its coffee and other exports, as well as pearls from nearby islands.

AFGHANISTAN—Barren tablelands, deep ravines and snow-covered mountains leave

The Gateway to India was erected to commemorate the landing of King George V and Queen Mary in 1911.

Afghanistan an unproductive land. Lying as a barrier between Siberia and India, it has been the scene of many invasions and conquests but the war-like Afghans have never been completely vanquished. Cereals, fruits and vegetables are grown only in small areas under irrigation, and the fat-tailed sheep—a native of the country—furnishes meat and a butter substitute.

PAKISTAN—Pakistan is divided into two widely separated sections. The larger part, West Pakistan on the Arabian Sea, consists of the fertile Indus valley, the extremely rugged Northwest frontier and arid Baluchistan. Cereal raising and cotton production are concentrated in the Indus Valley which possesses one of the oldest and most efficient canal irrigation systems in the world. East Pakistan, on the Bay of Bengal, occupies the lower Ganges-Brahmaputra delta and the Assam highland foothills. This nation, while almost wholly Mohammedan in religion, is influenced politically and culturally not only by the Islamic world to the west but also the neighboring Hindu civilization of India.

INDIA—For over four thousand years, India has been at the mercy of marauding and conquering races. Unlike many lesser coun-

tries, who have successfully thrown off the yoke of oppression, India, until recently, has always been subject to foreign rule. As a result it is a confusion of races, castes, and religions, with a civilization ranging from the highest type of culture to the most primitive. In 1947 India was granted independence and now takes her place among the important powers of the globe.

Except for the rocky slopes of the mountains, the soil is fertile and supports the largest agricultural population in the world. Like the farmers of France, a large majority of these people live in small villages surrounded by tilled fields. And, while primitive methods and equipment are used, surprisingly large crops are raised. Disastrous droughts, due to the vagaries of the weather, and the famines which followed, have been partially relieved by government sponsored irrigation works and the construction of railroads and motor roads.

SIKKIM, NEPAL AND BHUTAN—These three small independent states are shut off from the outside world by the Himalayas. Several of the world's highest mountains, including Mount Everest, are in northern Nepal. Their inhabitants are energetic people who raise cattle, wheat, rice, tobacco and spices which they export in exchange for necessary manufactured goods, sugar, oil, etc.

CEYLON—The island of Ceylon has been called the "Pearl of the Orient." Situated off the southern coast of India it is famous for its tea, precious stones and tropical beauty. The broad coastal strip which surrounds the central mountains is, for the most part, fertile and produces a luxuriant vegetation. Although the climate is tropical, sea breezes temper the heat.

INDOCHINA—This southeastern peninsula of Asia includes a part of Burma, Thailand, Cambodia, Laos, Vietnam and part of the Federation of Malaysia. Much of the peninsula has heavily forested valleys and mountain ridges of the Himalayas running the length of the land. This is the great rice-producing region, and most of the world's natural rubber comes from here. Rainfall is heavy in the entire area and the land is very productive. In the dense forests are valuable stands of prize woods, teak, ebony and other trees used for their wood or gum. Agriculture is the chief industry throughout the peninsula but there are many important deposits of valuable minerals. Modern methods of agriculture and mining have been introduced. Singapore, situated on an island at the extreme southern end of the peninsula, commands one of the most important sea routes in the world.

THE MALAY ARCHIPELAGO — The world's largest group of islands extends from Sumatra to the Philippine Islands off the coast of China, and includes many thousands of islands. With the exception of the Philippines, and parts of Timor, Borneo and New Guinea, the archipelago was ruled for hundreds of years by the Netherlands.

INDONESIA—Colonization and development begun by the Dutch in the XVIIth century has resulted in the richest and most important island group in the world.

Most of the islands are mountainous and of volcanic origin. At one time they were a part of the mainland connecting Asia with Australia. Java is the most productive and highly developed of the East Indies. It is one of the most densely populated regions in the world. Much of the land is divided into native farms and large plantations. The plantation crops are chiefly for export.

Next to Greenland, New Guinea and Borneo are the largest islands in the world. Sumatra and Celebes are next in size in the East Indies. Much of the mineral wealth of these islands is yet untouched. Borneo is crossed almost in the middle by the equator and few white people occupy the island because of the humidity and heat. Petroleum is an important resource of Borneo, Sumatra and Java, and two small islands adjoining Sumatra have valuable deposits of tin. Bali, while one of the lesser islands, has been one of the most publicized, and is favored by tourists as a tropical paradise.

PHILIPPINE ISLANDS — More than seven thousand islands, the Philippines, like other

Mt. Fuji, Japan.

islands of the Malay Archipelago, are the tops of drowned mountains protruding from the sea. There are well watered fertile plains between the mountains. Being near the equator the temperature is never very low. Although the days are warm, the nights are usually cool. Some of the many volcanoes in the Philippines are still active and the islands are subject to earthquakes.

CHINA—Chinese civilization is of greater antiquity than any other existent world culture. It has shown great powers of survival and has possessed the ability to absorb all foreign influences without losing its own identity.

The Chinese people are patient, industrious, and have great physical endurance. They are among the world's best farmers, having grown more food for longer periods on the same land, without exhausting the soil, than any other people. They take naturally to mechanics and are fine traders and business men.

With the possible exception of Africa, China has the largest undeveloped natural resources in the world. There are rich de-

Indonesia Information Office

Asian art has been stimulated by many technical and cultural institutions.

posits of coal, with China ranking second to the United States in total reserves. Iron ore reserves are large enough to meet its needs for many years to come. It is believed that China has one of the most valuable deposits of copper, and tin has been a leading mineral export.

China is a land of garden farmers and the soil is cultivated intensively. Few animals are raised, which conserves acreage for food crops. Hence the Chinese diet consists almost entirely of vegetable products. In a relatively mild climate people can subsist on less food than in a colder region. Rice is the most important crop but almost every known crop is raised.

Inner Mongolia, Tibet and Sinkiang are outer provinces of China. Until the building of railroads and motor roads they were reached entirely by caravan routes. This region has extreme temperatures and is largely desert. The Great Wall was built to keep the Mongols out of China. Tibet, until recently opened up to British trade, excluded all foreigners. Sinkiang consists almost entirely of a desert basin.

MONGOLIA—Lying between China and Siberia, this country consists largely of an arid plateau composed mainly of the Gobi Desert. In the northwest are high mountains whose streams flow into numerous sizable lakes. The Mongolian people are almost entirely a nomadic race who wander from place to place seeking new pastures for their herds of cattle.

JAPAN—The chief feature of the country is its mountainous character, for each island has a mountainous backbone. Mt. Fuji, the highest mountain, reaches 12,389 feet. One of the most notable physical features is the Inland Sea or Japanese Mediterranean. It is almost entirely landlocked and surrounded by chains of volcanoes, of which few are now active. The climate is temperate and healthful, with abundant rainfall.

Only 20 per cent of the land can be cultivated and the balance is largely mountainous, with frequent destructive earthquakes and volcanic activity. While minerals have been a major factor in her industrial growth, Japan is not well supplied with them. The only large mineral deposits are coal and copper, with some gold, silver and lead. The petroleum produced falls far short of her needs.

The low standard of living and the small amount of land suitable for cultivation have made farming highly intensive. A large percentage of the farms are only an acre or two in size and most of the farmers are forced to carry on some other occupation to exist.

Manufacturing has risen rapidly in Japan with the production of textiles leading. Because of low wages and nearness to the Oriental market, Japan has been able to compete in cheaper goods to the disadvantage of other countries.

KOREA—Korea's strategic position between the Asiatic mainland and Japan has made it an historic pathway for invasion. Coveted at different times by China, Russia and Japan, she lost her independence early in the century to the Japanese Empire. During the second World War, Korea was promised her independence, but the end of the fighting brought her only division between the great powers and later renewed military conflict.

Physically and economically Korea is divided into two contrasting natural regions. The agricultural heart of the nation is south of the thirty-eighth parallel, producing chiefly rice and barley. North of the parallel, industry and mining of coal and iron predominate.

INDEX OF PRINCIPAL CITIES OF THE WORLD

This alphabetical list of cities and towns gives statistics of population based on the latest official census reports or mo re-cent reliable estimates. Each line begins with the name of a place, followed by the name of the country or state, the population, the index reference and plate number. This index reference gives the location of the city or town name on the accompanying map plates. The name is found within the square formed by the two lines of latitude or longitude which enclose each of the co-ordinates—i.e. the marginal letters and numbers. In the case of maps consisting entirely of insets, the name is found near the intersection point of imaginary lines connecting the co-ordinates.

Where space on the map has not permitted giving the complete form of a name, the extended form is shown in the index. Where a place may be known under different names or by various spellings of the same name, the different forms have been included, to a large extent, in the index. Where an alternative spelling in parentheses is shown on the map itself, the first name gives the local official form, the conventional form following in parentheses.

* Capitals of countries, states and provinces.　　　　　† Population figure includes suburbs.

Aabenraa, Denmark, 14,219 ....B 3 43
Aachen (Aix-la-Chapelle),
　Germany, 169,769 ....B 3 42
Aalborg, Denmark, 85,800 ....B 3 43
Aalesund (Ålesund), Norway,
　19,170 ....A 2 43
Aalst (Alost), Belgium, 45,092....C 6 44
Aarau, Switzerland, 17,045 ....D 1 45
Aarhus, Denmark, 119,568 ....B 3 43
Abadan, Iran, 226,083 ....E 3 56
Abbeville, France, 21,744 ....D 2 40
Abécher, Chad, 9,877 ....L 9 63
Aberdare, Wales, 39,044 ....E 5 39
Aberdeen, Scotland, 185,379 ......E 2 38
Abidjan,* Ivory Coast, †180,000...E10 62
Abilene, Tex., 90,368 ....E 5 162
Abomey, Dahomey, 16,906 ....G10 62
Acámbaro, Mexico, 26,011...........E 4 77
Acapulco, Mexico, 48,846 ....E 5 77
Accra,* Ghana, †491,060 ....G10 62
Acireale, Sicily, Italy, 44,330......E 6 47
Adana (Seyhan), Turkey, 230,024..C 2 56
Addis Ababa,* Ethiopia, 400,000...O10 63
Adelaide,* South Australia,
　†587,957 ....D 7 66
Adelboden, Switzerland, 2,881......C 2 45
Aden,* South Arabia,
　†97,760 ....E 7 56
Aduwa, Ethiopia, 6,000 ....O 9 63
Agaña,* Guam, 1,642 ....E 4 68
Agen, France, 30,639 ....D 5 41
Agra, India, 462,020 ....C 2 59
Agrigento (Girgenti), Sicily, Italy,
　†47,094 ....D 6 47
Agrínion, Greece, 24,763 ....E 6 51
Aguascalientes, Mexico, 126,222....D 4 77
Ahlen, Germany, 40,485 ....B 3 42
Ahmadabad, India, 1,149,918 ......C 2 59
Ahmadnagar, India, 119,020 ....C 3 59
Aix, France, 55,398 ....F 6 41
Aix-les-Bains, France, 17,324 ......G 5 41
Ajaccio,* Corsica, France, 40,829..F 7 41
Ajmer, India, 231,240 ....C 2 59
Akita, Japan, 203,661 ....N 4 60
Akola, India, 115,760 ....C 2 59
Akron, Ohio, 290,351 ....G 3 144
Akureyri, Iceland, 8,957 ....C 2 37
Akyab, Burma, 42,329 ....E 2 59
Alajuela, Costa Rica, 19,564 ......C 3 76
Alameda, Calif., 61,316 ....J 2 90
Alausí, Ecuador, 6,659 ....E 4 70
Albacete, Spain, †74,417 ....F 3 46
Albany,* N.Y., 129,726 ....N 5 143
Albany, Western Australia,
　10,526 ....B 6 66
Albi, France, 31,672 ....E 6 41
Albuquerque, N. Mex., 201,189.....C 3 140
Alcamo, Sicily, Italy, 41,471........D 6 47
Alcoy, Spain, 39,417 ....F 3 46
Aldershot, England, 31,260 ....F 5 39
Alegrete, Brazil, 33,735 ....J 9 73
Alençon, France, 24,299 ....D 3 40
Aleppo (Haleb), Syria, 425,029.....C 2 56
Alès, France, 20,259 ....E 5 41
Alessandria, Italy, †92,291 ....B 2 47
Ålesund (Aalesund), Norway,
　19,170 ....A 2 43
Alexandretta (Iskenderun),
　Turkey, 63,736 ....C 2 56
Alexandria (El Iskandariya),
　Egypt, 1,497,026 ....M 5 63
Alexandria, La., 40,279 ....E 4 114
Alexandria, Va., 91,023 ....L 3 169
Alexandroupolis (Dedeagach),
　Greece, 18,712 ....H 5 51
Algiers,* Algeria, 329,700 ....G 4 62

Alhambra, Calif., 54,807 ....C10 91
Alicante, Spain, †121,527 ....F 3 46
Aligarh (Koil), India, 185,020......C 2 59
Aliquippa, Pa., 26,369.................B 4 154
Al Ittihad, S. Arabia ....E 7 56
Alkmaar, Netherlands, 43,606......E 2 44
Al Kuwait,* Kuwait, †119,472......E 4 56
Allahabad, India, 411,955............D 2 59
Allenstein (Olsztyn), Poland,
　64,300 ....E 2 49
Allentown, Pa., 108,347 ....L 4 155
Alleppey, India, 138,834 ....C 4 59
Alma-Ata, U.S.S.R., 455,000........L 5 54
Almelo, Netherlands, 50,775 ....J 3 44
Almería, Spain, †86,808 ....E 4 46
Altagracia, Venezuela, 7,362........F 1 70
Altamura, Italy, 38,231 ....F 4 47
Altenburg, Germany, 51,805 ....E 3 42
Alton, Ill., 43,047 ....A 6 105
Altoona, Pa., 69,407 ....F 4 154
Amarillo, Tex., 137,969 ....C 2 162
Ambala, India, 76,204 ....C 2 59
Ambato, Ecuador, 52,713 ....E 4 70
Amboina (Ambon), Indon.,
　46,403 ....H 6 61
Ambriz, Angola, 2,196 ....J13 64
Amecameca, Mexico, 12,271 ....F 1 77
Amersfoort, Netherlands, 70,458...F 3 44
Amiens,* France, 101,677 ....E 3 40
Amman,* Jordan, 244,599 ....D 4 58
Amoy, China, 224,300 ....P 7 55
Amraoti, India, 137,875 ....C 2 59
Amritsar, India, 376,295 ....B 1 59
Amsterdam,* Neth., 864,749........E 3 44
Amsterdam, N.Y., 28,772 ....M 5 143
Ancona, Italy, †99,678 ....D 3 47
Anchorage, Alaska, 44,237 ....D 3 84
Ancud, Chile, 7,390 ....F12 72
Anderlecht, Belgium, 94,677........D 6 44
Andermatt, Switzerland, 1,523.....D 2 45
Anderson, Ind., 49,061 ....F 4 106
Andizhan, U.S.S.R., 129,000 ....L 5 54
Andorra la Vella,* Andorra,
　1,100 ....G 1 46
Andria, Italy, 63,937 ....F 4 47
Angers, France, 109,614 ....C 4 40
Angmagssalik, Greenland, 612......C11 36
Angoulême, France, 46,924..........D 5 41
Ankara (Angora),* Turkey,
　646,151 ....B 1 56
Annaba, Algeria, 88,920 ....H 4 62
Annapolis,* Md., 23,385 ....H 5 119
Ann Arbor, Mich., 67,340 ....F 6 123
Annecy, France, 42,304 ....G 5 41
Anniston, Ala., 33,657 ....G 3 82
Annonay, France, 12,559 ....F 5 41
Anshan, China, 548,900 ....K 3 60
Antâkya (Antioch), Turkey,
　45,848 ....C 2 56
Antequera, Spain, 29,855 ....D 4 46
Antibes, France, 24,730 ....G 6 41
Antofagasta, Chile, 87,860...........F 8 72
Antsirabe, Malagasy Rep., 18,683..R16 65
Antung, China, 360,000 ....K 3 60
Antwerp (Antwerpen), Belgium,
　253,295 ....D 5 44
Anzhero-Sudzhensk, U.S.S.R.,
　116,000 ....M 4 54
Anzio, Italy, 9,084 ....D 4 47
Aomori, Japan, 202,211 ....N 3 60
Apeldoorn, Netherlands, 78,961....G 3 44
Apia,* Western Samoa, 25,000.....J 7 69
Apolda, Germany, 33,439 ....D 3 42
Appleton, Wis., 48,411 ....J 7 171
'Aqaba, Jordan, 9,228 ....D 5 58
Aracaju, Brazil, 112,516 ....N 6 71

Araçatuba, Brazil, 53,363 ....K 8 71
Arad, Rumania, 112,139 ....E 2 50
Aragua de Barcelona, Ven.,
　8,255 ....H 2 70
Araraquara, Brazil, 58,076 ....L 8 71
Arbroath, Scotland, 19,533 ....E 2 38
Archangel (Arkhangelsk), U.S.S.R.,
　256,000 ....F 2 52
Arendal, Norway, 11,324 ....B 3 43
Arequipa, Peru, †162,500 ....F 7 70
Arezzo, Italy, †74,245 ....D 3 47
Argentan, France, 11,724 ....D 3 40
Argenteuil, France, 82,007 ....A 1 40
Àrgos, Greece, 16,712 ....F 7 51
Arica, Chile, 43,344 ....F 7 70
Arles, France, 29,251 ....F 6 41
Arlington, Va., 163,401 ....L 3 169
Arlon (Aarlen), Belgium,
　13,272 ....G 8 44
Armavir, U.S.S.R., 111,000 ....F 5 53
Armentières, France, 23,168 ....E 2 40
Arnhem, Netherlands, 124,611......H 4 44
Arras, France, 40,969 ....E 2 40
Artemovsk, U.S.S.R., 61,000 ....E 5 53
Artigas, Uruguay, 17,684 ....J10 73
Aš, Czechoslovakia, 9,684 ....B 1 48
Asahikawa, Japan, 188,309 ....O 3 60
Asansol, India, 103,405 ....D 2 59
Aschaffenburg, Germany,
　54,131 ....C 4 42
Aschersleben, Germany, 42,196....D 3 42
Ascoli Piceno, Italy, †49,070 ....D 3 47
Asheville, N.C., 60,192 ....E 8 144
Ashkhabad, U.S.S.R., 170,000......J 6 54
Ashland, Ky., 31,283 ....M 4 113
Asmara, Ethiopia, 132,000 ....O 9 63
Asnières, France, 81,747 ....A 1 40
Asti, Italy, †60,217 ....B 2 47
Astrakhan, U.S.S.R., 294,000.......G 5 53
Asunción,* Paraguay, 281,007......J 3 73
Aswân, Egypt, 47,466 ....N 7 63
Asyût, Egypt, 117,067 ....N 6 63
Atbara, Sudan, 34,700 ....N 8 63
Athens (Athênai), Greece,
　†1,852,709 ....F 7 51
Athlone, Ireland, 9,624 ....C 4 39
Atlanta,* Ga., 331,314 ....D 3 98
Atlantic City, N. J., 61,657 ....E 5 139
Aubervilliers, France, 70,592........B 1 40
Auburn, N.Y., 36,667 ....G 5 142
Auckland, New Zealand, †448,365..L 5 67
Augsburg, Germany, 208,659.......D 4 42
Augusta, Ga., 71,507 ....J 4 98
Augusta,* Me., 21,680 ....D 7 117
Aurangabad, India, 87,579 ....C 3 59
Aurillac, France, 23,179 ....E 5 41
Aurora, Ill., 63,715 ....E 2 104
Austin,* Tex., 186,545 ....G 7 163
Auxerre, France, 28,949 ....E 4 40
Avellaneda, Argentina, 329,626....O12 73
Avellino, Italy, †41,509 ....E 4 47
Aversa, Italy, 33,809 ....E 4 47
Avignon, France, 64,581 ....F 6 41
Ávila, Spain, †26,807 ....D 2 46
Avranches, France, 8,828 ....C 3 40
Ayacucho, Peru, 21,454 ....F 6 70
Ayr, Scotland, 45,297 ....D 3 38
Azul, Argentina, 28,609 ....J11 73
Babol (Barfrush), Iran, 36,194.....F 2 57
Bacău, Rumania, 60,570 ....H 2 50
Badajoz, Spain, †96,317 ....C 3 46
Badalona, Spain, 40,983 ....H 2 46
Baden bei Wien, Austria, 22,484....D 2 48
Baden-Baden, Germany, 40,029....C 4 42
Bad Ischl (Ischl), Austria,
　12,703 ....B 3 48